DISPLAYS OF POWER

STEVEN C. DUBIN

DISPLAYS OF POWER

Memory and Amnesia in the American Museum

New York University Press • *New York and London*

NEW YORK UNIVERSITY PRESS
New York and London

Library of Congress Cataloging-in-Publication Data
Dubin, Steven C.
Displays of power : memory and amnesia in the American museum /
by Steven C. Dubin.
p. cm.
Includes bibliographical references and index.
ISBN 0-8147-1889-2 (cloth : acid-free paper)
1. Museum exhibits—Political aspects—United States. 2. Museum
techniques—Unites States. 3. Culture conflict—United States.
4. United States—Cultural policy. 5. Popular culture—Political
aspects. 6. Political correctness. I. Title.
AM151 .D84 1999
069'.5—dc21   98-58108
                         CIP

New York University Press books are printed on acid-free paper,
and their binding materials are chosen for strength and durability.

Manufactured in the United States of America

10 9 8 7 6 5 4 3 2 1

Time heals all wounds,
Smoothes, cleanses, obliterates;
History keeps the wound open,
Picks at it, makes it raw and bleeding.
                    —Janet Malcolm, 1993

Contents

Illustrations

Prologue and Acknowledgments

Unwed mothers in nineteenth-century Italy could avert public disgrace by leaving their infants at the *ruota*, a revolving table built into the walls of foundling homes. A woman placed her child on the wheel and turned it, and the baby would anonymously enter the security of the institution. This device is light-years from contemporary tabloid talk shows, where pregnancies generated by all manner of unions and scientific techniques are casually discussed without social censure.

Brooklyn, New York, 1996: miraculously, a cloistered Carmelite convent persists in the troubled Crown Heights neighborhood. No one knows for sure what goes on inside; there is not even an accurate count of how many nuns make their home there. A barrel-shaped revolving wooden cabinet called a *turn* is their link to the outside world, the site where people place bags of groceries to sustain the unidentified sisters. They leave prayer requests on the turn as well. But as much as the Monastery of Our Lady of Mount Carmel embodies life in the sixteenth century, it cannot entirely escape the twentieth: graffiti blemishes its gates and walls, the telltale marks of a gritty urban culture.

Today there is virtually no place and no person immune from the influence of American culture. It relentlessly seeps into every social crack and crevice in the United States certainly, but throughout the world as well. This was dynamically illustrated for me at New York's La Guardia Airport one day in 1997. A Hasidic Jewish man arrived in the waiting area, three children in tow. He carefully settled the two boys into seats, supplying a toy for each. For his daughter he produced a special surprise out of one of his bags: a new Barbie. He unwrapped the doll to the girl's delight, and she too was quickly immersed in play. The father, meanwhile, retreated to a corner of the room. There he draped his shoulders with a prayer shawl, wrapped his forehead and arm with the ceremonial *T'fillin*, and proceeded to *daven*, or recite his traditional daily prayers. It would be difficult to imagine a more splendid blending of the sacred and the profane than this family's varied activities.

This book is about contemporary cultural fusions, about how we depict the present and remember the past. It focuses on museums, places that the *Oxford English Dictionary* tells us were originally sacred to the muses and, as such, were detached from the mundane world. Today that is clearly no longer the case.

A casual conversation at a dinner party in Brooklyn in 1994 pushed my interests in a direction I could never have foreseen. By happenstance, I was recruited to work on a museum exhibition. Thus do careers sometimes develop. Along the way, I have alternately bored and grossed out nearly everyone I know with what I've learned. But gradually they too have been enlisted into the cause, clipping news items, furnishing videotaped goodies, or phoning in relevant tidbits of information. First and foremost, I salute Elizabeth Childs and John Klein for hosting the event that unwittingly kindled this project. And I thank Rich Nassisi, Linda Marie Bastone, Dean Stein, Jim Saslow, Terry Liebman, Norma Howard, Angela Messina, Betsy Immergut, Judith Schultz, Vera Zolberg, Barry Schwartz, Sarah Lauzen, Ken Burkhart, Susan Weiss, Dennis Wheaton, Les Kurtz, Annette Oko, Marilyn McLaren, Jennifer Hunt, Valencia Wallace, Connie Lobur, and Milo Miller for a variety of contributions.

I am grateful, too, to the entire staff of the Purchase College-SUNY Center for Instructional Resources; they never fail to come through with what I typically present to them as urgent requests. Moreover, Joyce Hellew and Mary Carroll did a fine (and speedy) job of transcribing my taped interviews. Although many of the people I met through this project were very generous in sharing material with me, I particularly appreciate the contributions of Melinda Hunt, Brendan Fay, Peter J. Swales, and Benny Andrews. They fattened my files and greased the wheels so that I could get certain things done with fewer hassles. Bless you, hoarders of documents!

My former editor, Cecelia Cancellaro, altruistically initiated the contact with my present editor on my behalf. Not only that, she picked up the tab for lunch at the same time she made this offer! I feel very indebted to her. And I am so pleased that she hooked me up with Eric Zinner and New York University Press. To my mind, a good editor is one who remains unflappable when an author floats all manner of *meshuggeneh* ideas—like proposing book titles in Yiddish, for example. Eric has taken all my cockamamie suggestions in stride and has continued to succor the more sensible aspects of this book. He has stayed the course, even when it might have seemed his author was drifting.

The *New Art Examiner* gave some of my ideas their first public airing, and later published an excerpt from one of the chapters. I value their advocacy and admire their commitment to providing a critical forum for art and social issues. I am particularly grateful to Ann Wiens and Kathryn Hixson for presenting my work in their journal.

Like most museum personnel nowadays, I had to hustle to find money to underwrite this project. In the end it came mostly from my own bank account. However, I was happy to receive a few modest contributions, which offset some of the transcription costs and the fees for rights and permissions, including a Purchase College Faculty Support Fund Grant, a grant from New York State/United University Professions, and a subsidy from Purchase College academic vice president Gary Waller.

I relished two residences at the Ragdale Foundation, an artists' retreat in Lake Forest, Illinois, which were tremendously important in the development of this book. I *shvitzed* during the record-breaking heat of the summer of 1995, but I also produced the essay that launched this project. And I trudged through Ragdale's snowy prairie countless times during the winter of 1998, a glorious way to unwind from a month's worth of productive days of working on the final chapters. The staff and the residents continuously create a unique, evanescent community based on mutual support and respect. It has been a privilege to share it twice, briefly. And I thank Cindy Infantino of the Lake Forest Library as well, for cheerfully and capably helping me answer many wacky questions.

Two people merit special mention. I probably regard Gary Schwartz's insights into life inside the academy (and beyond) more highly than anyone else's. They are invariably astute, and I am also constantly amused by them. Moreover, in an age of increasingly complex technologies, ours remains a steady, decidedly old-fashioned, and cherished epistolary relationship. Gary Schwartz is *sui generis*. He once observed that I am attracted to art "that reveals who hates who." I hope he finds that this book successfully amplifies that theme.

James Boyles has closely followed the progress of this project from its beginnings. He has variously acted as a sounding board, a reference librarian, and a cheerleader. Time and again our conversations have plucked me from the solitude of research and writing, and have refreshed and recharged my work. James has been extremely loyal and unfailingly kind. He is a good colleague and a good friend.

For all their support and encouragement, this book is for them: Gary Schwartz and James Boyles.

I

Introduction

Museums as Contested Sites

THE TIME: SPRING 1997. The place: outside the Russian embassy, a few blocks from the White House. The stakes: the future of East-West relations. A tense standoff drags on for days, while diplomats and other top-level negotiators scramble to defuse the situation and avert disaster. Was this a James Bond plot for the millennium? Perhaps another blockbuster sci-fi thriller?

The situation was all too real. But what was the problem: A proposed trade embargo? Human rights abuses? Nuclear disarmament? At issue were the Romanov family jewels and other royal ephemera, $100 million worth of it, crated up and packed into a mammoth moving van after pleasing crowds at the Corcoran Gallery of Art. The truck was boxed in by two cars bearing Russian diplomatic license plates. They refused to budge. And there the siege continued for nearly a week, as both Russian and American intermediaries debated whether the treasures could proceed to the Museum of Fine Arts in Houston or would instead be shipped back to Russia.

It was extremely difficult to fathom exactly what was going on. It seemed, however, to have something to do with deciding who in Russia should profit from the fees paid for the loan of these objects, and who controlled them. In the center of all this backroom intrigue was a Russian "mystery man" representing a new breed of post–Cold War entrepreneur, wheeling and dealing his way across the globe.

If you move beyond the inherent preposterousness of this situation, you can understand how it demonstrates that cultural matters increasingly have important political implications. Moreover, political matters are easily spun into cultural artifacts. For instance, Cold War relics become hot collectibles. When speaking of spacesuits and paintings of mushroom clouds, a dealer declares, "There's something sweet about it. . . . The Cold War is already looking antique." And the zany documentary *East Side Story* unearths the history of forty years of Soviet and Eastern bloc movie musicals, socialist schlock from behind the Iron Curtain, if you will. After presenting a cavalcade of film clips of singing pig farmers, tractor drivers, and factory hands from the "workers' paradise," the filmmaker slyly asks, "Who knows how things could have turned out if Socialism had just been more fun?"[1]

In this view, a political doctrine failed not because of theoretical flaws or chronic problems of official corruption, economic deprivation, and the suppression of individual liberties. Instead, it wasn't diverting enough, it didn't "have legs." It wasn't so much a case of Paine and Jefferson versus Marx and Lenin, but Hollywood versus East Berlin or Bucharest. And that, we know, is no contest.

More and more, symbolic politics is replacing realpolitik. People butt heads over representations and portrayals. They struggle for their interpretation of some historical moment to win out. They crusade to control what others know and feel about certain issues. For want of a better term, these are the so-called culture wars of the late 1980s and the 1990s that have commanded so many column inches of newsprint, prompted endless commentary on television and radio talk shows, and exposed innumerable worn spots in our social fabric.[2]

Politics does enter in to these tussles, particularly when legislators grandstand on behalf of truth, justice, and the American way. These are prime occasions to wrap oneself in virtue and try to deflect attention away from more concrete matters. In many instances these debates generate more heat than light. Once they've subsided, little has been fundamentally changed. But analogous to a "tagged gene," the marker for a certain hereditary trait but not the source of it, these cultural battles reveal tremendously important information about the body politic. They alert us to where the fault lines lie in our society.

One distinct variety of cultural war has centered on museums. Virtually sacred spaces in the past, museums have become hotly contested battlegrounds. But what we are currently witnessing in such places is rooted in our history. The terms of today's debates have important sources in the relatively recent past. In fact, one particularly controversial museum exhibition, *Harlem on My Mind* at the Metropolitan Museum of Art in 1969, displays most of the major features of more contemporary struggles. Certain strategies, arguments, and defenses may have been fresh then, but they have become common-places today.

You can't dream up scenes like the Great Russian-American Jewelry Truck Stalemate. You don't have to: they have been popping up with surprising regularity for the better part of a decade. *Displays of Power* will have a dual focus, then. In one respect this book will examine symbolic politics *as a process*, based on confrontations that flare up with great intensity and may then fade into relative obscurity over a brief interval. This captures the museum at its most evanescent, when the nature and tenor of the symbolic battles that are waged in and around these places can impact on their public identity and the ways they conduct their business. But the book will also investigate museums *as enduring institutions*. These are organizations that persist long after the shouting dies down.

Museums are important venues in which a society can define itself and present itself publicly. Museums *solidify* culture, endow it with a tangibility, in a way few other things do. Unflattering, embarrassing, or dissonant viewpoints are typically unwanted. For example, local politicians, leaders of the tourism industry, and members of the Italian American community fought against a "Chicago's Roaring '20s" museum for years, convinced that accenting the rat-a-tat-tat image of crime and corruption bordered on group libel. Or take Japan, where a museum specializing in wartime history commemorated the dead without addressing sensitive subjects such as the involuntary prostitution of other Asian women, slave labor, and monstrous medical experiments during World War II.[3] If museums stray from "making nice," they risk a confrontation with those who have a certain image to shield or an alternative image they would prefer to project.

The stories I will be telling are stories about power: losing it and gaining it, exercising it and resisting it. Museums have always featured *displays of power*: great men, great wealth, or great deeds. The emphasis could be on the spoils of war, victors in the marketplace, or man as the crown of creation. In all these instances, museums have ratified claims of superiority.

But nowadays, new ways of looking at and understanding the world can involve academic power plays. New entitlements symbolize political changes that can become fresh subject matter. Identity politics becomes operative in some instances, but not in others. Class is a critical factor in certain cases, in which social and corporate elites, "knowledge workers," or community-based groups struggle in various combinations. I will not attempt to force these examples into a single theoretical box; it is impossible to reduce all the variations of controversy into simply one pattern. There is, instead, a broad range of possibilities.

The responses contemporary exhibitions provoke are *displays of power* too. These responses are either defensive, trying to hold back the tides of change, or offensive, assertively demanding change. A variety of groups now challenge what museums are doing and press their distinctive claims for what they would like to see presented. *Displays of power* thus embody both action and reaction.

The timing of the controversy is crucial. In virtually every example I discuss, the outbreak of conflict occurs when power is shifting and the relative status of different groups is in flux. For example, *Gaelic Gotham: A History of the Irish in New York* emerged when the size of the Irish population and its political influence were seriously declining in comparison to other ethnic groups in New York City. *Sigmund Freud: Conflict and Culture* was proposed when psychoanalysis was losing favor because of advances in pharmacology, the impact of managed health care, and the pummeling that Freud and his theories have taken by revisionist scholars. *The West as America: Reinterpreting Images of the Frontier, 1820-1920* was developed at the same time that the promise of the mythical West had been debunked in crucial respects by writers, filmmakers, and the harsh realities of an uneven economy. *The Last Act: The Atomic Bomb and the End of World War II* provided an arena where the "victory culture" of an ingenuous older generation collided head-on with cheeky postmodernism.[4] Each of these disputes is symptomatic of much larger conditions, the visible footprints of the march of history. But rather than discussing these various episodes in strictly chronological order, I have arranged them with a thematic logic instead.

It's no exaggeration to claim that history and revisionism are central motifs of the 1990s, on both personal and social levels. Americans have become obsessed with reexamining who they are, where they've come from, and what they've done. In fact, if people feel they own anything today, it's their personal history. Just witness the much-remarked-on proliferation of memoirs published during the 1990s. Or consider the response to the memorial work of Melinda Hunt and Margot Lovejoy. Their ill-fated proposal for a collaborative public art installation entitled *Just Outside the City*, invoking the mostly forgotten potter's field beneath New York's City Hall Park, troubled certain constituencies within the African American community. For Hunt, a potter's field is "A great pot of history with people all smooshed up. But today no one wants to be smooshed together; every group wants to be distinct."[5] "Who, *me*?" their critics seemed to be saying. "*My kind of people certainly wouldn't be buried in a place like that!*"

The authenticity of lived experience is a powerful credential to invoke, and it is virtually impossible for someone else to rebut without seeming arrogant or insensitive. While many people may generally feel that a wide gulf exists between them and what goes on in museums, they can quickly surmount that distance if they feel they are being misrepresented in an exhibition. Moreover, the "*Roots* phenomenon" adds a group dimension to this sense of ownership. Perceived distortions can become fighting words, intolerable "dissing" that activists must redress to salve bruised egos and restore a sense of respect.

Museums and their exhibitions have become controversial sites in a number of respects over the past few years. They no longer merely provide a pleasant refuge from ordinary life, nor are they simply repositories of received wisdom. Museums have moved to the forefront in struggles over representation and over the chronicling, revising, and displaying of the past. Museums today differ greatly from their predecessors.

The sixteenth- and seventeenth-century *Wunderkammer*, for example, combined mechanical devices, shells and stones, skulls and bones, carvings, globes, books, paintings, and artillery in one chamber—a hodgepodge of whatever struck the fancy of an aristocrat or wealthy merchant. Or there are spectacular, sprawling collections like the eighteenth-century Teylers Museum in Haarlem, the Netherlands, room after room crammed to its skylit ceiling with fossils, gems and crystals, Old Master drawings, and H. G. Wells–type technology. But museums today are much more specialized, generally featuring either art, history, or natural history.

These distinctions are easy to outline on paper, but in the real world there is, of course, some overlap. Nearly anything can form the basis for an exhibition or a collection, from the National Cryptologic

Museum (highlighting technology that safeguards information) to the Fragonard Museum (displaying *écorchés*, or flayed cadavers of man and beast); museums that feature comic books, advertising icons, toilets, or nuts; places that commemorate Norman Rockwell, Dan Quayle, or the "American Dream."[6]

Contemporary museums are potentially accountable to diverse constituencies instead of being subject to the whims of a single wealthy patron or collector. They are buffeted by intellectual fads and trends, as Patrick Murphy, the director of Philadelphia's Institute of Contemporary Art, addresses with mock exasperation: "Now not only are you a looker at art, but you must be a looker of art either from the Lacanian camp, the Baudrillardian camp, the Derridian camp (or the Branch Derridians, as they're referred to), who knows, even the Pavlovians. But it's almost creating a hermetic language of a priesthood."[7] The practice of history is influenced by many of the same social and intellectual trends, and by the vigilance of groups who challenge how they are depicted, or the fact that they are displayed at all.

Even natural history museums feel the tug of new ideas and new demands. According to an official at the Smithsonian Institution, the nineteenth-century "paradigm of progress is rapidly shifting. . . . No longer viewed as the vertical masters of a natural order over which we were given dominion, Western peoples increasingly view themselves as participants in a horizontally interconnected ecological system and an interdependent, pluralistic cultural system."[8] That recognition has arrived none too soon: natural history museums, like others, have come under increasing scrutiny. Critics of "teddy bear patriarchy"—Great White Fathers who killed, stuffed, or had artists sculpt specimens of other animal species or human races—reveal the racist, sexist, and colonialist roots of many of the founders. Journalistic exposés highlight turn-of-the-century conduct that is contemptible by today's standards. For example, New York City's American Museum of Natural History once displayed living Eskimos, a painfully embarrassing revelation. An additional detail reveals shameful practices that have no place in contemporary museums: a young Eskimo boy accidentally viewed his own father's skeleton on exhibit after the man and most of his cohorts died there of tuberculosis. Such institutions now self-consciously try to consult with and include people as subjects, not treat them as mere objects.[9]

Moreover, museums also struggle to survive in a complex world of competing organizations, all jockeying for funding, publicity, and paying customers. Museums have had to learn to hustle to support their programs. The most obvious example is the growing importance of museum stores, which have become a multimillion-dollar source of revenue. They now offer everything from temporary tattoos and coffee mugs emblazoned with reproductions of their prime treasures, to pasta in the shape of Rodin's *Thinker* and baseballs bearing the "autographs" of artistic heavy hitters.[10]

In 1997 the American Museum of Natural History took this a step further to market *Endangered! Exploring a World at Risk*. It launched a major ad campaign and also initiated a tie-in with the retail giant F.A.O. Schwartz to sell plush toy versions of the different species featured in the exhibition. That same year the museum also blew the dust off years of tradition and premiered a flashy new dinosaur display. *The Lost World* shared its title with the Steven Spielberg film; the exhibition employed the extensive know-how of movie prop makers; and it installed theatrical lighting to grab the attention of media-savvy youngsters and their parents. It was reviewed as extensively and enthusiastically as a summertime blockbuster hit.

A great deal has changed since Joseph C. Choate, a founding trustee of the Metropolitan Museum of Art, implored the dignitaries gathered for its 1880 dedication to generously endorse this new venture:

> Think of it, ye millionaires of many markets—what glory may yet be yours, if you only listen to our advice, to convert pork into porcelain, grain and produce into priceless pottery . . . and railroad shares and mining stocks . . . into the glorified canvas of the world's masters, that shall adorn these walls for centuries. The rage of Wall Street is to hunt the philosopher's stone, to convert all baser things into gold, which is but dross; but ours is the higher ambition to convert your useless gold into things of living beauty.[11]

Yet on closer examination, have certain matters changed so significantly? Museums always have been reliant on benefactors, and benefactors often possess ulterior motives for their largesse: they may be seeking self-aggrandizement or trying to neutralize their reputations as heartless capitalists. In the latter part of the twentieth century they have been joined by corporations or government sponsors that wish to appear attuned to the public's needs and hope to exchange monetary capital for cultural currency. For example, the German menswear designer Hugo Bass sponsors exhibits and an annual prize bearing his name through the Guggenheim Museum, while Cartier, Fabergé, and Christian Dior have all underwritten shows featuring their companies' products at the Metropolitan Museum of Art. When the Met hurriedly assembled an exhibition of the fashions of the slain designer Gianni Versace in 1997, the sold-out, celebrity-studded opening-night gala raised millions of dollars for the museum and was heralded as the social event of the decade. All these activities blur the lines between commerce, hucksterism, and culture.[12]

Just a few years ago, the culture wars primarily focused on specific artists who belonged to marginalized groups or practiced newer art forms. Artists like Robert Mapplethorpe, Andres Serrano, and Karen Finley were cited again and again as fiendish schemers who were ripping off taxpayers and threatening the American way of life. Those individual artists were relatively unprotected by supportive institutions and were therefore extremely susceptible to attack.

Museums, whether they feature art, history, or something else, have become a principal target instead. In the earlier phase of conflict, it was easy to dismiss the attacks on artists as affecting only provocative outcasts. Nowadays, issues revolving around representation and responsibility, the control of expression, and elitism versus populism have infiltrated mainstream establishments, places that embody America for its own citizens and for the rest of the world.

While museums might seem much better equipped to defend themselves, they too are extremely vulnerable. They are beholden to others in more ways than individuals are. They have multiple pressure points, organizational nerve endings connected to funders, exhibit sponsors, trustees, curators and administrative staff, audiences, and the legacy of historical mandates. These are powerful constraints, each one potentially decreasing the institution's degrees of freedom. Museums are more anchored than individual artists, which can be a mixed blessing. They are certainly not wholly independent to operate as they wish.

To reiterate, museums are not sealed in a bubble. What goes on generally in the culture affects how they operate; how they do their work likewise affects related cultural activities. Why, exactly, have museums in particular become battlegrounds? First, there is the legacy of community empowerment and self-determination that surfaced in the 1960s in poor people's movements, civil rights activities, and anti–Vietnam War protestors' support for the North Vietnamese as waging a populist struggle against Western domination. To Jane Mc-Namara of the Museum of the City of New York,

> Museums have brought some of it on themselves. In the late '60s and '70s museums started to look around and say, "Wait a second, we want to involve people in the community." And I think what's happened is you invite people in, and then you have to be able to deal with the consequences, create boundaries and relationships that are productive. And I think that's what's happening now, trying to figure out where those lines are.[13]

A second factor is the "new social history." Historians have cast their nets in a broader and deeper arc since the 1960s. No longer settling for the exclusive accounts of the highly profiled rich and powerful, they now cast for "history from below." Historians are much more attuned to previously untapped and unconventional sources of information and artifacts, and many are committed to re-creating the overlooked lives of the common person. That too provides a challenge for today's museum.

As Jan Ramirez, also of the Museum of the City of New York, reflects, "The new social history has been a very positive but very challenging thing for us in the history museum. Many of us have inherited collections that on first blush are not going to let all that many people find themselves in them." She continues,

> If you're going to structure exhibitions so that people of a variety of backgrounds can come and find themselves, you are going to have to jostle people. Because you know, in creating room for one group to come and find themselves, you're eclipsing the traditional story that you were telling for another. And they may be your benefactors. And how do you then develop new benefactors, because you always have to have not only financial support, but vocal moral and political and social support for your institution.[14]

Sherrill D. Wilson directs the Office of Public Education and Interpretation of the African Burial Ground. When backhoes digging the foundation for a new skyscraper in downtown Manhattan in 1991 disturbed the centuries-old slumber of what was known in the colonial era as the Negros Burying Ground, they exposed much more than human skeletons. They laid bare the racial breach that has long divided this country. The intense struggle between the "descendent community," government officials, and scientists for control of the remains demonstrates that the controversies over representation that this book focuses on stretch far beyond museum walls. Wilson notes that in the past "people everywhere would like to say, 'George Washington took a piss right over there.' 'We'll build a shrine. We'll build a monument.' Right there you're creating vested interest. But today we believe everybody's played a role in creating history."[15]

Moreover, the fact that cultural issues became so controversial in the late 1980s and early 1990s has had an unforeseen consequence. The general public heard much more about such matters than it had in the past because of congressional debates over the National Endowment for the Arts and the National Endowment for the Humanities, extensive media coverage of outré artworks, and even court cases involving indictments on obscenity. The public also became more aware that in certain instances it was picking up part of the tab for this material. Culture is accorded additional importance today, even if it also seems increasingly problematic. More people appear to be concerned about the direction cultural production is taking and how much *they* are paying for it.

Without doubt, museums are becoming democratized. The historian Edward T. Linenthal argues that contemporary museums are more like forums than temples.[16] Frequently these days, different groups press their distinctive claims there. At present, groups define their identities by claiming an exclusivity of oppression or citing singular legacies, traditions, and experiences. That leaves little room for exploring common ground. Nevertheless, encounters between groups are increasing on this turf. A cacophony of demands often leads to an elaborate call and response of charges and countercharges that rapidly picks up speed and intensity.

This state of affairs obviously did not crystallize overnight. Duncan F. Cameron of the Brooklyn Museum viewed these tensions in embryonic form when he made these startlingly prescient observations in 1972: "Our museums are in desperate need of psychotherapy. There is abundant evidence of an identity crisis in some of the major institutions while others are in an advanced state of schizo-

phrenia." Writing during an era of widespread social protest and upheaval, Cameron was a firsthand witness to what was happening
when museums initially opened their doors to broader audiences
and made their exhibition schedules more inclusive. He also predicted the type of conflict that has become habitual in recent years
when he made the following distinction: "[T]he forum is where the
battles are fought, the temple is where the victors rest. The former is
process, the latter is product."[17] Cameron believed that these two
missions should not be blended. But they have, of course, with ex-
plosive results.

This leads to questions that generally surface in discussions
around contemporary museums: "*Should* the community be involved
in exhibitions?" "*Do* people have a right to offer input or to exercise
oversight, especially when the subject directly relates to them?" But I
don't intend to pose *shoulds*. The awesome doors to these institutions
have opened up to a degree, so that they are no longer as rarified as
they once were. People now feel entitled to participate in these venues, and it would be very difficult to seal them up tightly again. I am
interested in examining the consequences of these developments
rather than assigning one position supremacy over another.

To my mind, the most important points are these: Why do exhibits rouse such passion? Why do groups feel that so much is at
stake in what is depicted in museums and how it is presented? When
do these controversies erupt? What do they demonstrate about more
fundamental social issues? Why can't exhibitions just be dismissed as
irrelevant or simply wrong? The frequency, intensity, and specific
timing of these struggles are what pique my interest the most.

Examining culture is never simply a case of "what you see is what
you get." Reaching a thorough understanding of cultural phenomena
requires conducting several layers of analysis. First one must understand the creator's intention. Whether making a painting or assembling a museum exhibition, the designer has certain meanings in
mind, messages that s/he wishes to communicate. Sometimes these
can be elusive. Sometimes even the creators may not be fully conscious of their own motives, or they become apparent only later. Even
so, this is merely the first stage in generating meaning. Culture is dynamic, always in transformation. As Picasso argued, "when [a paint-
ing] is finished, it goes on changing, according to the state of mind of

whoever is looking at it. A picture lives a life like a living creature, undergoing the changes imposed on us by our life from day to day."[18]

Second, one must understand the social context, that "life from day to day." This entails "the stuff" creators draw on to generate their work. Race, gender, social class, current events, and history are prime examples. Of course, in our own time, these subjects are all disputed. The family no longer has a solitary model like the Cleavers or the Nelsons. The West is now seen as an arena of greed, exploitation, and incipient class and race warfare, not just a field of heroic dreams. Even heroes—maybe especially heroes—are being toppled. Explorers like Columbus are as likely to be reviled as conquerors as they are to be honored as discoverers.

Finally, there is reception, or what the viewer brings to the exchange. Audiences come crammed with preferences, biases, pleasant and unpleasant experiences and memories, which all channel how they understand their world. Audiences may in fact "get it," just as an artist or curator intended. But there is also a great deal of room for possible slippage. For example, a controversy developed in Boston when a gas company prepared to repaint a rainbow design on a large storage tank, something of a local landmark. Some Vietnam veterans objected, claiming that they spotted the likeness of North Vietnam's Ho Chi Minh in the blue stripe.[19] Many others were frankly puzzled by this claim of special sight.

The original artist in this case was Sister Corita Kent, well-known in the 1960s and 1970s for her breezy watercolors and humanistic, inspirational poetry. If any art should pass muster with middle Americans, one would expect it to be Corita Kent's. But Kent was a bit more complex than her work immediately suggests. She went beyond cloying daily meditations. She also opposed the Vietnam War. That fact may have acted as a filter on the vets' perception.

They were as confident of their vision as were the three young cousins who claimed to see the Virgin Mary hovering in the skies over Fatima, Portugal. But to what extent do such people project their personal needs, interests, and anxieties onto a scrim? Artists and museums are much more self-reflexive about the issue of reception today. One of the most exciting consequences of the Robert Mapplethorpe controversy is that the cycle of assessment and reassessment of the artist's work continues. Glenn Ligon's contribution to the Whitney Museum of American Art's 1993 biennial was *Notes on the*

FIG. 1. Fred Wilson, *Truth Trophy*, 1992. Courtesy of the artist and Metro Pictures.

Margin of the Black Book: the artist arranged two long rows of Mapplethorpe photographs along the walls. Sandwiched between them were two rows of framed quotations revealing every shade of opinion about this body of work. The viewer was nudged first toward one political, aesthetic, or philosophical position and then another, with a dizzying multiplicity of voices. Ligon has helped insure that no one response is the last word.

The contemporary artist Fred Wilson redirects his audience's attention to issues of colonialism and racism underlying museum practice. In *Mining the Museum*, his "intervention" at the Maryland Historical Society, Wilson combed through the collections of this staid, nineteenth-century collection and mounted his own displays. In *Cabinet Making, 1820-1910,* Wilson set up a selection of Victorian chairs as an audience of mute witnesses to a whipping post. In *Metalwork, 1723-1880,* he filled a vitrine with ornate silver serving pieces surrounding slave shackles. These wry, deadpan taxonomies first mask and then uncover the significance of museum classifications. One room featured a trio of portrait busts of famous white men set across from a trio of three empty black pedestals. They all flanked a globe embossed with the word "truth." In other spots Wilson wrote new wall labels to name and highlight previously overlooked black figures in paintings, and changed the overhead lighting to steer a viewer's attention to where *he* desired they look.

In Wilson's words, "I disrupt the standard way of looking at museums. . . . Museums pride themselves on being objective, and they don't want you to believe that there's a view that they're producing. And so to sort of pierce that is what they're all afraid of. It's really [about] how it's been done and how they want to keep it."[20] Wilson reveals how reception is typically molded along certain lines and not along others. He forces viewers to question both institutional and personal biases, their effect on what we see, and the meanings we ultimately attach to what we're viewing.

Can we speak of shaping perceptions and not address the role of the media? Media accounts are commonly pivotal in constructing, amplifying, and sustaining the types of controversies that flare up in museums and around memorialization. In many instances, these events provide an ongoing saga that the media can revisit again and again. Bottom line: the media can't resist these juicy stories, and few people can resist the media's glare. In fact, they often wave their arms wildly to be caught within its range. The precise role the media play warrants close scrutiny, especially where it appears to fan the flames or helps pump up the volume on the rhetoric.

Moreover, the role of ideologues of various stripes is also critical in these controversies: ideologues frequently contribute to how these public tussles are scripted and how they are ultimately played out. But note: the impulse to quash expression is not the exclusive domain of either the political Right or the Left. As the cultural critic Kobena Mercer argues, "the new social actors of race, gender, ethnicity, and sexuality are just as capable of antidemocratic politics as the old social actors of class, party, and nation-state."[21]

The absolutist mind-set has been a perennial subject for academics and cultural observers, from the "authoritarian personality" developed by Theodor Adorno and his colleagues, to such distinctions as the "rigid versus fuzzy" mind, noncosmopolitans versus cosmopolitans, or the culturally conservative or orthodox versus cultural progressivists.[22] All these concepts address the differences between uncompromising or flexible stances toward the world, and the ability or willingness to tolerate difference and social change.

Ideologues polarize issues *in extremis*. Their activities make traditional distinctions, such as a political continuum extending from right to left, seem obsolete. That line is now being bent into more of a horseshoe shape. As a result, many of those in the center may be pulled toward the extremes at either end. However, no matter how pitched these battles become, there's always a great mass in the middle that will remain relatively oblivious to and unaffected by the issues.

There are, of course, professional ideologues, individuals whose lives are dedicated to mounting crusades against dissimilar values and beliefs. Many of these individuals have become quite well known through their public statements and activities. But I argue that any of us can act on the inclination to behave as an ideologue when our own buttons are pushed. Being an ideologue is a stance people can assume and then abandon. It is not necessarily fixed for all time. In fact, when you speak directly to someone acting in this manner—especially away from the pressure of the conflict—they often present rational accounts of their motives and concerns, and make everything they're thinking and doing seem perfectly reasonable. The conduct ideologues engage in is obviously situational as well as psychological.

I have personal as well as professional reasons for writing this book. For the past decade or so I have written and lectured extensively about cultural controversies. To use an imprecise term, my academic life has focused on "censorship," and freedom of expression issues. My many bulging file cabinets attest to my fascination with these matters.

In 1994 I made my first formal foray into the world of museums when I became a member of the curatorial team for *Art, Design, and Barbie: The Making of a Cultural Icon,* an exhibition slated to tour nationally and internationally. After nearly a year of challenging work with an energetic and talented group of people, I was summarily dismissed at the eleventh hour by order of Mattel, which, I belatedly discovered, was footing the bill. Furthermore, every word I'd written for the catalogue was rejected because it was deemed "unflattering" to Mattel's premier product. Matters that I knew about intellectually I suddenly understood experientially. I too had "been there." I had become a different kind of expert.

As the journalist Janet Malcolm observes, "The writer, like the murderer, needs a motive."[23] But I have no interest in producing yet another book about Barbie. Nor is this an exercise in revenge; I have secured that already through a series of articles I've written, including the essay "How I Got Screwed by Barbie: A Cautionary Tale."[24] Rather, to borrow an idea from the anthropologist Claude Lévi-Strauss, I argue that Barbie is "good to think with." That is, my personal experiences with Mattel taught me a great deal about contemporary patronage, about the current state of museums, about culture high and low, and about the collision of different perspectives in the somewhat mystifying process of generating cultural goods and cultural meanings. In other words, my experience was not an isolated one.

The terrain to be explored in *Displays of Power* is exacting and confusing. There are no precise road maps to follow, no landmarks by which to gauge your progress, no one source to depend on as a guide. The ground—that is, the moral high ground—seems to shift frequently. Accusations of intellectual fraud, McCarthyism, or censorship whiz back and forth. When you speak directly to major players, you get the impression that the other side is rigid and uncompromising and, of course, is at fault. That is, until you hear the competing story. It's almost like being a war correspondent where the combatants are continually switching uniforms.

I've come to understand that all my informants are thoughtful, and indeed earnest, about what they believe in. But I have spoken with them away from the heat of battle, when they've been expressly minding their manners. When they confront their foes, it's another story. And it's often yet *another* story once it's processed through the various lenses of the media.

It would be markedly easier to write about these conflicts if there were obvious heroes and equally obvious villains. But that is certainly not the case. To one person, revisionism may offer an equitable and overdue way to set the record straight. Yet to another person it can seem misguided and excessive, merely a way to even old scores. One side calls for openness and participation in the curatorial process, an appeal to democratic action; the other sees this as heavy-handed, uninformed, and unprofessional interference. Both, however, are defending important principles. One faction argues that "fairness" and "balance" are desirable and within grasp; another counters that those axioms don't always apply to cultural matters. My goal is to understand how and why people invoke these diverse principles when they do, and to look at when they are willing to go to the mat for them. I intend to let as many voices speak as I can, and then probe the various messages that are being dispatched.

2

Crossing 125th Street

Harlem on My Mind Revisited

Gershwin. He comes from another oppressed people so he understands.
—George C. Wolfe, *The Colored Museum*

FOR THOSE AMERICANS who lived through the 1960s, the tumult
and the excitement, the sense of things falling apart or beginning
anew, the fervor, the naïveté, and above all the emotionally charged
rhetoric are all easily recalled. For those who did not experience this
era directly, it can be conjured up without much difficulty. Scan any
issue of the *New York Times* during this period. You can reanimate the
zeitgeist as easily as a baby boomer once added water to produce the
mysterious sea monkeys commonly advertised in the back of their
comic books.

Pluck a day from the calendar—let's say, January 31, 1969. Three
hundred students occupied the administration building at the University of Chicago, enraged over the dismissal of a popular Marxist
sociology professor. On the campuses of San Francisco State and the
University of California, Berkeley, police on foot and on horseback
broke up demonstrators lobbying for ethnic studies departments.
Also in California, Sirhan Sirhan, the accused assassin of the presidential hopeful Senator Robert F. Kennedy, challenged the composition of the grand jury that indicted him for the 1968 murder.

Governor Nelson Rockefeller recommended stiffer penalties
against unions of public employees after strikes and slowdowns the
preceding year by city teachers, sanitation workers, police, and fire-
fighters crippled New York City. Youth violence was front-page news.
School desegregation lurched along fitfully between reform and re-

sistance. S. Dillon Ripley, the head of the Smithsonian Institution, acceded to the demands of Lady Bird Johnson that a portrait of her husband be consigned to storage; three years earlier, then President Johnson had declared the likeness of him by the artist Peter Hurd to be the ugliest thing he ever saw.

A pervasive sense of upheaval and crisis was sustained internationally as well. The perplexing and divisive war in Vietnam raged on. The bloody Tet offensive had been launched exactly one year earlier, intensifying American apprehension about military involvement in Southeast Asia. In Iraq, the hangings of fourteen people accused of spying for Israel evoked worldwide condemnation, while the trial of thirty-five additional individuals—including 13 Jews—on similar charges generated great concern.

All these events provide a backdrop for a local story that had been garnering attention for weeks. In a front-page, top-of-the-fold report that day, a headline declared, "Museum Withdraws Catalogue Attacked as a Slur on Jews." The museum in question was New York City's Metropolitan Museum of Art, and the show was *Harlem on My Mind: The Culture Capital of Black America, 1900–1968,* possibly the most controversial American exhibition ever mounted. In fact, the *New York Post Magazine* credited it with sparking the biggest public flap since Marcel Duchamp's *Nude Descending a Staircase* shocked visitors to the 1913 Armory show.[1] In 1969 this exhibit or its catalogue infuriated blacks, horrified Jews, purportedly smeared the Irish, slighted Puerto Ricans, teed off artists and art critics, and propelled the Jewish Defense League, the Black Emergency Cultural Coalition, and members of the right-wing John Birch Society all into upper Fifth Avenue to man picket lines in front of the Met.

Harlem on My Mind is a landmark. It opened the doors of cultural institutions to multimedia technology. It helped define the blockbuster exhibition. It launched at least one person's career, but hobbled several others'. And, depending on whom you listen to, it either insulted Harlem residents and black artists, shattered significant racial barriers in museums, or frightened these institutions away from addressing racial topics for years to come. As is true for any watershed event, each of these observations captures some bit of the truth.

Harlem on My Mind also provides a template for the museum-centered controversies that followed in its wake, many of them surging over the social landscape like a *tsunami* a quarter century or so later.

Features that are common to these events in the 1990s actually have deep sources: the acute breach between groups occurring along racial, ethnic, generational, and ideological lines, the dig-in-the-heels, take-no-prisoners bombast, and the demands for accountability in the use of public funds as a way to leverage control over content may all be commonplaces today, but they were relatively fresh developments in 1969. In hindsight the inevitability of this conflict becomes excruciatingly clear: *Harlem on My Mind* pushed on an array of civic pressure points, inducing cries of pain in several quarters.

With its imposing Beaux Arts facade, squatting on the rim of Central Park, the Metropolitan Museum of Art oversees tony Fifth Avenue like a dowager queen. With the appointment of Thomas P. F. Hoving as director in April 1967, the Met embarked on a tumultuous ten-year odyssey that tested its prim and poised reputation. Hoving was not shy about tweaking noses. He granted that the initials *P.F.* stood for "publicity forever," thus inviting association with the hucksterism of a P. T. Barnum. In a lengthy cover story in the *New York Times Magazine*, the art reporter Grace Glueck dutifully noted his "modishly-longer hair" and the dismissive moniker "Tom Swift and his Electric Museum," coined by a detractor dissatisfied with Hoving's fledgling stewardship.[2]

Hoving brought a blend of charisma, youthful good looks, and ambition to his position, akin to what John F. Kennedy had used to turn Washington, D.C., into Camelot, and that John Lindsay was also exploiting as mayor of New York City. He bore a distinguished pedigree and splendid credentials: he was the son of the chairman of Tiffany's, he held multiple degrees from Princeton, and during the five years he spent at the medieval collection called the Cloisters, he worked his way up to the position of curator. At the age of thirty-six, Hoving left his briefly held post as New York parks commissioner—where he turned the city into the staging ground for what some critics felt was threatening to become an unremitting Happening—to assume control of the country's wealthiest museum. Chartered in 1870, the Met was also among the oldest and most conservative. *Making the Mummies Dance*, Hoving's controversial chronicle of the years 1967 to 1977, takes its title from a remark made to him by Mayor Lindsay when he first took the helm, sensing that Hoving would breathe new life into the venerable institution.[3]

Tom Hoving wanted the museum to be "relevant." He wanted the museum to be "now." Soon after he came aboard, a Department of Contemporary Arts was established for the first time, headed by the young Henry Geldzahler, whose social circles intersected with Andy Warhol's Factory and the pre-Stonewall gay demimonde. It looked as though the Met was no longer going to be merely a temple to the sacred past.

According to Joseph Noble, the vice director for administration under Hoving, "When Tommy came he wanted to do a show, but it had to be quick. And that meant it had to be something from within the house, stuff we had in the Metropolitan. He came up with a damn good idea. He called the show *In the Presence of Kings*. And it was all royal paraphernalia."[4] Featuring crowns, scepters, suits of armor, and even the kennel of Marie Antoinette's pet dog, that show fell foursquare within the museum's symbolic boundaries. It became a success. Not so the display of James Rosenquist's enormous ten- by eighty-six-foot Pop Art mural *F-111* early in 1968. In this billboard-sized painting, the fighter-bomber provides the backdrop for a smattering of Technicolor images such as a smiling girl under a hair dryer, an angel food cake, and a twisted mass of spaghetti. Linking smug materialism with militarism, its antiwar sentiments played off three history paintings hanging alongside: Poussin's *Rape of the Sabine Women*, David's *Death of Socrates*, and Emanuel Leutze's *Washington Crossing the Delaware*. The mini-exhibition was blasted by the prominent critics Hilton Kramer and John Canaday, for whom this contemporary behemoth had invaded hallowed space.

That mini-show was a teaser, a brief foreshadowing of the trouble that would follow. Noble recollects that "Tom wanted to do something that he could really put his imprimatur on, and not just have something that was around the Metropolitan anyway." When Hoving first announced *Harlem on My Mind* at a staff meeting, the curator-in-chief, Theodore Rousseau, said, "'Oh, that's wonderful. I've got some wonderful paintings. Which Harlem do you mean?' Tom laughed and said, 'The one north of us.' And Ted shut up and he never opened his mouth again about *Harlem on My Mind*." Rousseau may have perked up his ears at what he initially assumed would be a survey of the golden age of Dutch painting. Soon enough, it would become clear that they were all greeting a new breed of dog that would prove to be lame at this hunt.

■

It was actually Allon Schoener's brainchild. Schoener, who was trained as an art historian, produced over one hundred television programs for the San Francisco Museum of Art in the early 1950s. He was an aficionado of new communications technology, deeply influenced by Charles and Ray Eames,[5] and then by the writings of Marshall McLuhan. Later as the director of the Contemporary Arts Center in Cincinnati, Schoener produced *Cincinnati Plus and Minus*, his first venture in creating an exhibition as a total cultural environment. Schoener also masterminded *The Lower East Side: Portal to American Life (1870-1924)* at New York City's Jewish Museum while he was the assistant director there in 1966, and he then became the visual arts director of the New York State Council on the Arts (NYSCA).

The Lower East Side show integrated sound, image, and text to re-create the teeming immigrant Jewish ghetto. It enveloped the visitor in a startlingly different way with slide projections, films, photo murals, and recordings, and was both a critical and popular success. On the face of it, there was every reason to expect that Schoener could achieve something similar with Harlem. The reality proved to be much more complex.

The texts making up the Lower East Side show and its catalogue drew heavily from the writings of immigrant Jews themselves. The documentary images were not only photographs, but paintings bearing signatures such as Walkowitz, Soyer, Gross, Epstein, and Weber. In other words, Jewish artists were well represented. Moreover, by this time large portions of the Jewish community had moved on from the immigrant experience, geographically and financially. The Jewish Lower East Side was generally yesterday, not today; it was sufficiently in the past to serve as prime symbolic real estate for nostalgic reflection. The exhibition also provided an occasion for self-congratulation, a tangible measure of how far one ethnic group had progressed to realize the American Dream.

It was a different story in Harlem, which had long been, and continued to be, a largely impoverished, segregated quarter that offered few escape routes to blacks. According to Schoener,

> Well, the Lower East Side show was sort of a sentimental meditation on life at another time, and it didn't have a political agenda. And the Harlem show had a very clear-cut political agenda. I mean, the objective of the exhibition was to create an awareness that didn't exist.

So it questioned some very fundamental attitudes. And it dealt with what is still a major issue in American life, racism.[6]

Racism was unmistakably in the forefront of the public's consciousness in 1968 while *Harlem on My Mind* was being designed. That same year, the Black Panther minister of information, Eldridge Cleaver, published his searing book *Soul on Ice*; the American athletes Tommie Smith and John Carlos gave the Black Power salute on the winners' platform during the Mexico City Olympics; and the Reverend Martin Luther King, Jr., was assassinated in April in Memphis, sparking riots in Washington, D.C., Chicago, Kansas City, Newark, Trenton, Hartford, and a bloody roster of other cities, dashing many people's dream of an integrated, nonviolent society. Moreover, links between blacks and Jews, forged out of a shared sense of oppression and minority status and through extensive collaboration in the civil rights movement, were rapidly coming uncoupled. Growing militancy and the desire for self-determination by more vocal segments of the black community made the martyrdom of the black and white civil rights activists Michael Schwerner, Andrew Goodman, and James Cheney seem a part of ancient history, even though they had been murdered in Mississippi only four years before. Both blacks and Jews increasingly turned inward, blacks wishing to control their own fate, and Jews focusing on Israel, Soviet Jewry, and other concerns directly affecting their brethren.

In New York City, black-Jewish tensions exploded in a spectacular way in the Ocean Hill–Brownsville section of Brooklyn. The issue was the decentralization of control of the schools. The rhetorical context is exquisitely captured in a letter to the editor published in the Harlem-based *New York Amsterdam News*, signed simply "Black Brother":

> The beautiful soul blacks want some power. . . . Obviously the whole white power structure will shut down all schools . . . if it is necessary to keep the niggers in their place. [T]ough beautiful soul blacks . . . are incapable of being anti-Semitic. That kind of jive shows the sick minds of some poor whiteys. . . . The blacks have been up against the wall for a good while now. And they ain't afraid. "How long blues" is a part of the black experience and now the cats talk about black-stone-soul. Struggle with it brothers and sisters. Better grave than slave![7]

In this particular Brooklyn district, one of three experimental sites introducing decentralization, a locally elected community governing board transferred out a group of teachers and administrators. The neighborhood was 95 percent black and Puerto Rican; all the transferred teachers were Jewish, as was much of the membership and the leadership of the United Federation of Teachers, including its pugnacious leader, Albert Shanker. (As several commentators noted at the time, whites typically interacted with minority ghetto residents only in their capacity as landlords, business owners, teachers, or welfare workers; many times these people, experienced as exploiters, were Jews.) The UFT called three strikes in 1968, shutting down most of the schools for fifty-five days. It was a battle very much staged in the media's glare: charges and countercharges sailed back and forth on the nightly news as each side exposed the boundless corruption and villainy of the other.

The black community was primed for a fight against what it perceived to be an oppressive, alien, ineffective bureaucracy. Jews felt betrayed for all their sincere efforts, and very much under assault. Accusations of "mental genocide" were met by epithets such as "Black Nazis," "hoodlums," "extremists," and "vigilantes." The constant polemic dominated both the print and broadcast media.

At one juncture, a virulently anti-Semitic tract was placed in some teachers' school mailboxes in Brooklyn. Slamming white instructors as "Money Changers," the leaflet threw down the gauntlet of black nationalism:

> If African American History and Culture is to be taught to our Black Children it Must be Done By African Americans who Identify With And Who Understand The Problem. It Is Impossible For The Middle East Murderers of Colored People to Possibly Bring To This Important Task The Insight, The Concern, The Exposing Of The Truth That is a *Must* If the Years Of Brainwashing And Self-Hatred That Has Been Taught To Our Black Children By Those Bloodsucking Exploiters and Murderers Is To Be OverCome.[8]

Shanker publicized the contents, giving the document an influential public life. Later it was discovered that the leaflet bore the endorsement of a parents' community council that did not exist, as well as other fraudulent details. Its exact origins remained a mystery.[9]

This struggle created a huge breach between New Yorkers, and the repercussions continue to be felt even now. Shanker's obituary in the *New York Times* nearly thirty years later was headlined "Albert Shanker, 68, Combative Leader of Teachers, Dies," and an editorial soon thereafter called the "school wars" of 1968 "corrosive," leaving a "painful legacy."[10] In a city known for its belligerent style, this struggle over the schools was especially nasty. It reflected a climate of suspicion and mistrust that already existed between whites and blacks, and also helped set the terms of the debate over *Harlem on My Mind*.

This was Allon Schoener's exhibition: "I ran the show, and there's no question about it. I mean, it was my concept and my direction." His proposal was to present a sixty-year panorama of Harlem history divided into six sections, roughly by decade. Photographs were to be enlarged to gigantic proportions, audio speakers would broadcast period music and the voices of Harlem residents, and slide projectors would flash images at a staccato pace, creating a dynamic, pulsating environment. Visitors would sample a broad array of sights, from poverty to glitz: everyday street scenes, private homes, commercial life, exuberant dancers, glamorous sports figures and celebrities, political demonstrations, and chaotic riots. The final statistics are impressive: seven hundred photographs (some as large as fifty feet long and eighteen feet high) and five hundred projected images.

Harlem on My Mind was publicly announced on November 16, 1967, at a press conference attended by Mayor Lindsay, Hoving, and the Honorable Percy E. Sutton, president of the borough of Manhattan. In the press release, Hoving emphasized the Met's "deep responsibility" to facilitate communication and a creative confrontation between whites and blacks. He argued that this signalled not a rupture with the Met's past, but continuity: just as Rembrandt or Degas revealed particular worlds to their audiences, so too would *Harlem on My Mind*. In a classic gesture of *noblesse oblige* seasoned by '60s liberalism, Hoving declared, "This isn't going to be a white hand-out to Harlem. The Museum's role is simply that of a broker for channeling of ideas. You might say we're attempting to tune in on something we've been tuned out on."[11]

Two points made that day became hotly contested later. One was the notion of "community participation," a goal that many people in

FIG. 2. 1900–1919 section of *Harlem on My Mind* exhibition, 1969. People standing in front of the photo enlargement begin to merge with the image. From the collection of Allon Schoener. Used by permission.

Harlem felt was never fully realized, even though notables such as Sutton and Jean Blackwell Hutson from the Schomburg Collection of Negro Literature and History were among those listed as "cooperating and participating" in the enterprise. Furthermore, *Harlem on My Mind* was initially announced in the press release as including paintings, prints, and drawings, along with photographic and sound documentation. But Schoener alleges it was never his intention to incorporate these media; he abandoned that possibility, basing his decision on the impression that the painting gallery in the Lower East Side show diminished the interactive and enveloping ambience he so eagerly sought. Ultimately he came to believe that "paintings are from another world. They've stopped being a vehicle for valid expression in the 20th century. I believe in art as process, not as artifacts."[12]

Moreover, he states that he never saw nor approved the language in the press release. As he recollects, "I was always clear with everyone from the start."[13] Schoener's most ambitious designs always shattered expectations of the museum experience, such as when he filled up a renovated barge with material related to the 150-year history of the Erie Canal, and then hauled it to communities from Albany to Buffalo via tugboat. His concept for *Harlem on My Mind* was a form of "electronic theater," where more traditional media were outmoded and out of place.

Black artists considered this aesthetic choice a slap in the face. For them it was an uncomfortably familiar scenario, corresponding to a painfully long history of closed doors in the art world. Just as the issues of discrimination, blocked opportunities, and exclusion had tremendous currency for blacks generally, they carried special poignancy for black artists. Few of them had penetrated the commercial gallery or museum world, and most felt obliged to represent the history and experiences of their community in their work, an aesthetic ghetto that trussed them stylistically and thematically. What at first seemed like a promising possibility, a natural setting to feature their work, quickly soured.

This was a pivotal and baffling period for black artists. The writer Ishmael Reed was deeply suspicious of white artists taking up some social causes while ignoring others that were equally pressing: "many pimps of misery . . . although publicly 'crying the blues' about Vietnam have never given a black artist a Hershey bar let alone invite[d] him to set up his work in a gallery."[14] Nonetheless, group shows of black artists had become suddenly fashionable in the late 1960s, much like miniskirts, bell-bottom pants, and Indian print bedspreads. This was particularly the case with university-affiliated galleries and other modest spaces, but not major museums. The artistic status quo seemed to be changing grudgingly, incrementally, while leading institutions were still perceived to be largely aloof from these matters. As the artist and activist Benny Andrews quipped, "We're a trend like pop and op. . . . We're the latest movement. Of course, like the others, we may be over in a year or two."[15]

About three months before *Harlem on My Mind* opened, black artists were incensed that the Whitney Museum of American Art presented *The 1930s: Painting and Sculpture in America,* and included no blacks. This provoked an angry editorial and a cartoon, which both ran in the *Amsterdam News,* each incredulous that the museum could represent that era without recognizing the many black artists working then. For many blacks it confirmed an all too familiar motif. Even so, a defensible curatorial logic in fact existed: the goal of this exhibition was to highlight the modernist artists who labored primarily "underground" during a time generally noted for its representational and politically partisan work.

Critics in the black community attributed enormous power to this exhibition, as if it were the last word about the period. Yet Hilton Kramer applauded the show in two substantial reviews in the *New York Times* because he felt it added a different perspective to the received wisdom, tipping the balance away from an exclusive focus on social realism in the 1930s. To Kramer's mind, it resurrected an important bit of history that had been buried. But that argument seemed lame to those who'd felt consistently neglected in the past. Henri Ghent, the director of the Brooklyn Museum's community gallery, helped organize *Invisible Artists of the 1930s* at the Studio Museum in Harlem to redress the injustice, and defensively countered Kramer's position in a lengthy letter to the editor, where he argued, "What seems most apparent in Mr. Kramer's article is the all-pervading concept that what is white must necessarily be *superior*."[16]

What was in fact going on was a failure to communicate effectively and a failure to listen, on all sides. Rationalizations honed by years of isolation or bitter experience dictated people's responses as much as the evidence in front of them. Remarkably, soon thereafter, each side to this debate joined the chorus of opposition to *Harlem on My Mind,* admittedly for different reasons.

The battle over the legacy of the 1930s was being fought just as *Harlem on My Mind* entered its final planning stages. Hoving and Schoener aimed for an innovative show, one that broke new ground. Black artists merely wanted to be invited in, to finally become a part of the action. When this didn't occur, the painter Benny Andrews launched the Black Emergency Cultural Coalition (BECC) from his Beekman Street loft, the group that coordinated black demonstrators against the exhibition. He poignantly recalls, "Ideally I would have liked to have been an insider, with my nose pressed against the glass, looking out at those dirty people walking around in the cold with the police all around them."[17]

Coalition building failed in this instance. Allon Schoener had three black staff members, who signed off on every aspect of the project. But one hailed from Chicago and another was from Milwaukee, so some Harlemites treated them as suspiciously as they did Schoener, who is white. Schoener cultivated ties with Mel Patrick, an assistant to the powerful and respected Harlem politico Percy Sutton. But Schoener claims that local political opportunists tried to grab a piece of the action and became angry when they were rebuffed. For example, he alleges that Ed Taylor, the head of the Harlem Cultural Council, came to his office soon after *Harlem on My Mind* was announced and demanded, "'Either you hire me as your associate director on this project or your ass is going to be in a sling.' He said, 'I'll fix you.' And he did." Barely two months before the opening, the Harlem Cultural Council publicly withdrew its support, citing a breakdown in communication and a failure to include the Harlem community beyond rubber-stamping decisions made elsewhere. Hoving has written, "Schoener was a genius, but he was also protective of 'his' show and reluctant to allow outsiders to participate." However, he concurs that Taylor was a "firebrand" and presented "unreasonable demands." Schoener told Taylor to "fuck off."[18]

Schoener also recalls a lunch he had with Jean Blackwell Hutson from the Schomburg library and John Henrik Clarke, a Harlem-based historian of the neighborhood, associate editor of *Freedomways Magazine,* and director of the Haryou-Act Heritage Teaching Program. The lunch was held a week or ten days after the encounter with Taylor. At first Clarke reminisced that he had been a *shabbas goy* as a kid, and then "He looked me straight in the eye and said, 'You're another downtown Jew who's come up here to rip us off. Go away.'" In a gem of understatement, Schoener says, "I got the signal at that point that this was not something that was going to be a totally rosy picture. We were going to run into static."[19]

Furthermore, when the curatorial team approached the photographer Roy DeCarava about contributing work to the exhibition, he demanded a separate room featuring his work. That suggestion, too, was rebuffed, because it did not jibe with the chronological narrative of *Harlem on My Mind*. To Schoener, "It became trench warfare after that." Benny Andrews, who confronted Hoving at an early announcement of the show, complained that the concept was more like an exposition than an exhibition, reminding the artist nowadays of automobile trade shows: "It had nothing to do with advancing art; it strictly had to do with something else. . . . [T]he show was like *Life* magazine blown up. It was just an historical thing. It had nothing to do with art." By the time the exhibition opened, the list of its enemies had become longer and longer. Individuals whose hopes to become a part of this show had withered, individuals who rejected its inventive character, and individuals offended by certain passages in the exhibition catalogue all harbored deep suspicions about the finished product.

In many respects the catalogue overshadowed the exhibition. At the very least, it expanded the range of those taking offense to this venture. The catalogue was ready before the show officially opened its doors on January 18, 1969. Schoener gave copies away to friends as Hanukkah presents, and they were also distributed for publicity purposes. A week to ten days before the opening, Schoener received a call from a representative of the American Jewish Congress. The man told him that a meeting of Jewish leaders had been called to discuss the book, and that they were intending to compel the Met to withdraw it from sale. Joseph Noble, Hoving's vice director for administration, also recalls that about the same time synagogues throughout the city publicized a Sabbath sermon entitled "Metropolitan on My Mind." Soon thereafter, a rabbi condemned Schoener to his face as a "traitor to the Jewish people," and the Jewish Defense League (JDL), formed during the recent school strike, demonstrated in front of his apartment building.

The source of the problem was an introductory essay, originally written in 1967 as a term paper by a seventeen-year-old high school student, Candice Van Ellison, a lifelong Harlem resident. Van Ellison's essay about Harlem came to Schoener's attention when the girl worked at the New York State Council on the Arts as part of the Ghetto Arts Corps. He felt it presented a fresh, young voice. But several passages deeply troubled members of the Jewish community. In particular, they singled out Van Ellison's statement that "Behind every hurdle that the Afro-American has yet to jump stands the Jew who has already cleared it." Citing the friction between blacks and Jews, and blacks' negative experiences as customers in Jewish-owned shops, domestic workers in Jewish homes, and lower-level government workers with Jewish superiors, Van Ellison concluded, "our contempt for the Jew make us feel more completely American in sharing a national prejudice."

She took aim at other groups as well. Van Ellison highlighted black/Irish frictions because of the alleged brutality of Irish cops. She argued that "It was also disconcerting that Blacks, who were actually American citizens, could never have gotten the jobs on the city's police force as the Irish immigrants so easily managed to do." Moreover, she disparaged Puerto Ricans for riding the crest of black civil rights efforts, becoming beneficiaries of antidiscrimination campaigns without expending much effort of their own, and commanding a lion's share of public housing apartments.

But the Jews mobilized like no other group to condemn the catalogue. With the wounds from the Ocean Hill–Brownsville struggle still festering, and with the specter of executions of Jews in Iraq, this invective was extremely disquieting. It confirmed the worst fears of many Jews about a serious national and international outburst of anti-Semitism, a new Holocaust in the making. The American Jewish Congress, for example, ran a full-page statement of concern in the *New York Times*, "A Call to Negroes and Jews." It was peppered with words and phrases such as "the big lie," "[the alleged] conspiracy of the Jews," "slander," "group libel," "scapegoating," and "vicious slur." But the conclusion was a plea for moderation and unity: "We dare not fall prey to the divisive tactic that seeks to pit Negro against Jew, Jew against Negro. The victim will be justice. The dupes will be ourselves."[20]

Adding more fuel to the fire was a controversial broadcast on the New York City listener-supported, Pacifica-licensed radio station WBAI-FM on December 26, 1968. That night the poem "Anti-Semitism," penned by a fifteen-year-old girl, was presented on Julius Lester's program (a show with the self-mocking title "The Great Proletarian Cultural Revolution"). The poem was recited by Leslie Campbell, a black junior high teacher who had been center stage in the Ocean Hill–Brownsville battle and who was the author of an article entitled "The Devil Can Never Educate Us." The poem, "dedicated" to Albert Shanker, reads, in part:

> Hey, Jew Boy, with that yarmulke on your head
> You pale-faced Jew boy—I wish you were dead;
> I can see you Jew boy—no you can't hide,
> I got a scoop on you—yeh, you gonna die.
> I'm sick of your stuff; every time I run 'round,
> You pushin' my head deeper into the ground;
> I'm sick of hearing about your suffering in Germany,
> I'm sick about your escape from tyranny;
> I'm sick of seeing in everything I do
> About the murder of six million Jews;
> Hitler's reign lasted for only fifteen years—
> For that period of time you shed crocodile tears.
> My suffering lasted for over 400 years, Jew boy,
> And the white man only let me play with his toys.
>
> ▪   ▪   ▪
>
> Guess you know, Jew boy, there's only one reason you made it—
> You had a clean white face, colorless and faded.

On a subsequent Julius Lester broadcast, a student from Ocean Hill–Brownsville asserted, "[Hitler] didn't make enough lampshades out of them."[21]

The poem advances a hierarchy of misery and oppression that has a familiar ring in the 1990s, and it presents some of the same sentiments expressed by Van Ellison in an uncannily similar way. Much like Schoener, Lester believed that the feelings of this girl were valid and should be heard. But by publicly airing such spiteful sentiments at this time, he helped undermine interracial collaboration and mutual identification through shared pain. Rather than expediting productive communication, the broadcast of the poem abruptly shut it down.

Reflecting on these events twenty years later, Julius Lester said he had been "naive," an explanation that several principal players in the *Harlem on My Mind* controversy later used to defend *their* actions. But he also revealed a deeper grasp of what was at stake:

> [Jews] needed to know that if they wanted blacks to care about Jewish suffering, they had to care about black suffering. As crude and obscene as the poem was, I heard in it an excruciating paroxysm of pain. It was pain expressed as anger at Jews, many of whom found identity by borrowing suffering from the Holocaust while remaining blithely blind to the suffering of black people around them and actively opposing the political means blacks used to alleviate a portion of that suffering.[22]

After numerous death threats against Lester, a JDL demonstration outside WBAI, and a demand by the president of the City Council that WBAI's license be suspended, the UFT filed a complaint against the station with the Federal Communications Commission (FCC) in January 1969. That in turn sparked a vigorous debate over freedom of expression. As in many discussions of this sort, people are generally more eager to invoke the First Amendment in defense of views they are already comfortable with, rather than views they find upsetting. The FCC dismissed the complaint two months later. It ruled that Lester's own remarks over the course of several shows, in consideration with the comments made by some of his callers, were protected under the Constitution and satisfied the fairness doctrine.

Calls for repressive action also targeted the *Harlem on My Mind* catalogue. Hoving wrote a preface that sounds guileless yet condescending today. He speaks about the maid of "sunny disposition" and the "sour" chauffeur of his childhood in Manhattan's Silk Stocking district, and of his mother's adventurous slumming in Harlem nightclubs.[23] But Hoving came under fire when politicos jumped into this fray. Mayor Lindsay, having to continuously appease various groups and put out emotional brushfires throughout the city, ordered an aide to call Hoving and convince him to withdraw the catalogue. City Council members, meanwhile, threatened to cut off financial support to the Met, a potential loss of millions of dollars a year earmarked for operating expenses.

To placate the politicians, Hoving first solicited a statement from Candice Van Ellison to be inserted into the catalogue. She obliged by stating that "any racist overtones" inferred from her essay were "regrettable." This was accompanied by Hoving's own *mea culpa*, declaring that he hadn't recognized the "racist *under*tones" (emphasis added), and "deeply apologized" for his "error in judgment": "her essay was not appropriate as an introduction to the catalogue and should never have been used as such." Even Bennett Cerf, the publisher of Random House, professed to be sorry that this had happened. But these statements didn't completely satisfy City Hall, possibly because no one actually repudiated the essay. Bowing to continuing pressure, Hoving ordered all the remaining softbound copies to be embargoed in the Met's basement. They were eventually distributed to libraries and community groups, whereas the hardcover version continued to be sold.

Schoener was adamantly nonrepentant: "'It is not inflammatory or anything else,' [Schoener] said. 'It states a fact. And if the truth hurts, so be it!'"[24] Furthermore, he decried this as "bookburning," evoking searing images from Nazi Germany. A *New York Times* editorial concurred: "[To suppress the catalogue] would be book burning without the flames, an even greater offense to American traditions than anything in the book." A humorous newspaper account of an "uptown cat" visiting the exhibit dismissed the charges of anti-Semitism in the catalogue: "'That,' retorted Soul Brother, 'is like denouncing the victim in a disaster area for picking his nose.'"[25]

In the midst of all this, a significant, surprising detail was uncovered by an investigative report published in the Upper East Side community newspaper *Park East*, and subsequently picked up in the general press: Allon Schoener ordered Candice Van Ellison to remove all the footnotes and quotation marks from her original essay to make it more concise and more readable. As it turned out, the composition did not spring purely from an angry young black girl, but relied heavily on the influential book *Beyond the Melting Pot*, by Nathan

Glazer and Daniel Patrick Moynihan. Even her much-reviled observation about anti-Semitism being the glue that bonded blacks to various other ethnic groups came from this scholarly source.

Recasting a theoretical argument as a venting of personal opinion changed the tone and the meaning of Van Ellison's work considerably. That editorial misstep on Schoener's part intensified the condemnation and compromised his credibility: "This is the stuff from which natural saboteurs are made," an editorial writer sarcastically declared, "and if the C.I.A. has any brains it will send him to Peking to make a documentary show about the glory of the Red Guards. It would set China back a decade."[26] The specter of book burning was raised by one other source: right-wing demonstrators protested the sale of "communist" books in a bookstall set up at the Met during the run of the exhibition. Bowing once again to pressure, Hoving removed books with the imprint of International Publishers and Merit Publishers, including works about W. E. B. Du Bois, Frederick Douglass and Kwame Nkrumah and books written by the radical historian Herbert Aptheker. The president of International Publishers sent Hoving a letter in protest, indicting what he regarded as "McCarthyite tactics," to no avail. He invoked the memory of a period of intimidation and creative gridlock that cultural foes commonly lob at one another.[27]

But this was only the sideshow. The main attraction was at the Met itself, both in its galleries and on the adjoining streets. Exhibition openings are typically a time of anxious anticipation: Will the public like what they see? Will the critics approve? But the intensity of that ordinary apprehension was cranked up several notches by events during the preceding days. The Black Emergency Cultural Coalition started demonstrating at the Met nearly a week before the show was publicly unveiled. Next, only about half the guests invited to a Thursday evening preview of *Harlem on My Mind* appeared at the museum, and those who did were greeted by BECC members imploring them to spurn the formal dinner and join them on the picket line instead. One observer reported hearing shouts of "Oh, Thomasina!" "Aunt Jemima, don't go in, there's no SOUL in there," and "Sellout! Sellout!" Sure enough, some of the visitors took the protesters up on their offer: "People in their little tuxedos came and joined us. And a lot of

FIG. 3. Protester outside the Metropolitan Museum of Art's *Harlem on My Mind* exhibition, 1969. Used by permission of *Modern Photography*.

the time they were white people. [Meanwhile] there were black people in African garb going in."[28]

The following day, an unknown vandal scratched the letter *H* into ten paintings in the Met's collection, including a Rembrandt. Met officials and the public speculated on what the graffito meant: Harlem? Hoving? Honky? Although there was no permanent damage to any of the works, it set the museum on high alert. Then, according to Joseph Noble, "Hoving pulled the old political trick. 'When the shit hits the fan, get out of town.' He jumped on a plane with his wife and went down to Bermuda or the Bahamas or someplace."

Saturday, January 18, 1969: a large group of black protesters was marching up and down on the wide sidewalk north of the Met. A group of Jews had staked out the area directly before the broad front stairway of the museum. Positioned down at the south end was a much smaller group of people from the John Birch Society, upset that W. E. B. Du Bois, a man they scorned as a communist, was featured in the exhibit.

The passage of time makes it impossible to accurately calculate numbers, but some memories rouse upwards of a thousand impassioned picketers. Benny Andrews candidly recalls how the combative style of the times required groups to pump up the volume of their rhetoric and strike a militant pose if they wished to get their point across and be noticed by the media:

> At that time "coalition" was a very strong term. And really it was surreal, because we always had ultimatums. There was no its, ands, or buts. Because you couldn't rationalize things. Rationalization had been the whole process anyway. So if you're going to start sitting down speaking the pros and cons, you were just going to be washed away. So you just had to be either totally radical or you were going to be washed away.

There were limits, however: Reginald Gammon, a BECC member, recalls, "There was a guy we threw off the picket line because he was passing out red sheets saying, 'Bomb the Metropolitan!' We wanted to be in this place eventually! He was a total nihilist."[29]

Cops kept these different contingents a reasonable distance from one another. But it was a boisterous, chaotic, and utterly unprecedented sight at a cultural institution. As Joseph Noble recounts the scene,

The Jews start to chant. And they're yelling in unison, "No Auschwitz here. No Auschwitz here." They had worked themselves up
into hysteria that this was the beginning of a planned denigration of
the Jews, which ultimately would lead to their segregation and an
Auschwitz. I mean, you know, [the end of] World War II wasn't that
old by that time. Less than twenty-five years.

With an atmosphere this politically charged, it's no wonder that the
reviews and commentary on *Harlem on My Mind* generally devoted
less time and space to evaluating what was actually on view, and directed much more attention to assessing the *idea* of the show. Reviewers for the most part prejudged it along racial, political, generational,
and aesthetic lines, and bored away at it with whatever weighty literary devices they had at their disposal. They outdid themselves by creating the catchy headline, the witty turn of phrase, the ultimate put-
down. Meanwhile, the Met was registering record crowds, on some
days having to close its doors early because the museum was filled to
capacity.

Blacks who attacked *Harlem on My Mind* frequently raised the issues of paternalism, self-determination, and the symbolic ownership
of a group's history and identity. The photographer Roy DeCarava,
whose demand for his own room in the exhibition was dismissed as
incompatible with the show's concept, roundly rejected its legitimacy: "I have no confidence in the people doing the show, and I did-
n't want my pictures wrongly used. The fundamental thing is that
blacks want to say their own things about themselves. White people,
no matter how sympathetic, can't do it." The artist Reginald Gammon
likewise condemned the choice of Schoener as the curator, declaring
with a sense of resignation, "They always pick somebody else to do
your life." The three BECC cochairs—Andrews, Ghent, and Taylor—
were quoted in the *New York Times* as denouncing "'the white man's
distorted, irrelevant and insulting' picture of Harlem."[30]

All these remarks could have been borrowed from another cultural struggle that was playing out at the same moment over the film-
ing of William Styron's best-selling 1967 novel, *The Confessions of Nat
Turner*. As Styron describes him, Nat Turner is a complex mix of conflicting attributes. Among other things, he has a fleeting homosexual
encounter when he's young, and although celibate, he lusts for white
women. He emerges from these pages as an admirable, if somewhat

reluctant, hero. But in an era of "black is beautiful," ghetto uprisings, and the macho posturing of the Black Panthers, this version of the story upset blacks who wanted idols who were not encumbered by feet of clay.

The aforementioned John Henrik Clarke edited and published *William Styron's Nat Turner: Ten Black Writers Respond* to counterbalance the fictionalized view. In that volume, the writer and editor Lerone Bennett, Jr., roundly condemned the portrait he confronted: "The man Styron substitutes for Nat Turner is not only the antithesis of Nat Turner, he is *the antithesis of blackness*. . . . a Hamlet-like white intellectual in blackface" (emphasis added). Moreover, the psychiatrist Alvin Poussaint noted that Turner's "speech sounds more like Styron's than that of an heroic black slave of nineteenth-century America," while the Schomburg staffer Ernest Kaiser dismissed the novel as "a witches' brew of Freudian psychology, [Stanley] Elkins's 'Sambo' thesis on slavery and Styron's vile racist imagination." The political scientist Charles V. Hamilton, who condemned the book as a "betrayal" rather than a "portrayal," concisely captured the heart of the matter in his title, "Our Nat Turner and William Styron's Creation." This was, above all else, a proprietary issue. When the story was being filmed, the Black Anti-Defamation League negotiated an agreement with the producer and director to abandon Styron's title, supplement the Styron version with additional material, base their cinematic tale on "the real facts," and present a "positive image."[31]

When picketers at *Harlem on My Mind* strapped on sandwich boards declaring "On the Auction Block Again—Sold Out by Massa Hoving," or writers (black *or* white) referred to the show as "an urban plantation" or "The Electric Uncle Tom," they too were endorsing this view that enduring, white-dominated institutions unjustly dictate the prevailing image of the black world. As Benny Andrews remarks, "The Met was like the Vatican. No one would imagine you'd have the gall to do [make statements such as] that." The novelist Charles Wright summed up the situation bluntly. He accused the blacks associated with assembling the show of being "two-dollar whores," and he dismissed his visit to the Met as "an afternoon of dungburgers." "[E]motionally—this photo-audio happening forced the skin on my testicles to contract as in cold weather."[32]

Coverage of the exhibition and all the associated controversy in the *Amsterdam News* was somewhat spare, and hardly emotionally overwrought. Quite possibly "hard news" stories such as proposed cuts to public aid and severe financial strains at local hospitals were simply more pressing. One editorial in particular was a reasoned appeal for everyone to step back and calmly examine how extremists—both black and Jewish—had been allowed to dominate various racially charged debates, with the help of opportunistic politicians and "hysterical" people in the media.[33] Some letters to the editor expressed forceful opinions in these pages, to be sure, although an early one expressed bewilderment at how people could disapprove of the show before it had opened.

But as Benny Andrews sees it, "Some of the people who we hear a lot of are people who do drastic things. People who are rational, they just don't make the news, and they're probably more right. Anyone who is very extreme, if they're successful at it, they get attention." Certain individuals indeed surface as spokespersons in these contested instances, through self-interest, sheer doggedness, the visibility of their institutional affiliations, or their expertise at snagging the attention of the media. But while some people become passionate over certain museum exhibitions, many remain oblivious to what the controversy is all about, and others take away something positive from these shows. This points up the obvious folly of claiming that "the black community" did *this*, or "the black community" felt *that*. No such monolithic entity as "*the* black community" exists, just as it's inaccurate to refer to "the Jewish community," "the Irish community," or any other. There are, instead, *communities*, marbled with contradictions.

For example, the Harlem minister (and congressman) Adam Clayton Powell praised *Harlem on My Mind* in the sermon to his congregation at the Abyssinian Baptist Church the day after the exhibition opened because, in his words, it showed "what we came from." The Reverend Henry Dudley Rucker of the New White Rock Baptist Church, on the other hand, condemned it "because it revived aspects of Harlem history that were 'better off dead.'"[34] Same show, same "community," but widely different evaluations in this, just a small sampling of prevailing opinion.

And how do we understand black voices such as that of Bill Miles, a noted documentary filmmaker who made the acclaimed four-hour series *I Remember Harlem* for PBS in 1981? Miles hadn't bothered to go

to the Met in 1969. For him, "My world was all up in Harlem. Everything was going on right there."[35] The Metropolitan Museum of Art
lay beyond the customary boundaries of his mental geography, so
that what was happening there—even if it was expressly about the
district where Miles lived—was irrelevant to him. Then there's the
artist Fred Wilson, who was taken as a teenager by his father and recalls seeing "Big kind of images, graphic, graphic, graphic. I remember enjoying it. At the time it was a big, beautiful museum exhibition
and it was something to be proud of. Now I'd be more critical, but at
the time it was certainly the first of its kind and seemed important."[36]
What about Dawoud Bey, who had never seen a photography exhibit
before he viewed *Harlem on My Mind*? It launched him on his own career as a documentary photographer of Harlem, seeking to emulate
James Van DerZee. And what about Van DerZee himself, the most important "discovery" of the exhibition?

Van DerZee (1886-1983) was a storefront photographer with no
formal training who had documented life in Harlem since the early
part of the century. His work ranged from portraits of common people, to distinctive groups like Moorish Jews and the followers of Mar-
cus Garvey, to celebrities such as Bill "Bojangles" Robinson, Jack
Johnson, Florence Mills, and Father Divine. But he was a virtual unknown outside Harlem. That all changed when Reggie McGhee from
the *Harlem on My Mind* staff drifted into his studio one day; he was
immediately wowed by the impressive size and breadth of Van
DerZee's collection.

Van DerZee made the largest contribution of photographs to the
exhibition. He was paid more than $2,000 for his part in the show and
the catalogue ("That kind of money" he had "never seen before for
photography"). He was also the beneficiary of new demands for his
services and was cascaded with honors: he was invited to the White
House to receive the Living Legacy Award from the president, he was
selected as a Fellow for Life of the Metropolitan Museum, and honored by the National Geographic Society and the American Society of
Magazine Photographers. Several books were published about him
and his work as well. The first, compiled and edited by McGhee and
published by Grove Press, featured an interview with him conducted
by Candice Van Ellison. In another interview published in 1980, he reflected, "I don't know if it [*Harlem on My Mind*] was the turning point
or the starting point of my career. . . . I guess I appeared to be like

FIG. 4. James Van DerZee, *Daddy Grace*, 1938. © Donna M. Van DerZee. Used by permission.

'Alice in Wonderland.' It was quite a thrilling sight for me to see the photographs hanging there."[37]

That was well and good for Van DerZee, but these rewards brought nothing to a larger group of creative blacks who insisted that the status quo in the art world had not changed appreciably. A case in point: the Black Emergency Cultural Coalition. For the most part, the members of the BECC were in their early thirties, mostly without gallery representation, mostly without family obligations. According to Benny Andrews, "We had nothing to lose, so we could be radicals. We could afford to be radicals."[38] For a while, it seemed as if the Met was moved by their argument that the work of black artists deserved to be showcased in the museum. A front-page article in the *Amsterdam News* declared that "A Black Show Is at the Museum." It didn't read "A Black Show Is Being *Proposed*," or "A Black Show Is Being *Developed*." Rather, it authoritatively announced *The Inner World of the Black Movement*, with a roster of eight artists (incorporating none of those active in the protests), and running for six weeks beginning February 18.[39]

Yet the exhibition never materialized, for reasons that are not entirely clear. Joseph Noble maintains that "The black artists withdrew. The black artists wanted to be in the big show. And [because of] the fact that they were being segregated and put into the rear of the bus, as second class citizens, they stood up and wouldn't play." Schoener, on the other hand, attributes the failure to the fact that a young and inexperienced staffer at the Met was placed in charge, and she in turn entrusted the project to a Harlem gallery owner who was also not very capable. What *is* clear is that the institutional commitment to follow through from the conception of this idea to the finished product was never made.

The interest in mounting public rejoinders did not fade. It merely moved across town. The BECC began meeting with officials at the Whitney Museum in April 1969 to organize an exhibition of black artists, partially "in penance" for their absence from the show on the 1930s. Those talks resulted in *Contemporary Black Artists in America* in 1971, but the BECC picketed the museum, and seventeen artists withdrew, in protest that a black curator was not employed. The "Rebuttal Show" was held at the Acts of Art Gallery, a black-curated response to museums that many artists felt still failed to take them seriously. However, Lawrence Alloway, writing in the *Nation*, took issue with the concept of such "special interest" shows as proposed at the Met and later at these other locales. He feared that this would invite yet other groups to apply political pressure to museums and prompt a torrent of ill-conceived exhibits: "How about: 'Salon de Backlash,' an annual poor whites' art show . . . and 'Cop Art,' arranged . . . by the Police Athletic League."[40]

Hale Woodruff, an elder statesman of black artists, lamented that the situation that black artists faced was unlikely to change in the near future because blacks were not generating their own distinctive critical scholarship. Speaking as a panel member at "The Black Artist in America: A Symposium," he argued, "We need a writer to make us known. . . . Scholarship from our college men and others has gone into the social movement and civil rights. Look at your jazz critics, they're white, and most of your drama critics are white. Even your writers, like Baldwin and so on, aren't concerned with us."[41] As Woodruff was keenly aware, during an era when blacks were mobilizing to transform the racial order, strategic resources could hardly be funneled in vast amounts to championing the cause of art.

In a basic respect, *Harlem on My Mind* addressed social issues through cultural expression. But critics, whatever their ideological allegiance or aesthetic bent, intoned the same disdainful mantra throughout their reviews of the show: "it's sociology, not art," "it's sociology, not art." An exhibition born of the liberal faith of the 1960s was harshly condemned by a majority of those who had access to print, as if a huge cross-section of critics had been converted to some powerful cult of negation.

Even so, criticism coalesced along some particular, predictable lines. One division is represented by those people who rejected the multimedia, communications-environment concept of *Harlem on My Mind* as too strong on gimmicks and gadgetry and too populist. To these people, Schoener had issued an aesthetic call to battle when he wrote in his editor's foreword to the catalogue, "the individual who responds to an experience becomes as important in the communication process as the one who organizes it. In other words, the audience itself becomes a creative force. Participation implies more effective communication. This suggests a new aesthetic hierarchy."[42] Not only was this philosophy tantamount to heresy for defenders of the traditional artistic faith, but Schoener and Hoving had the nerve to bring it to life in, of all places, the Metropolitan Museum of Art. For defenders of elite culture, this exhibition was a defilement. Moreover, it represented a threat to their authority.

The art critic John Canaday wrote a haughty and deeply ambivalent polemic in the *New York Times* about how he wasn't qualified to review *Harlem on My Mind* because the Met "is making its debut this Saturday as a museum of sociological documentation." Since the Met had drifted so far from its artistic mission, Canaday could not bear to view or evaluate the results: "It would be presumptuous of me to review the Metropolitan's show on the only grounds that are important—its thoroughness and veracity as a social document. As far as 'Harlem on My Mind' is concerned, I herewith sign off."[43] Canaday's "nonreview" was a barely disguised and very forceful condemnation of the legitimacy of the entire enterprise.

Canaday was dismissive, as if an absurd, annoying thought had crossed his mind and was not worthy of notice—except he couldn't easily thrust it aside. His stance was almost exactly replicated in an aesthetic squabble that occurred in 1995, a debate initiated when the critic Arlene Croce adamantly refused to see the choreographer Bill T. Jones's *Still/Here* because it was what she termed "victim art" (it was a multimedia show that showcased people with life-threatening illnesses, including AIDS). She repudiated the performance as "a messianic traveling medicine show," and argued that "By working dying people into his act, Jones is putting himself beyond the reach of criticism. . . . I can't review someone I feel sorry for or hopeless about."[44] She too carped disagreeably at considerable length. In essence, both she and Canaday were announcing that they simply refused to consider admitting nascent expressive forms into an established artistic pantheon. At the same time, they were acknowledging that these new creations challenged the limits of their own critical expertise.

Katherine Kuh added her sense of violation to Canaday's. She underscored the mandate of art museums to preserve and present art and "offer us islands of relief." She deplored what she termed "borrowing Madison Avenue techniques" and offering "oversimplified sociological banalities" as beyond the Met's ken, and pondered "Why photographs should decorate ceilings and leap off columns, why lights should imitate psychedelic frenzy." Hilton Kramer also chimed in with disgust. Beginning with the almost obligatory disclaimer of interest—"it hardly seems a proper subject for criticism at all"—

Kramer condemned the show as "an event that belongs to the history of publicity more than to the history of art," and wondered why Hoving "felt compelled to abandon art for a cheap form of photo-audio journalism." But Kramer threw his best punch in the following passage, where he demanded an accounting by the man ultimately responsible for this travesty:

> [T]here can be no doubt that in mounting the *Harlem on My Mind* exhibition Mr. Hoving has for the first time politicized the Metropolitan, and has thereby cast doubt on its future integrity as an institution consecrated above all to the task of preserving our artistic heritage from the fickle encroachments of history. . . . We have a right to know, I think, exactly how far Mr. Hoving intends to carry this process.[45]

By installing new technologies in the hallowed galleries of the Met, and by introducing previously overlooked subjects, Schoener and Hoving symbolically knocked traditional art off its pedestal. What is more, this exhibition possessed no significant market value, it offered no promise of an enduring economic afterlife once it closed. This posed an immeasurable threat to all those who had a stake in the art world as a system that validates claims to greatness and inherent worth—and cashes them in—from artists to critics to galleries to museums. If this exhibition was mainly information and an imaginative style of presentation, then where was the enduring product? How would this new "commodity" impact on everything that came before, known as "art"? Where did one become credentialed to evaluate it? Reputations, jobs, investments, and profits were at stake, and *Harlem on My Mind* threatened to collapse the gold standard and devalue the shaky currency of this realm.

Whereas black artists hoped that museum doors would open wider to them, the *Amsterdam News* wished that *all* extremists would tone down their rhetoric and back off. While conservative cultural critics wanted to turn their backs on this show and simply deny its existence, some politically progressive white reviewers desired a harder-hitting, grittier, more authentic exhibition: "How come . . . not a single cockroach or a rat?" asked A. D. Coleman in the *Village Voice*. "Now that would have been a radical achievement—a room devoted to the vermin of Harlem, with still photos, slides, and films of roaches, lice, and rats crawling over babies, adults, food, tooth-brushes, to the accompaniment of a tape playing, over and over, the obscene scuttling noises of rodents in the walls."[46]

Coleman was nurtured in a left-wing, pro-labor household and cut his own political teeth in the civil rights and peace movements in New York City. He believed he was asking questions about inclusive-ness and representation in his photography reviews that paralleled the central concerns of his activism: "Who has power?" "Who does-n't?" "How can it be shared more?" For Coleman, was *Harlem on My Mind* exploitative by intent? No. Was it exploitative as executed? Probably, because for him it embodied a "typical bleeding-heart do-gooderism that makes unconscious assumptions and doesn't ask peo-ple what *they* want."[47] However, in this racially charged atmosphere (or, during most times) one can just imagine how a "bugs, rats, or crap" exhibition at an elite institution might be received by residents of Harlem or by trustees or white liberals, for that matter.

Dismissing *Harlem on My Mind* as "a staggering display of honky chutzpah," a "visual version of slumming . . . [that] skims the surface . . . without ever probing to the horror beneath," Coleman continued to assail the exhibition in subsequent reviews. He acknowledged the "discovery" of Van DerZee as "One of the few positive effects" and proposed a solo show of the photographer's work at the Met as a way "to begin atoning for past sins." He also supported Roy DeCarava's refusal to participate on anything but his own terms, and crowed about a DeCarava show that confirmed the man's talent. But the most significant phrase in everything Coleman wrote pertaining to *Harlem on My Mind* appeared in his original assessment: "on purely aesthetic and technical grounds, 'Harlem on My Mind' rapes photography re-peatedly without even bringing that medium anywhere near orgasm. (The Metropolitan Museum of Art is a bad lay.)"[48]

The present-day reader recoils—at least I do. But what's impor-tant about this quote is how it points up the fact that racism was the great concern of the moment; sexism wasn't. Proving yourself to be "right on" in regard to one issue did not automatically guarantee being sensitive to others. According to Coleman, no one ever took him to task for this statement. He now attributes it to a certain "punk-iness": "I look back with some chagrin that this bit of cultural lunacy had hooked into my unconscious. I see traces of sexism and homo-phobia in my earlier work and ask 'How did they get there?' 'How could I think that was funny?'" He was obviously asking these questions by 1979, because when he collected ten years of reviews for publication as a book, he edited his previous thoughts. The latter version simply reads "on purely aesthetic and technical grounds, 'Harlem on My Mind' violates photography repeatedly." Period, end of paragraph.[49]

In the intervening years, the impact of feminism had heightened Coleman's consciousness so that his enduring concerns about representation and the biases of speaking either as an insider or an outsider led him to revise his own writing. But Coleman stands by his criticisms in the main, and feels that "the politics of depiction," which is today a regular part of the dialogue in the art world, was somewhat prophetically raised in the discussions around *Harlem on My Mind.*

One of the strongest voices to be heard along these lines was that of the historian Eugene D. Genovese. Labeling the exhibition "an abortion," he declared that only "legitimate groups" in Harlem had the right to interpret the legacy of Malcolm X, for instance. What Hoving and his representatives had done was "intrude themselves" into a community they knew little about. But his most stinging indictment came at the end of his article: "All paternalism rests on good intentions, and the paternalism of New York's *grande bourgeoisie* is not better or more well-intentioned than that of the ill-fated Southern slaveholders. In some ways it is much less palatable. The slaveholders, after all, had the wisdom and decency to own their niggers outright before they presumed to run their lives."[50]

Soon afterwards, similar concerns surfaced in a debate over Bruce Davidson's photos of East Harlem. Davidson was extremely careful to not exploit his subjects, but since he was a white man documenting the lives of Puerto Rican residents of East 100th Street, some critics judged his work to be "limited," although not automatically invalid. At the very least, this and other projects raised questions about power, access, and social responsibility, in addition to considerations of artistic merit.[51]

Harlem on My Mind was neither fish nor fowl. Its uniqueness sent reviewers scrambling for ways to describe and understand this new creature. For Amy Goldin, "The show's format suggests the March of Time in blackface"; Lawrence Alloway concluded, "The general effect is of a Voice of America broadcast added to 'The Family of Man'"; and James R. Mellow chided it as *"Uncle Tom's Cabin in the Sky."* For each of them, this was a crossbreed, spawned from somewhat undistinguished stock.[52]

Few critics pushed beyond sheer bluster to develop precise arguments based on what they actually saw. Amy Goldin was the rare observer to note that "The near-absence of photographs showing any economic relationship of Negroes to whites is extremely misleading. . . . The result is a highly deceptive impression of the autonomy of Harlem life."[53] This is certainly not as eye-catching as her other remark, but it is a solid observation about a serious omission, part of her extremely methodical critique of the show. A few others analyzed specific rooms in the exhibition, what worked there and what didn't: audio components that didn't complement images, attempts to set a particular mood that misfired, confusion resulting from the bombardment of too many images or too many sounds.

But for the most part, *Harlem on My Mind* took on the role of a Bobo Doll, attracting the punches of anyone who cared to step up and register their dissatisfaction. But try this experiment. First think about such snappy quotes as "freeze-dried Harlem that does not even hint at flavor," or "it tells us too much about the white man's Negro and not enough about Harlem's blacks."[54] Then examine the catalogue for yourself, either a surviving original copy or the reissued version from 1995. Even minus the direct experience of the "electronic museum theatre," it is difficult to deny the importance of the achievement of *Harlem on My Mind* In the final analysis, for all the exhibition's flaws or naive miscalculations, the catalogue's dedication, "To the people of Harlem—past, present and future—as a record of their achievements," is a sincere reflection of what's contained inside.

The media kept stirring the pot. Reporting on the minutiae of *Harlem on My Mind*—inside and outside the Metropolitan Museum—both the print and the electronic media kept these events continually in the public eye. And why not? There were racial tensions, ethnic strife, a wealthy landmark institution, panicked politicians, and *action*: vandalism, angry denunciations, militant demonstrations, and the potential for further fireworks at any moment. The coverage by newspapers and magazines, as well as television and radio, was vast.

What's more, some people learned how to play to the reporters, striking a mutually beneficial bargain: those with little power got much-desired attention, and the media got an appetizing story. "My experience with the media is it's almost like riding a horse in a rodeo, you know," Benny Andrews observes.

> The problem with it is that once you tame the horse, the media is no longer interested. They look for a horse that bucks. And your job is to get off now and do a calf. And then after you rope the calf and tie the feet you got to get up again, because no one's going to hang around, now that the calf is lying on its back. Well, that's the rhythm that you get to know.

The more accomplished the wrangler, then, the more likely he or she is to be noticed and ultimately remembered.

Because of his leadership role in the BECC, Benny Andrews was singled out as a spokesperson and frequently invited to appear on television. But in an electronic age, and as a commentator on a multimedia-driven exhibition, Andrews presented an interesting anomaly: he talked the talk of black nationalism, but the force of that dogma was somewhat subverted by his extremely light-colored complexion. More than once, he fell short of being a news director's vision of what a bona fide black radical should look like. During a time when the politics of representation was being actively debated, this apparent disjuncture between appearance and reality could be disconcerting— to black militants who wished to bolster a certain public image, as well as to white extremists, who believed they could easily spot their enemies.

Andrews didn't always wait for the media to appear on their own. He sometimes summoned them. He reports that he called the major networks about upcoming BECC activities. As the group matured, it also held press conferences. Moreover, Andrews claims that on occasion the media didn't wait for news to occur unassisted: he maintains that one of the major networks guaranteed airtime to the BECC if it would publicly oppose the artists participating in *Contemporary Black Artists in America* by demonstrating outside the Whitney Museum in 1971. Recall that this was a show the BECC helped broker, but later withdrew from because it lacked a black curator. Andrews states that he and his comrades refused to become a part of a staged skirmish that would pit black against black. This remained a more private struggle, played out beyond the camera lens.

To be fair, articles appeared during this time that could be characterized as attempts to cool things out. For example, the *New York*

Times ran a story showing young black men in yarmulkes, part of a dance troupe comprised of black Jews representing a multiracial group calling itself Hatzaad Harishon, "first step" in Hebrew. The spokesperson earnestly stated, "We're looking for a mutual meeting ground, a place where white and black Jews can come together and discuss common problems." The *Times* also asked twelve black artists, writers, and arts administrators to address the question "Can Black and White Artists Still Work Together?" Not surprisingly, no consensus was reached. (A generation later, the debate continues: in 1997 the critic Robert Brustein [who is white] and the playwright August Wilson [who is black] faced off over issues of opportunity and inclusion, Wilson arguing for the creation of more all-black troupes. The *Times* once again sampled opinion from a dozen professionals in the field.) But these stories could hardly offset the passions reported (and aroused) in the more typical media coverage.[55]

Without a doubt, *Harlem on My Mind* was political dynamite. The danger was heightened because it opened in January of a year in which a mayoral election was scheduled for the fall. And it involved politically ambitious people. There was speculation, for example, that Hoving might be using the directorship of the Met as a stepping-stone to something higher. Might he become a running mate with Mayor Lindsay for City Council president? Perhaps even mount a direct challenge to Lindsay's reelection run for the mayor's office? By reaching out to the black community with *Harlem on My Mind,* Hoving might be trying to accumulate capital he could use in the near future. At least that's what many people at the time thought.

The only catch was that the exhibition blew up in Hoving's face. At some moments he was accused of being an anti-Semite; at others, a racist. Hoving nearly lost his job over the fiasco. Furthermore, any political aspirations he might foster now seemed absurd. As Joseph Noble recalls it, when Hoving returned to the museum after he missed the first few days of the show's run, he was briefed on the chaotic situation. "Shit," Hoving shouted. "I couldn't even be elected dogcatcher." Noble replied, "Tom, you couldn't be elected garbage collector."

Mayor John Lindsay was also caught in the cross hairs. Had *Harlem on My Mind* become an uncontested success, it could have helped to mend some of the damage his office suffered from the prolonged battle over the schools. Instead, both blacks and Jews were affronted, and others on the sidelines were aghast at how turbulent the city had become. Damage control became the order of the day. One of Lindsay's Democratic political challengers, for example, jumped on the opportunity to denounce Van Ellison's essay. That pressured Lindsay to do the same, in order to maintain the stride in the political horse race. In fact, the withdrawal of the catalogue became a fence-mending priority for Lindsay and his cronies.

Lindsay's political vulnerability and the challenge of preserving his complex coalition of supporters were clearly understood at the time. Lindsay was reported to have said in exasperation, "You Jews have made me use up all my Negro credit cards." The iconoclastic journalist I. F. Stone remarked, "John V. Lindsay is in trouble because he suddenly finds himself Mayor of a Southern town."[56] One more reason *Harlem on My Mind* was so controversial, then, was that it became another scene in a larger political drama.

Even the exhibition's title pushed some people's buttons. It was taken from a song written by Irving Berlin in 1933, a lament by a black woman being "kept" in France: "I've a longing to be low-down/And my 'par-lez-vous,'/Will not ring true,/With Harlem on My Mind." Charles Wright panned the song as "masochistic," and proclaimed that "It is in extremely bad taste, an insult to blacks."[57] Others agreed with him in print. But just look at what's happened in the intervening years. A 1994 exhibition of James Van DerZee's photographs at the Smithsonian Institution was called *Harlem on His Mind.* A 1997 news feature on the director of the Upper Manhattan Empowerment Zone, which aims to economically revitalize Harlem, was titled "Harlem on Her Mind." A 1997 article on stereotyping in fashion photography singled out *Paper* as "One magazine that consistently gets it right. . . . Its fashion shoots labeled 'Banjee Girl' and 'Harlem on My Mind' were deeply attuned to the subjects' heritages."[58] In short, the phrase has shed its former distastefulness and has entered the lexicon. One of the best indications of this is the fact that Allon Schoener was commissioned by the Schomburg Center for Research in Black Culture to assemble a 1996 photographic calendar. You guessed it—the title was "Harlem on My Mind."

How have Schoener and others fared since 1969? Schoener retreated to Vermont after a couple of years and still operates his own consulting firm there, mainly working as an independent curator and a writer. He thinks of *Harlem on My Mind* as "revolutionary" and the most important thing he has done in his life. Yet he admits, "We all bumbled it. The biggest regret I have in retrospect is that it's hard to imagine that one could have been so naive about some of the things that happened, because they seem so obvious now. I mean, they seem so improper or wrong or not astute." He also regrets not being recognized as an innovator: "I was and still am a pariah in the museum world."

Thomas P. F. Hoving continued as director at the Metropolitan Museum of Art until 1977. Like Schoener, he too runs his own consulting firm, specializing in the arts and communications. When *Making the Mummies Dance* was published, critics skewered it as mean-spirited and mendacious. But according to Schoener, "he didn't fuck up any worse than anybody else did [regarding the exhibition]. And you've got to give him credit for having made this possible. It would not have happened if he didn't have the vision. And he also took a rap on it." Joseph Noble took over the helm of the Museum of the City of New York in 1970 and retired from the directorship in 1985. His first exhibition was *Drug Scene*, a show that had the potential to roil viewers but was instead a success.

The Black Emergency Cultural Coalition continued to lobby to get more black artists shown in museums and more blacks placed in curatorial positions. It also began offering drawing classes to prison inmates, inaugurated at Manhattan's "Tombs" in 1971. Ten years later these programs were going strong in prisons throughout the country. The Metropolitan Museum of Art now owns two Benny Andrews paintings; he's realized his dream of being on the *inside*: "All through this I was trying to be a creative artist. I never wanted to do any of this protest stuff. I did this because it needed to be done."

What, in the final analysis, is the legacy of *Harlem on My Mind*? The exhibition meant many things to many different people. For instance, it signifies an opening salvo in the continuing debate over "high" and "low" culture. Not only was photography deemed somewhat of an upstart form of expression to most museums and many critics in 1969, but this show was being presented in the Metropolitan Museum of Art, after all. This medium's exotic quality was further accentuated because the show's subject broke new ground, and its high-tech presentation made it seem more of an incursion. Defenders of quality and traditional standards jumped forward; a few of them, like Hilton Kramer, have been doing that for a long time now. The sense that the cultural hierarchy was being challenged—with the fresh potential for some forms of expression and their advocates to gain ground, while others risked losing it—was an important aspect to this struggle.

Harlem on My Mind also forced museums to represent minority communities. For Fred Wilson, "I think it was great that Hoving did it. It showed the museum's Achilles heel in a kind of wonderful way, because it acknowledged something and then it opened the flood gates for attack on a broader base." But in reality, those doors and gates may have opened merely a crack. As time has passed, there has been a ghettoization of minority artists to ethnically specific museums, which offer more opportunities for marginalized groups than major institutions do.

Many of the goals of the Black Emergency Cultural Coalition concerning inclusion and expanding the administrative and curatorial structures of museums to include minorities have yet to be realized. There are some notable exceptions, to be sure. Thelma Golden, a Whitney Museum curator until recently, emphatically states that "The reason I have my job is because of *Harlem on My Mind*. [And] Lowery Sims [who, like Golden, is black] often says she got her [curatorial] job at the Met specifically in 1973 because of the controversy." Golden continues, "Had the protests not happened, I'm not sure the Whitney or other institutions in this city would have changed. It galvanized most museums to get to the place where in 1990 I could work here and do the things I do. But it took twenty years."[59]

The struggle over this exhibition was so intense that it may have made other museums think twice about tackling something similar. For Allon Schoener, "It created the opportunity for these ethnically specific museums to be created, and maybe it also scared the major cultural institutions forever. Or maybe it wasn't a question of scaring them, but maybe what it did was prove to them that if they moved into these territories, it was too dangerous."

The extensive media attention focused on Thelma Golden's exhibition *Black Male: Representations of Masculinity in Contemporary Art* (Whitney Museum of American Art, 1994) confirms this to a degree. Golden feels she was breaking new ground in this show because it approached race as a topic, not as a condition: the artists were linked by common subject matter, not by belonging to the same racial group. But many critics pummeled the exhibit, complaining that too much of the material confirmed established stereotypes, or that it represented a politics of the moment, not art. Golden was unfazed. As a curator in a museum that showcases contemporary art, she believes that such reactions are predictable and largely irrelevant. But many other museum professionals and their institutions are not so thick-skinned. And many more would rather avoid controversy than view it as a necessary cost of conducting their business.

A case in point: twenty-five years later the exhibition *Back of the Big House: The Cultural Landscape of the Plantation,* curated by John Michael Vlach, a professor of American studies and anthropology. In the more than half dozen books Vlach has either written or edited, he has explored folk art, African American folk art and architecture, and plantation life. His work is a superb example of the "new social history." Vlach's book *Back of the Big House: The Architecture of Plantation Slavery* (1993) presented the landscape of southern plantations as texts to "read" and interpret. He drew on two unique and largely untapped sources of material deposited in the Library of Congress: a stockpile of photographs and architectural renderings produced by the Historic American Buildings Survey (HABS) mainly in the 1930s, and narratives collected by interviewers from the WPA Federal Writers' Project of the lives of surviving former slaves, dating from the 1930s and 1940s as well. His interpretive skills have also been honed through years of field research on these environments.

Vlach dubbed his methodology "historical ethnography," combining architectural history with social history. The HABS material provided the visual raw material; the slaves' words animated these spaces with vivid and authentic sounds. Vlach's passion for his data is evident as he counsels his readers, "Look at the pictures. Pore over the drawings. Check their details. Do it carefully, and you can develop almost a tangible sense of the buildings that once sheltered the everyday routines of slaves."[60] There can be no doubt that this is an engaged scholar. Vlach is devoted to redressing historical oversights. He is also a white scholar committed to altering the ways we understand our built, as well as our social, environment.

In part, Vlach interprets plantation structures and their spatial relations. We recognize his partnership with academics who identify

with the marginalized when he asks us to reconsider the typical fig-
ure/ground relationship of this territory: "A master's house was 'big'
only if it had smaller buildings nearby."[61] He thereby requires us to
shift our accustomed viewpoint and appreciate that the plantation
was an *ensemble* of buildings, in dialogue with one another. Moreover,
he examines various strategies the slaves used to take some control
over these spaces for themselves, to humanize and personalize them.
Here he employs concepts such as "resistance," "accommodation,"
"autonomy," "community," and "identity." Simply put, he explores
the ways slaves were able to make themselves at home, even within a
repressive context.

The success of the book led to a traveling exhibition, commissioned by the Library of Congress (LOC). But the two projects were
not exactly the same: the exhibit added more of a human dimension,
especially through photographs of former slaves. The slave narrative
collection, it turns out, included about three hundred such photos,
and Vlach also borrowed images that were privately held. It was "an
emotional breakthrough" for him to match a real face to someone
whose words he'd been working with for a long time.[62] As with one
of the examples he included of the ex-slave who remembered working from sunrise to sunset—"can see to can't see"—Vlach feels that
these people "continue to preach to us."

The exhibition contained six major subdivisions: "The Plantation
Landscape," "Slave Tasks," "Slave Quarters," "Slave Skills and Tal-
ents," "Slave Religion," and "The End of Slavery." Self-empower-
ment, dignity, and defiance permeated the display. It concluded in a
heartening manner, with testimony about emancipation and a final
image of a row of abandoned slave quarters.

Back of the Big House: The Cultural Landscape of the Plantation was a
success at the sites that hosted it before it appeared at the Library of
Congress itself in December 1995. It was extremely well received
everywhere else it toured, too—primarily university museums and
historic homes. (In fact, it became one of the most popular exhibits
the LOC has ever sent on the road.) More to the point, it garnered a
positive response everywhere *except* the LOC itself, where officials
took it down within hours of its debut there.

Black employees, and some white ones as well, complained that
"it lacked perspective and balance," or they were disturbed by the

"broken dialect." Estimates of the number of people voicing concern ranged from twenty to sixty.[63] But instead of exploring these charges, senior-level administrators, led by Winston Tabb, the associate librarian for library services, quickly capitulated and closed the show. The LOC Librarian James H. Billington casually dismissed this as "a complete non-story," and avoided the hard issues by writing it off as a petty, private matter: "no one wanted a family quarrel—particularly in this holiday season."[64]

Jill Brett, the LOC public affairs officer, concurs: "Rather than trying to get everybody together and talk it through and kind of heighten the rancor, we felt it was just better to lance the boil." Tabb stands by his decision: "To have taken down an exhibition that was never intended to have been put there in the first place, to me is a non-story. The real story would have been if we had tried to suppress the exhibit, which clearly we did not. We were quite happy it went to additional places. We did not disown the exhibition."[65]

But this is "the nation's library," after all, and the way it conducts itself has far-reaching consequences for other institutions. And the story was eminently newsworthy, even attracting international attention. Reports were published in France and Sweden, for example, and discussions were held on NPR affiliates in Germany and South Africa. To many observers, these responses seemed dismissive, rationalizations rather than explanations.

The controversy turned out to be a boon for Washington, D.C.'s Martin Luther King Memorial Library, a public branch that embraced the exhibition, and where "It's definitely generated more interest than any other exhibit we've had," the MLK's exhibit coordinator remarked.[66] According to Vlach, people attending the opening at the MLK were primed to view some sort of historical dynamite; "they expected to see blood, but the event turned into a love-in." For most of those who carefully examined the exhibition, there was nothing offensive, and much that was affirming, about the black experience. Yet at the LOC, a black employee had described a picture of a white overseer on horseback brandishing a shotgun that was particularly upsetting to him: "It reminded me of the white overseers here at the Library of Congress looking down over us to make sure we're in the fields doing our work." As with the Vietnam vets who imagined Ho Chi

Minh's face on a Boston gas tank, this was also a fantastic projection. There was no gun in the photo.[67] How could such misperceptions and apparent cowardice be occurring at the country's premier library?

Minority employees, it turns out, have nicknamed the LOC "the Plantation" or "the Big House," especially since the passage of the 1964 Civil Rights Act. Many of them feel trapped in clerical and menial jobs. Some of them filed a complaint with the Equal Employment Opportunity Office in 1975, providing the basis for a class action racial discrimination lawsuit, *Cook v. Boorstin*. The case straggled along for so long that it was eventually renamed *Cook v. Billington*, to reflect the Librarian's successor. A court finally ruled on the plaintiffs' behalf in the amount of $8.5 million just three months before *Back of the Big House* was displayed. But that was not the end. The case dragged on because of outstanding appeals; monies were not dispersed until early 1997.

Even though discrimination was confirmed in this workplace, the conditions were not yet suitably developed for healing to commence. This site, where approximately two out of every five employees are black, was saturated by a heightened sense of injustice and insensitivity. Vlach, whose wife is an LOC employee, notes that "the poison, the stink of no payment from the court order has changed the environment." As a result, certain people lugged frayed and cumbersome emotional baggage along with them when they viewed the exhibition, which appeared without advance word just outside an employees' cafeteria.

It was more than some employees felt they could bear, given the history of this place. But their instantaneous response seemed to betray a defense mechanism that first develops out of necessity, but lingers long beyond its usefulness. Besides, they knew how to snap their fingers to get the administration's attention. The last thing those in charge wanted were further claims of breaches of racial etiquette. Today's protocol in settings such as the office precludes honest and forthright discussion between the races. As a result, people often steer clear of engagement, even when that compromises cherished principles such as freedom of expression. It was, as a *Washington Post* editorial correctly identified, a "hair-trigger reaction" in a place where people were nervously walking "on tiptoe."[68]

A black editor at the *Washington Post* charged that this protest against the exhibit was "cultural blackmail" and extortion. His position was shared by Byron Rushing, a black Massachusetts state legislator who once directed the African Meeting House Museum on Boston's Beacon Hill, and who consulted on this show. Assessing Billington's easy surrender, Rushing declared,

> This is a white man panicking. The black staff people that objected to this have an agenda—to annoy white people. But the director is a silly white man. He doesn't say "I'll have a dialogue with you." The thing he does, which is racist, is he does not assume that there would be any other black people on the staff of the library who would have a different view.[69]

Rushing gets to the heart of the matter. In this instance, blind outrage was coupled with knowing exactly how to get the Man's goat.

But both sides were losers. The LOC lost face with the general public, professional librarians and academics, and undoubtedly many of its employees. This incident compounded the bad press the LOC had received for postponing a proposed Freud exhibit just over two weeks before, when critics assailed it due to what they perceived as dictatorial control by "the Freud establishment" (see chapter 4). The sociologist Todd Gitlin dubbed this and other incidents of conflict avoidance on the part of the LOC and the Smithsonian Institution "profiles in cowardice."[70]

Winston Tabb offered the authorized "defense" to supplement Billington's nonchalance over the demise of *Back of the Big House*. In a letter to the editor published in the *Chicago Tribune*, Tabb cited the lack of advance preparation or explanation to support the exhibit, and its allegedly "ambiguous title." He also threw in what sounded like a choice bit of bureaucratic obfuscation: "This exhibit was designed to travel, not to be installed at the Library of Congress."[71]

As Irene (Burnham) Chambers, the head of the Interpretive Programs Office, explains, the LOC was sponsoring a half dozen traveling exhibitions at the time. Her supervisor, before Winston Tabb took over those duties just two weeks prior to this incident, decided that these shows deserved to be highlighted inside the building: "We also are doing this" would be the message. With the transition of power being so recent, Chambers had not told Tabb of the plan. That's why Tabb adopted the position he did. But keep in mind, no one foisted this show on the LOC. This was not imported matter;

the LOC initiated it. It was based on its own holdings. And at no other site were such issues of ambiguity or outreach raised.

LOC employees were also losers. *Back of the Big House* was an exhibition that potentially enlarged the understanding of slavery for any viewer. For black Americans in particular, it had the potential to enhance their identities as survivors. Included among the viewer comments from the MLK Library presentation is clear evidence of the show's positive impact. One woman wrote, for example, "The exhibit moved me to tears. It was important to see how my ancestors lived, survived and overcame. I'm bringing my husband and kids back to see it." Another visitor offered this evaluation: "Thanks for letting me decide on the merit of this exhibit. History for most Blacks is a painful and emotional study, but it is what happened. It serves for me as a reminder of the strong people that are my past and resolve that I too must endure."[72]

What is particularly lamentable is that a number of alternative strategies could have easily been adopted to address the dissent while keeping the exhibit in place at the LOC. For one thing, adjacent space could have been provided for people to write their responses, turning it into an interactive event with a contemporary component. It also could have been debated in the *Gazette*, the LOC's in-house organ. One employee published a frank condemnation of the LOC's response in the "Forum" section of the newsletter. When that was countered by the editor's lengthy rationalization, an employee wrote in a later issue that it was inappropriate for the editor to become a mouthpiece (and apologist) for management. That same issue of the *Gazette* published another letter on the subject by a black employee whose interest was piqued when she first saw the exhibition being installed. She was later saddened that she would not have the opportunity to view it *in toto* herself.[73]

Here, then, was a ready-made forum. Vlach reports that a black historian colleague of his attempted to speak with employees who had been identified in the media as opponents, and Vlach also proposed holding a teach-in to confront their concerns. But neither proposal was given much opportunity to evolve. Employees who were critical of this exhibition completely dug in to their positions and refused to engage in a dialogue.

LOC officials *did* take charge in one respect. Bothered by the title, they excised *Back of the Big House* from the exhibition's name. That

FIG. 5. *The Cultural Landscape of the Plantation,* 1996. Brochure from a traveling exhibition sponsored by the Library of Congress. Photograph by Bart Dellarmi.

phrase raised hackles only at the LOC, because of its peculiar institutional history. Sadly, this sacrifice was an empty action, no more than a small, symbolic cut. During the eight days it took to transfer everything and set it up at the MLK Library, the LOC re-shot and remounted the first panel with just *The Cultural Landscape of the Plantation*. But the complete name of Vlach's book remained in the very next panel.

Tabb admits he wasn't personally aware of this sobriquet employees used for the LOC until the protest erupted. "There might have been no way for us to have known this in advance, had this not happened," he contends. But Jill Brett insists that longtime employees—black and white—were aware of the reference. Moreover, Tabb worried that since the exhibit was placed just outside this cafeteria, literally "in your face" as you stepped off the elevator, it was seen as an intentional affront. That fell foursquare within Tabb's new domain. For his part, Vlach considers the missing words "a dueling scar," proof of the virtue of his project. One of Vlach's biggest sources of gratification and confirmation is the ritualized exchange that developed between him and the secretary of the LOC's interpretive history section. She routinely inquires when he visits, "How's *our* exhibit?" She delights in hearing reports that it has been garnering positive responses. To her mind, the continuing success of the exhibition "sure makes LOC look stupid." That woman, incidentally, is black.[74]

Museums and other public exhibition spaces have become more politicized since *Harlem on My Mind*, as the example of *Back of the Big House* amply demonstrates. They are increasingly subject to the whims of politicians who contemptuously use them for target practice. Museums can be censured when crusading officials turn the issues presented within their galleries into questions of morality, decency, or patriotism. Museums can also be threatened with a tightening of the purse strings when public funds are involved. This infusion of financial support, and the control it introduces, was just accelerating when *Harlem on My Mind* debuted. Moreover, as we've just discovered, pressure groups of all sorts are also important. Alliances based on race, gender, religion, region, generation, occupation, and other interests have proliferated during the past twenty-five years, resulting in a much remarked upon balkanization of American society. This was already apparent in nascent form with the many groups that found fault with different aspects of *Harlem on My Mind*. Visualize once again the cadres of protestors outside the Met and you will have caught a glimpse of the future of American public life. Today museum staffs cannot focus exclusively upon their subjects; they must pay much closer attention to the social ecology in which they are embedded. Many people who generally care very little about museums use them as a jousting ground for extracultural concerns.

During the controversy surrounding *Harlem on My Mind,* the tremendous power attributed to symbols and representation and the urgent desire to rebut an image or demand restitution for perceived distortions demonstrated that the cultural sphere was displacing the realm of "pure politics" as a primary site of contemporary public debates and struggles. At the time it occurred, *Harlem on My Mind* and the response it evoked seemed *sui generis.* But in so many ways, *Harlem on My Mind* was the mother of them all, the harbinger of many more battles to be fought.

3

"The Troubles" in the New World

The Uncivil War over Gaelic Gotham

Freud . . . muttered in exasperation that the Irish were the only peo-
ple who could not be helped by psychoanalysis.
— Thomas Cahill, *How the Irish
Saved Civilization*

IRISH SELF-IDENTITY has always included a large component of
persecution, victimization, and the anguish of being silenced. In the
1995 film *The Secret of Roan Inish,* for instance, a man speaks to his
granddaughter of olden times:

> The English were still a force in the country then. They had the
> schools. It was their language and their ways that you had to learn
> there—or else. Was a new schoolmaster in the school one year. As
> stiff as a cat's whiskers, he was. Sean Michael wasn't a week in his
> class before he put the cinglum[1] about his neck, as a punishment of
> those days for speaking Irish within his ear shot.

Enraged by his schoolmates' shouts of "Idjit," "Idjit," the boy tore the
horse collar–like device off and attacked his schoolmaster, defiantly
screaming back in Irish.

This passage illustrates two themes, in fact. One is the centrality
of storytelling to the Irish, who have a powerful oral and written tradition that links new generations to a centuries-old legacy. The other
is the history of attempts to stifle Irish expression—and thereby disrupt their culture and crush their aspirations—as well as Irish struggles to defy such restrictions. Both of these themes were thrown into
sharp focus in the controversy over *Gaelic Gotham: A History of the
Irish in New York City,* an exhibition mounted by the Museum of the

City of New York (MCNY) in 1996. In this conflict definitions of community, community participation, and the immigrant experience and its various meanings were very much contested, just as the struggles over *Harlem on My Mind* and *Back of the Big House* brought up concerns about collective identities and their representation. As in still other controversies, these troubles broke out at a critical juncture: when the relative position of Irish Americans and their identity as a group were in transition.

Angela's Ashes, Frank McCourt's affecting, Pulitzer Prize–winning memoir of his hardscrabble upbringing in Limerick, carries on the tradition of vibrant Irish storytelling. But the book's phenomenal success and the author's newfound fame, later in life, recapitulate what has happened to the Irish generally in this country. While they faced enormous hardships and discrimination in the nineteenth century, the Irish also shrewdly consolidated political power. Tammany Hall, the embodiment of the ethnically dominated urban political machine, greased the wheels for Irish ascendancy in New York City.

A century later, the Irish have largely assimilated and achieved a remarkable degree of economic success in America. Irish chic currently translates into mass market appeal. Witness the proliferation of Irish-themed movies or the huge box-office receipts of Riverdance or of Michael Flatley's "Lord of the Dance," the traveling musical/tapping/clogging extravaganza that one critic indignantly called "about as Irish as the old Disney film 'Darby O'Gill and the Little People,'" and about as authentic as an imagined Disneyland attraction called Shamrockland.[2] Nevertheless, these are immensely crowd-pleasing entertainments.

But as noted in a bittersweet news feature in New York's *Irish Echo* entitled "A Fading Tile in the Gorgeous Mosaic?" the mass suburbanization under way since the 1950s has meant that the Irish influence in New York City has diminished considerably, as it has in other cities. Here are some sobering facts: from 1960 to 1970 the number of Irish-born New Yorkers declined 40 percent. In 1990, 7 percent of the city's population was of Irish ancestry, native or foreign-born, compared with about a quarter of city residents a hundred years earlier. The article sorrowfully observed, "Gone are the days of Irish dominance of New York City politics. Gone are the days of Irish families breathing life into every neighborhood." Then it posed the question,

THE TIGER'S SHARE

FIG. 6. H. Gillam, *The Tiger's Share*, c. 1875. Color lithograph. Museum of the City of New York. Used by permission.

"So, will New York's Irish soon go the way of New York's Dutch?"[3] In other words, will the Irish become another group to fade from prominence, to surface primarily as names on street signs and shallow annual ethnic tributes?

The notion that everyone is Irish once a year pitches an ethnic "big tent" unlike any other group's. But all is not necessarily well: the Irish have not struggled exclusively against invaders and colonizers. Take the St. Patrick's Day parade, frequently a focus of controversy. In the nineteenth century, two parades were sometimes held to accommodate different viewpoints. In more recent times, what the person on the street probably knows about the Irish in New York City involves the battle to keep ILGO, the Irish Gay and Lesbian Organization, from marching under its own banner down Fifth Avenue.

Founded in 1990, the ILGO first applied to march in the 1991 parade to the Ancient Order of Hibernians, the Catholic fraternal organization in charge. Two of the ILGO's founders, Brendan Fay and Anne Maguire, became fixtures on the local news. Their distinctive looks and the cadence of their speech confirmed their birthright. Their bold, no-apologies bid to participate attested to their resolve not to be silenced. The terms were thus set for a nasty public debate that has raged for several months each successive year.

After it was blocked in its initial attempt at inclusion, the ILGO marched with a sympathetic contingent in 1991, with Mayor David Dinkins walking alongside. The group was showered with beer and epithets. The ILGO was denied a place the next year too. In 1993 Cardinal John O'Connor angrily denounced a decision by the mayor and the police commissioner to name a new parade sponsor that would accommodate the ILGO's wish to participate (the cover of the *New York Post* showed the cardinal holding the majestic doors of St. Patrick's Cathedral, accompanied by the tabloid headline "Don't Try It!").[4] A federal judge upheld the right of the Hibernians to exclude the ILGO, and the Supreme Court ruled similarly in 1995 in a case involving a related situation in Boston. But mass arrests ensued during demonstrations in 1993, when angry ILGO members and their supporters protested the situation. Arrests have continued in decreasing numbers every year since.

To many observers, the parade has devolved into an opportunity for suburban dwellers to invade the city, drink, and carouse. Pete

FIG. 7. Carolina Kroon's 1993 photograph was incorporated into this New York City Irish Lesbian and Gay Organization (ILGO) poster in 1994. Used by permission.

Hamill dismisses the parade as "an annual celebration of vomit," and Jimmy Breslin notes, "They [the Irish] don't live or vote here and they don't like it here. Let them parade [elsewhere]."[5] However, such events retain a powerful symbolic attraction for the Irish throughout the United States: for example, although the population of Newark, New Jersey, is now less than 2 percent Irish, the city still mounts an annual St. Patrick's Day parade. And for reasons that are not exactly self-evident, the Japanese began holding their own parade in Tokyo in 1992. For Irish Americans, the parade is a residue that nostalgically symbolizes ethnic pride; for others, it is an excuse to party.

The extensive news coverage of the parade debates has angered the Catholic Church. It has been portrayed in an extremely negative light in most instances. The church hierarchy has been characterized as holding antediluvian ideas about sexuality that lead to hatred, misunderstanding, and discrimination on the official level. The sociologist Reverend Andrew M. Greeley counters that polling data consistently reveal Irish Catholics to be the most liberal gentile ethnic group in America.[6] Yet the stereotype of Irish narrow-mindedness has been renewed through the invective the rank-and-file hurl on the streets of New York City each spring.

The controversy over the parade broke out at the same time that a number of revelations were being made of child sex abuse by priests, and the church was losing its fight to block the distribution of condoms in public schools to help put the brakes on the AIDS epidemic. Moreover, popular culture frequently takes up the banner against the church. Sinéad O'Connor ripped up a picture of Pope John Paul II on *Saturday Night Live*; Miramax produced a film entitled *The Pope Must Die*. Such incidents have prompted the church to decry "Catholic bashing," evidence of what it argues is entrenched media bias against the church. An institution historically associated in the public mind in New York City with being Irish has, therefore, been feeling quite defensive.

All these matters provide the backdrop to *Gaelic Gotham*, an exhibition whose origins can be traced to 1989. At that time, a young local Irish American scholar named Marion R. Casey started organizing a small exhibition, *Keeping the Tradition Alive: A History of Irish Music and Dance in New York City*. It was mounted at the Museum of the City of New York in 1991, where Casey also successfully coordinated a series of related weekend events.

An additional contextual factor deserves mention: one of the most pivotal events of modern Irish history was, of course, the Great Potato Famine of 1845-51. An estimated one million people died from starvation and disease, and another million and a half were forced to abandon the country. During the 150th anniversary commemoration in 1997, British prime minister Tony Blair expressed regret over these events, not going quite so far as issuing an apology for English culpability. (This occurred at the same time that his American counterpart, Bill Clinton, raised the idea of apologizing for slavery.) That tragedy now bears considerable importance for Irish identity, much as the Middle Passage does for blacks.

In 1996 Irish Americans won a significant symbolic victory: the New York legislature mandated all state-funded schools to include the Great Famine in their curricula, alongside other considerations of human rights violations and genocide. The British refused to divert food for export to the starving Irish; their actions have been likened to the conduct of the Nazis during the Holocaust. Moreover, a proposal to erect a memorial in New York City's Battery Park (where the Museum of Jewish Heritage: A Living Memorial to the Holocaust opened in the fall of 1997) inched toward approval. The monument would commemorate the victims who arrived aboard "coffin ships," so-called because of the countless immigrants who perished en route to America. A feature in the travel section of the *New York Times* even highlighted famine places of interest for tourists, including a convenient website, www.famine.ie.[7]

In other words, the Irish have expended considerable effort over the past few years to have their own suffering presented equitably, on par with that of other groups. The famine becomes the Irish Holocaust, because it is the one term we have that bestows sufficient gravity on a situation to command and sustain the general public's attention. It stands as a critical linguistic marker, a yardstick that confers the legitimacy of suffering.[8] The linkage of past injustices with current conditions is splendidly displayed in a letter to the editor of the *Irish Echo* about the parade: "The mayor, the [police] commissioner and their homosexual constituents continue the *pogroms* against Irish Catholics begun in the 1600s by James I and culminating in the 1920s with the Special Constabulary designed to purge the Irish North of its Catholic population."[9] To reiterate, a dominant trope in Irish self-reflection is that the Irish temper has been shaped by centuries of op-pression. The challenge their descendants face today is to control the telling of that history, even if it means appropriating anachronistic concepts like "pogrom" and bending and twisting them into new forms.

Hindsight not only bestows twenty-twenty vision. It can also make you wince over the tragedy of miscalculated aspirations and dashed expectations. Those are exactly the feelings you have when you look at a 1993 *New York Daily News* article confidently predicting that "Irish eyes will smile at her exhibit." The "her" was Marion Casey, poised and grinning at the camera. The exhibit was *Gaelic Gotham*, with an anticipated budget of $250,000. But beneath the upbeat tenor of the report there was already a slight sense of unease on Casey's part: "I do get depressed because I think maybe only 10 people will care about what I do," she lamented.[10]

Casey's fears were somewhat misplaced. Although planning and executing this exhibition became extremely complicated, several things became evident. Casey has legions of supporters. They care deeply about what she does. She can count on them to rush to her de-fense when they feel she has been wronged. Moreover, the flap over *Gaelic Gotham* piqued people's curiosity; attendance expectations were exceeded. The tempest eclipsed Casey's worries that this show would be slighted or neglected, even though her ultimate role in it di-minished.

The *Daily News* article offers one additional hint at the problems to come. The notion of "her exhibit" proved to be very troublesome. In fact, it precipitated the dispute, which later transmuted into sev-eral distinct forms. As mentioned, Marion Casey successfully engi-neered a small exhibition in the MCNY's community gallery spot-lighting Irish music and dance in 1991. Because of that, she was hired as a consultant for the preparation of an application to the National Endowment for the Humanities (NEH) for a planning grant to under-take a much grander survey of over 350 years of Irish life in New York City. After that was secured, Casey was also pivotal in preparing a 1994 application for an NEH implementation grant. That too came through: $250,000 in direct aid and $50,000 in matching funds. The NEH contribution and the matching funds—$350,000 in toto—plus direct and indirect costs of the museum added up to a budget of just over $770,000 by MCNY calculations, far short of the original projection of $1.2 million.

At the initial stages, the show was called *Sweet Recollections of Home: The Irish and New York*. Once the grant was announced, the MCNY had to prune back the project to what was feasible and affordable. In fact, when MCNY director Robert R. Macdonald wrote to Casey with congratulations on securing the grant, he also stressed that the first order of business was to revise the budget. Casey assisted in that task. The "fancy interactive stuff" was scrapped. So was ancillary programming tied in with institutions such as the South Street Seaport and the Brooklyn Historical Society.[11] According to Jan Seidler Ramirez, who became the project director, working around such reductions is typical: "First you shoot for the moon, [asking for] everything you possibly want to do. But we're very good at living with less. We do that all the time."[12]

From December 1994 until late March 1995, the museum and Casey sparred with one another over job titles, mode of payment, and control. It's not difficult to understand why Casey felt proprietary toward this project. She nurtured it over several years. She suspended her doctoral studies in history at New York University to devote herself to it. Her friends and colleagues closely identified her with the proposed exhibition, as did the general public via the *Daily News* coverage. She was listed as "guest curator" on the NEH application. But moving from the proposal to the implementation phase, MCNY administrators increasingly emphasized the importance of a team effort, eclipsing what Casey had envisioned as her role as overseer.

In all the contracts offered to Casey, the museum continued to refer to her as a guest curator. But the MCNY cast her future position more as that of a consultant, who would be paid upon completion of specific tasks. Marion Casey believed she would be managing the project. She thus answered an MCNY request for a list of her proposed tasks with a broad "statement of responsibilities" instead. In that document she claims, "Marion R. Casey will be responsible for the integrity of *Gaelic Gotham*, in its whole as well as its component parts. *Gaelic Gotham*'s integrity includes the expression of (1) intellectual content, (2) artistic interpretation, and (3) image or public representation. . . . Marion R. Casey assumes, but is not limited to, all tasks generally covered by the term 'curator.'"[13]

MCNY officials supported an alternate model. According to Jan Ramirez,

> We've undergone a sea change, and work by the exhibit project team method. Marion Casey never would have had the independence to go off and write something and give it to us and say, "This is it, folks. Up it goes on the wall." She would have been part of a team constantly critiquing, looking, thinking, sorting, balancing, editing. And that's just the way we work with anybody.

Furthermore, Marion Casey wished to be paid biweekly as if she were a regular employee so that she could cover her bills. (Several of her allies attest that she lives "hand-to-mouth.")[14] She was concerned that she might be engaged in many of the tasks simultaneously, so that her income would be unpredictable at best. However, if you examine the list of tasks the museum presented in the draft contract it sent to Casey, the tasks seem sequential. Moreover, the deadlines listed for each task fell at the end of succeeding months, March to September 1995. From October until the exhibition opened in February 1996, the MCNY was offering a flat fee for continued services as well. In effect, the museum was offering regularity of payment, as long as Casey produced what she was being hired to do.

A number of letters passed between the parties trying to iron out these differences. Although the museum promptly answered Casey's many queries and kept pushing back the deadline for her to return a signed contract, the matter remained at an impasse. Significantly, the parties never spoke directly during this period. According to Edward T. O'Donnell, a young historian who became part of the curatorial team later on, "Marion had done heroic work. This is not just a career thing for Marion, it's a real personal, deep commitment to produce quality history about Irish Americans." O'Donnell has examined all the documentation of the contracts and the terms the MCNY tendered and that Casey subsequently rejected. He concludes that Casey was not "fired": "Firing is when you're told you may not work here." What he observed instead was that each written offer came back to the museum "with point by point by point by point, saying, 'I want, I need this. I need that. This is my interpretation of guest curator, yuppity yup.'"[15]

For example, Casey faxed a three-page letter to the museum on February 28, 1995, characterizing the proposed contract as "a very puzzling document." She then enumerated her points of contention and asserted her authority over such matters as supervising the installation of the exhibition, handling the press, and managing volunteer orientation tours. She anticipated that in the critical weeks just before *Gaelic Gotham* opened, she would need to be working full-time. The MCNY's reply came on March 2. Each point was clarified, and her role as guest curator *as part of a project team* was reiterated. Included in the list of twenty-two points was the explanation that "Preparation of the final edited script will be the responsibility of other consultants employed by the Museum."

Casey replied in another lengthy letter four days later. She saw the stewardship of the exhibition slipping from her exclusive command: "'other consultants employed by the Museum' will edit *my* script, proofread *my* label and text panel copy. . . . The point of view expressed in that grant application is *mine* alone. . . . [T]he Guest Curator is being cut out of any substantive role in the project a full nine months before the opening of the exhibition" (emphasis added). Marion Casey's concept of guest curator diverged widely from the one supported by the museum.

The most important sticking point became that of copyright. When the MCNY negotiated a contract with Casey in 1992, it specified that all the intellectual work done under its employ was the property of the museum. But the MCNY also understood that there would naturally be some overlap between Casey's dissertation research and her work for the museum. To that extent, the museum would "retain copyright to the form, but not to the intellectual content, of the work provided."[16]

In Robert Macdonald's eyes, this was work-for-hire, no more, no less. Casey was insisting on a broader role, and Macdonald balked. Keep in mind that negotiations dragged on for months, during the critical period for mapping out the exhibition in practical terms. This became tedious and annoying for everybody. When Casey proposed joint copyright for everything produced for the show, Macdonald felt that this was contrary to museum practice, and that she had crossed a line: "I said, 'That's it. We can't proceed on this. We are not going to give up the museum's rights.' A grant was given to the Museum of the City of New York. It was written by the museum. The hypothesis was written by the museum. Marion's research is in there, no doubt about it. But we paid her for it."[17] Casey and the museum terminated their relationship.

Macdonald's position really angered Angela Carter, the owner of the Irish Bookshop in lower Manhattan. Carter speaks deliberately but passionately. Her concerns continually circle back to issues regarding labor, women, and social class. Carter had seen firsthand what a fine job Marion Casey had done managing the exhibition on Irish music and dance. Carter was even one of a group of about twenty volunteers who raised funds and assisted with the weekend events associated with that earlier MCNY show. So she was enraged by the museum's treatment of Casey: "A lot of it was tremendous disrespect for women. I mean, 'Who is this girl, Marion Casey? She's just a difficult girl.' If it had been a man, it might not have been the same."

The freelance journalist Helena Mulkerns, who specializes in writing about the arts and the "New Irish," argues, "Macdonald didn't keep Marion on because she was *too* passionate, and would have seen the project through. She would have fought to have everything to be done perfectly. To have the best exhibition ever on the Irish in New York."[18] But that emphasis on perfection made it difficult for Casey to settle for less than the commanding position, which was not forthcoming.

Brother Emmett Corry, O.S.F., a retired professor of library science and an archivist, was similarly incensed at the MCNY. At the time, Corry was the president of the New York Irish History Roundtable, founded in 1984. Roundtable members are interested in Irish history and genealogy. The group numbers approximately five hundred members nationwide; about a hundred regularly come to meetings throughout a given year. The roundtable sponsors lectures and workshops and publishes a journal. Corry characterized Robert Macdonald's treatment of Marion Casey as "shabby," and felt Macdonald had done "a dastardly thing" by displacing her from the guest curator position.[19]

Listen carefully to the language of some people "on the other side," and you have to wonder whether Angela Carter's suspicions that gender played a role might not indeed have been correct. Robert Macdonald argues that various individuals and groups rallied around Casey because "Marion was their lassie." In fact, Casey is well known in certain Irish circles. At various times she has been an officer, board member, or active participant in such groups as the New York Irish History Roundtable, the Irish Institute, and the Columbia University Seminar on Irish Studies. To Macdonald, this was "chivalry gone mad." Ed O'Donnell uses the same imagery, charging that the people who waged a multipronged attack against the museum "to avenge" how Casey was wronged "get an A+ for chivalry and loyalty, and an F for quality and knowledge."

But does this reveal gender bias on the part of Macdonald and O'Donnell? Or could it instead reflect what they perceived as protective, paternalistic behavior displayed by Casey's supporters? Jack Salzman, another member of the final exhibition team, dismisses the idea that Marion Casey was treated badly because she was a woman. He sees her as a "bright prospect" whom some people "anointed as a martyr."[20]

Casey's fate does not seem unusual to David Lackey of Whirlwind and Company, the designers of *Gaelic Gotham*. He reflects that it is not unusual to conceive of an idea, and then not be given the central role one anticipated in carrying it out: "Whether it's because my name is Lackey, or whether because I've worked for public institutions all of my life, I'm used to that."[21] Robert Macdonald emphasizes that museum work is always a collaborative effort. "I don't know of one historical exhibit that is a quote individual effort," he notes. Moreover, as the principals in *The Last Act: The Atomic Bomb and the End of World War II* emphasized, museum exhibitions are not exclusively composed of ideas, but are visual and auditory experiences as well (see chapter 6). They do not merely present ideas and arguments, but must also convey impressions swiftly and precisely, through a variety of media.

Budgets, square footage, traffic patterns, and design do's and don'ts are all specialized skills, honed over many years of hands-on experience. They represent the pragmatic side of making an exhibition compelling, interesting, and understandable. Once the planning for a show proceeds to a certain point, the challenge is for a group of people to transpose a concept from the page into something tangible. To Macdonald, "An individual might be a very good academic, but have limited experience in the practical need to use things to interpret history. Material culture is limited in its ability to transmit ideas. You need a translator."

Many observers of what occurred around *Gaelic Gotham* were struck by how tenacious, argumentative, provocative, uncompromising, posturing, and unyielding Casey *and* Macdonald were. They both had stamina and stick-to-itiveness and were utterly convinced of the correctness of their own positions. The *Irish Echo* mused that this controversy was "a classic case of irresistible culturally persistent force meets immovable culturally persistent object."[22] It is true that the personalities of two individuals loomed large in this dispute, which consumed the time and attention of more and more people. Particularly because Robert Macdonald is the MCNY's director, what he said and did became the public face of the museum. In a basic respect, he became the MCNY. That is where this dispute transcended personalities. For David Lackey, "I began to understand how those sort of personal issues manifest themselves on an institutional level and become problematic. And we used to joke around [in the office] that we could begin to see how the conflict in Northern Ireland could persist. To me it became almost a microcosm."

The sense of outrage built as the news began to spread that Marion Casey would no longer have a hand in this exhibition, a show that many people felt she had conceived and then essentially single-handedly nourished. It affected her many friends and acquaintances, as well as people on the periphery. Casey now proposes a hypothesis about why her relationship with the museum was dissolved. "At the time I didn't understand what was going on. But with a lot of hindsight I think he [Robert Macdonald] had decided to get rid of all the witnesses who knew what the original grant was like. Because within short order he got rid of everybody else. . . . He completely had eliminated everyone who knew the truth."[23] By that she means anyone who knew about the original budget or the evolution of the exhibition's thesis and outline. This explanation casts Macdonald's actions as a diabolical power grab. It also completely deflects attention away from anything Casey did to seal her own fate.

The struggle between these two also triggered a clash of views regarding the contemporary relationship between a museum and the public. Jan Ramirez captures a key issue: "There was sort of an effort to equate no importance whatsoever to the professional staff at the museum. If anything, we were here to be passive vessels, to allow the community's voice to go unedited onto the wall." Was the MCNY to become a billboard, a venue where a group could temporarily squat and "do its own thing"? Or was the museum's staff in charge? Were *their* vision and *their* expertise going to triumph—informed, of course, by the input of others they would call in for advice and support?

"It's sociology, not art" became the mantra of the critics of *Harlem on My Mind.* "Ancestors" and "descendants" were continually invoked during the debate over the African Burial Ground. Likewise, the phrase "bait and switch" assumed center stage in the initial phases of the dispute over *Gaelic Gotham.* Critics wanted museum officials to be held fiscally accountable, to "show them the money."

The first public appearance of the "bait and switch" charge was probably in a letter to the editor published by the *Irish Echo,* where the writer alleged that "Macdonald convinced the National Endowment for the Humanities that it was buying a Rolls Royce but instead he plans to deliver a Hyundai."[24] Over the next seven months the charge surfaced in several other letters and articles in the Irish press and in more mainstream media as well. It thus gives the appearance of being a pre-scripted, orchestrated response—part of a campaign, in other words. What is fascinating is how resilient it remained: Kerby A. Miller, a professor of history at the University of Missouri-Columbia, still invoked it over two years later.

Miller was one of three distinguished historians of the Irish American experience who were consultants during the initial stages of the project. He suspects that federal money, taxpayers' money, was misappropriated by those working on *Gaelic Gotham.* Pocketed? Diverted elsewhere? Whatever. Miller wishes that an investigation would be conducted à la Watergate. "Follow the money!" he suggests. If a deep throat were to be located within the museum, the truth could be revealed at last: "If it went into a new limo for Macdonald, you've got him by the neck."[25]

Limos? Cheap imports? Shady accounting practices were thus the first line of attack. If Marion Casey wasn't getting paid what she'd been budgeted to receive originally, and if the flashier components of the exhibition had been eliminated, critics reasoned, the money must be going *somewhere,* slipping through the cracks between a once grand proposal and its scaled-back reality.

A group of people from the Irish History Roundtable decided to contact the National Endowment for the Humanities. They wanted

NEH officials to investigate whether the money that had been allocated was being used in conformity with NEH regulations. They were following the lead of numerous recent critics, particularly conservative politicians and religious fundamentalists, who have targeted the NEH and the National Endowment for the Arts. In essence, these people all demand a level of accountability regarding the public funding of culture far outstripping what the general public typically exercises. On the face of it, such calls for oversight are a profoundly democratic request. However, it is no accident that these appeals generally attempt to tightly regulate potentially disturbing ideas rather than scrutinizing military expenditures or subsidies to the tobacco and mohair wool industries, for example. In that respect, they increase the pressure on artists, performers, scholars, or museum professionals who wish to complete certain projects, often of a controversial nature.

Public funding makes each of us a stakeholder in what's produced through our taxes. The Museum of the City of New York has multiple connections to such funds. It is a private, nonprofit institution but it is housed in a city-owned building, as are many other New York City cultural establishments, such as the Metropolitan Museum of Art, the Brooklyn Museum, and the American Museum of Natural History. It receives nearly a fifth of its annual budget from the city for operating costs. The rest of the funds it raises on its own. Moreover, the MCNY regularly receives support from such public agencies as the New York State Council on the Arts, the NEA, and the NEH. According to Brother Emmett Corry, "Irish-American taxpayers' money was being used for something we had no input into at all. . . . We felt this group should have an opportunity to look at how our ancestry was going to be portrayed. This was our own area of expertise."[26]

These Irish Americans thus strongly believed that they deserved a hearing and had the right to demand clarification of what the MCNY was doing. Possibly, just possibly, they might expose some fiscal sleight of hand that would trip up the MCNY's plans for *Gaelic Gotham*. A roundtable member who works in a New York state government office called the NEH on at least three occasions, beginning in early April 1995. She worked behind the scenes at that time, and wishes to remain anonymous now. One person she spoke with was a project director at the NEH with whom Marion Casey had dealt previously. In fact, Casey suggested that this man would be the main person to contact. On subsequent calls she spoke with an assistant to NEH chairman Sheldon Hackney, and then with a woman whom she urged to make a formal site visit to the exhibition. If such a visit occurred, no formal report of it has ever been filed.

Referring to notes she took at the time, this roundtable member recounts that the project director explained to her that a grant is not as stringent as a contract, and that some degree of modification was permissible. Moreover, he told her that the NEH had funded what it saw on the application, and hoped it would be implemented. The NEH knew that the MCNY wanted to make changes, but did not wish to mediate between the museum and the public. Finally, he stated that the NEH had not been asked to approve a change in either director or guest curator, substitutions it would have to confirm.

According to this informant, "It was an out-and-out lie." Citing what she calls "shenanigans," she continues, "NEH never gave us a straight story. You have an ordinary citizen call the NEH, and you have them absolutely lie to you. Hackney basically palmed us off."[27] She is referring to the fact that Marion Casey later received NEH files via a Freedom of Information Act (FOIA) request. Casey and her supporters in the Irish American community thereby found out that Macdonald had discussed additions to the project team with the NEH and alterations in the exhibition itself—before the museum formally notified Casey that it would not agree to her contract demands, and before she was informed that she would no longer be associated with the project.

To supplement the phone calls to the NEH, Brother Emmett Corry had written to Sheldon Hackney. From Corry's perspective, "The NEH was complicitous. They knew what was going on, and they denied that there was anything going on." To Angela Carter, "The NEH was scrambling for survival. Not for funds for the humanities, but for their own jobs." With anger leading her to mix her metaphors, she declared, "I mean, they sold Marian down the drain."[28]

What they had in fact discovered was that the MCNY was not passively sitting around waiting for Marion Casey to agree to terms. Rather, Macdonald and his staff were laying concrete plans to implement the show. Macdonald cued the NEH in, to be sure that he was acting properly. For example, Macdonald informed the NEH on February 1, 1995, that Dr. Jack Salzman had agreed to join the project team. Casey and her supporters were not privy to this information at this time. Since there was no formal relationship between the parties at that moment, it would not seem appropriate to divulge it. But when Casey eventually received this material through her FOIA request, she interpreted it to mean that the museum was replacing her rather than adding to the roster of people working on *Gaelic Gotham*. Casey's supporters accepted her distinctive interpretation. According to the anonymous informant, "Supposedly museums are above board, and they [NEH officials] don't have to worry about museums. Well, that's a laugh and a half."[29]

Feeling frustrated, Casey's supporters sought additional muscle to make their interactions with the NEH more effective. They solicited the backing of several politicians, including Representative Peter T. King of Long Island and Senator Daniel Patrick Moynihan, as well as Schuyler G. Chapin, New York City's cultural affairs commissioner. Carter reports, "We wanted the politicians to go to the NEH and say, 'Do not give this money to this man and let him do this.'" Corry concurs: "We pushed those buttons to see if we could get some response. At that point, we wanted the show to be closed down, if they [the NEH and the museum] were not going to respond to our legitimate inquiries." But no politicians or public officials were willing to throw themselves behind this cause in a major way. (King and Moynihan each wrote letters of inquiry to NEH chairman Sheldon Hackney; Chapin encouraged the roundtable to work with the museum.)[30]

According to a scholar familiar with how the NEH deals with the gap between an original proposal and the ultimate execution of a show, "the museum director looks at the grant, and either decides to raise money to match the grant, or they scale down the exhibition to suit the money that was given. This revision process is par for the course. NEH assumes that this is understood, and there is no formal accountability process."[31] So while nothing might appear unusual to the MCNY or the NEH, the Irish Americans who were concerned about what was happening felt that their voices were being ignored and that their opinions didn't matter.

Frank Naughton, a college professor who became involved in this struggle at a later stage, feels that the museum acted unscrupulously. From his perspective, the museum proceeded in a dishonest way, and should have informed Casey and her supporters early on that it might ultimately mount something very different from the original proposal: "There are understandings [on the NEH's part] that people aren't going to meet proposal standards, but the money will be coming anyway." Naughton doesn't feel that Marion Casey was naive—for him, that would come uncomfortably close to blaming the victim—but he believes that she should have been clued in about the way things typically occur, so that her expectations would not have become so compromised. He is describing, then, a clash of cultures and a clash of understandings, where one side took for granted what the other side felt uninformed about. However, it's difficult to imagine that anyone could work in any phase of cultural production for any length of time without comprehending the realities and uncertainties of funding. It seems unfair to point the finger of blame in one direction only.

These community members feel they've been deceived and shortchanged. They view all the figures the MCNY has released about the costs of *Gaelic Gotham* as wildly inflated. According to the anonymous informant,

> We only know what's been said publicly. We don't believe a word of it. What a laugh; it couldn't have cost $700,000, or $900,000. There was nothing complicated, just stuff up on the wall. And most of it was from their own attic. You could practically choke on that. We don't think they ever told the truth about the money.

She, along with many others, also faults Macdonald for not aggressively fund raising so as to put on the finest exhibition possible. But this fails to acknowledge one of several ways the actions of the protestors affected the final outcome. According to Robert Macdonald, "Our ability to raise funds was severely curtailed because everywhere we went, so would the other people. Corporations and foundations said, 'Well, it might be [a] good [show], but we don't want controversy.'"[32]

People reacted in a variety of ways to the breach between Marion Casey and the MCNY. Two of the three original historical consultants, Ronald Bayor of the Georgia Institute of Technology and David Reimers of New York University, withdrew from the project. Kerby Miller's geographical distance limited his information about what was going on in New York. But when he received a copy of the letter of resignation of one of his colleagues, he called someone in New York to confirm what it said. Then *he* followed suit, pulling out as well in May 1995. Jack Salzman was appalled by what he believed was the blind faith of people who should have known better:

> The scholars never asked us any questions. Never called me. Just assumed (and these were people who I knew well) that if Marion said, "Don't go near the Museum of the City of New York exhibition, it won't be any good," they believed her. These scholars assumed that the voice of one person had to be correct. No one did what you're doing, trying to talk to everyone and find out what really went on.[33]

But according to Ed O'Donnell, this type of unreflective, knee-jerk response—the sort of reaction he would have expected from the media or from activists—extended far beyond the academic world: "When the word hit the street that 'Marion's been screwed,' people didn't say 'Tell me the details. Really? That sounds strange.' Everyone just said, 'That's outrageous. Our beloved Marion has been treated so poorly. She did all this work and then they fired her, you know.' And that gets the outrage meter soaring." O'Donnell remembers that Casey and a group of her supporters were calling "everybody I talked to" during the summer of 1995, "building this tremendous lobbying effort to increase the level of outrage."

Members of the Irish History Roundtable, of which Marion Casey was a past president, took the lead in attacking the museum and the exhibition. Angela Carter recalls that most of those active early in the controversy were in their sixties and seventies, and many shared strong union backgrounds. To their minds, this was a case of unfair labor practices. That is why they first went to the NEH, to discover whatever they could, and perhaps correct the museum's blunder at its financial point of origin. Carter notes that Marion Casey kept the roundtable well informed about the exhibition's progress over the years. Members were excited; "I knew absolutely everything [about developments]," she recollects. For Carter, this museum represented an alien environment, "an Anglo-Saxon world of New York, European high culture." She draws a direct line between oppression of the Irish in the nineteenth century and the ill treatment meted out by museum officials. Scorning the word "patrician," she declares, "I call them nativists who went to Harvard. You know, they're the same people who greeted my people in 1850, and they've just gotten a bit more money and polish since then. But as far as we're concerned, the relationship is no different."

Each time this ad hoc group initiated some action, members were forced to take up a collection to cover the costs of such mundane tasks as duplication and mailing. They were emotionally fueled by a profound sense of offense, but severely undercapitalized. What sustained them was the belief that this exhibition was tremendously important. It would be the largest such survey of Irish American history. It was their due. Carter explains, "There are two hundred ethnic groups in New York City. They [the MCNY] know of probably four or five. I mean, the blacks and Puerto Ricans were kind of forced on them because of geographical location. And I think the Jews and the gays are the only others they have represented. Otherwise it's Ladies' Mile and Broadway and Gilded Age New York, and the sixteenth century [sic] ancestors, who are all over the place."[34]

Carter is proud of the group's efforts. She believes they supported a fine, admirable scholar. Furthermore, "We made this exhibition controversial," she states with delight. "They were just not able to get away with it totally." Over the fall of 1995 the group's activities gradually dwindled. Later in the year another coalition of people emerged. The activist Brendan Fay felt that Casey had been treated "disgracefully," "shabbily," "unjustly"—"like crap." He recalls, "I passionately threw myself into organizing this crowd, but my hope was resolution."[35] He was going back and forth, speaking with Jan Ramirez and others at the museum, and meeting with people in the community. Fay called a meeting of those concerned at the Lesbian and Gay Community Services Center in Greenwich Village. For most of those who attended, it was their first time in this formerly dilapidated school building, which is still being spruced up since it was transferred from city ownership in 1983.

This grassroots effort drew people from the roundtable and elsewhere. Angela Carter became part of the group, as did Frank Naughton, a sociologist at Kean College in New Jersey. Naughton teaches comparative ethnic and racial relations. He also served as president of the faculty senate at Kean in the early 1990s, a time when ethnic conflict was acute on that campus. He felt that those experiences might be useful in resolving this controversy.

Over time, the group had a fluctuating membership of between five and fifteen people. They later switched to meeting at an Irish

FIG. 8. Hughson Hawley, *Men Laying Tracks at Broadway and 14th Street*, c. 1880. Gouache. Museum of the City of New York. Gift of Thomas Crimmins. Used by permission.

restaurant nearby. All told, they met about five times. Their most important and dramatic gathering was held on January 11, 1996, at Fitzpatrick's Hotel, an Irish-owned midtown Manhattan establishment favored by Irish businessmen, politicians, and travelers. Fitzpatrick's was a far cry from the community center where they'd begun. A press packet had even been assembled for journalists and other interested parties. Brendan Fay claims he heard about the meeting secondhand: differences had been emerging within the group and communication had become complicated. Once he had looked around, he wondered who was paying the freight. And he felt that some people were looking at him "like I had four heads" because of his outspoken gay activism. To Fay, the effort had shifted from the grassroots to something else.

The meeting lasted from between two to three hours and was attended by thirty to forty people, according to most estimates. All agree there were too many people stuffed into too small a room. According to Fay, at one point a reporter from the *New York Post* stood up and declared,

> If you want to get the attention of the media, forget letters and all of that." You need something juicy, he implied. Something like a call for closure: "Irish call for closure!" Well, it was like a cue. Somebody picked up the cue, and it was bang! on the table. I remember sitting there and thinking, "I can't believe what I'm witnessing." My heart sank. And I nearly wanted to cry.

To his mind, this was a position that would not allow the museum to compromise.

During the discussion the frustrations that had built up over months of confused and misunderstood attempts at communication between the museum, community members, the NEH, and various politicians and public figures finally coalesced. Fay describes the sort of dynamic that can take over in gatherings, a "sense of the meeting" that is nearly impossible to interrupt or derail once it gains momentum. Calling itself the Ad Hoc Committee of Concerned Irish-American New Yorkers, the group released a statement that said, "Attempts to hold meaningful discussions with the Museum regarding *Gaelic Gotham* have been sabotaged by Mr. MacDonald's insult and innuendo." It endorsed a resolution stating that "After prolonged discussion, the meeting participants voted to call on the Museum of the City of New York *to immediately cancel the exhibit*" (emphasis in the original).

The journalist to whom Fay referred was John O'Mahony, who had written an overview of the controversy in an article published three weeks earlier. He attended the meeting as a journalist, not as a community member. He remembers that people seemed "very lost," that they kept going off on tangents, that they were promoting various agendas. Others confirm that it was loosely coordinated, hardly a model of parliamentary procedure. O'Mahony was hoping there would be a better story; he wanted to expose Macdonald's behavior. But he felt the group was incapable of taking any firm action. Therefore, as he saw it, there was not enough for a follow-up article for a major daily newspaper. The way O'Mahony remembers it, he participated in the proceedings to the extent of calling for clarification of what was being discussed: Was there new information? What was to be the resolution of the evening's discussion? Would there be a boycott?[36]

But Brendan Fay's assessment of what occurred is quite different: "Fucking ethics of journalism were crossed here," he insists. O'Mahony's search for understanding—his attempt to uncover something newsworthy—catalyzed inchoate sentiments. John McInerney, a clinical social worker elected to be a spokesperson for the Concerned Irish, corroborates Fay's version of what occurred. He too recollects the call for closure, and the way the group took it up.

Frank Naughton remembers proposing a preliminary motion that was amended and subsequently passed. He avows that he had not talked it over with anyone beforehand; it was not "prepackaged." Rather, "I just thought things should be brought to a head." McInerney explains that the group sensed that it was being "stonewalled" by the museum. "We felt that we were basically a group of reasonable people who were being treated in an extremely unreasonable manner. We had to begin behaving somewhat unreasonably in order to get any kind of reasonable response. While we were calling for closure of the exhibit, we were aiming high, and expecting to get something less than that."[37]

Fay and one or two others were alone in withholding their support. "I understand the feeling around the table," Fay says, but "I have absolutely zero respect for it. And I'm sorry for all the people of intellect and the academics and the leaders of this. Some leadership, you know. Joining in silence. Irish people were silenced at one time. Had our tongues cut out and children were beaten for speaking their own language." He argued then that the group should declare its displeasure through protest, not closure. If the exhibit indeed turned out to come up short in their opinion, by all means mobilize. But Fay was foursquare against quashing anyone's freedom of expression:

> I would be the first to stand in front of that museum with a photograph of Marion Casey. I would chain myself to the door, do a sit-in, protest what's up on the walls. But the last thing I was going to do was to be part of a call for silence, because I've fought that all my life. And I've paid dearly. It's an issue that professionally and

personally I feel so strongly about, how human beings engage in silence and silencing. . . . It's a matter of life and death. And in the
Irish community, no less.

But his was a voice in the wilderness, as the sentiments for action
gathered steam and then barreled through the gathering.

To understand this group's vehemence, you must understand some
circumstances that preceded the meeting at Fitzpatrick's. The strategy of exposing the alleged "bait and switch" on the MCNY's part
was gradually abandoned. Even so, critics argued strenuously that
the size of the exhibit was being scaled back. In the end, museum officials claim that *Gaelic Gotham* gained square footage. But instead of
taking up the entire first floor as initially conceived, it spilled into the
lower level instead. Certain people were dismayed at what they saw
as the Irish experience being sent into symbolic exile. And the final
space calculation included the auditorium, where *Voices of the Irish*, an
audiovisual piece, played nonstop; some felt that this "padded" the
size estimate.

Furthermore, critics attacked the credentials of the new exhibition team the MCNY assembled. If the historians they respected
weren't running the show, these opponents couldn't be sure anyone
else was up to the task. This came out most clearly in articles published by the *Irish Echo,* and also in O'Mahony's article in the *New
York Post.* O'Mahony described the team as follows: "It's made up of
two experts in 19th-century American art, furniture, and silverware, a
scholar of Jewish history, an expert on Roman Catholic nuns in New
York and one in New York labor politics. None of these scholars, they
[critics] say, has sufficient background in the actual subject matter of
the exhibition."[38]

These dismissive descriptions pushed Ed O'Donnell's buttons.
He fired off an angry letter published in the *Irish Echo,* where he argued that everyone's credentials had been deliberately diminished
and distorted—including those of Bernadette McCauley, an assistant
professor of history at Hunter College-CUNY, the so-called expert on
nuns who teaches immigration and ethnic history and has done primary research on the Catholic Church and women, and ethnicity in
New York City. O'Donnell's letter carefully demolished the critics'
claims, but his fury was barely disguised when he chided "Miss

Casey and her cabal of zealous supporters" as "the chronically of-fended." O'Donnell argues,

> The *Irish Echo* essentially took the lines of the opposition and wrote
> it as "reporting." Their stating that I was a political and labor histo-
> rian was the equivalent of saying Marion Casey is an historian of
> suburbanization—as opposed to saying she's a scholar of Irish-
> American history and one of the things that she has focused on is
> middle-class mobility and migration to the outer boroughs of New
> York City.[39]

Part of what upset Jan Ramirez about this was that "Somehow there was the sense that this exhibition idea developed like Venus out of the head of Zeus." In fact, three years of consultation with Irish schol-ars and collecting institutions and archives had already occurred. She was confident that the new team could take over the helm, building on the groundwork that had already been done.

When the *New York Post* referred to "a scholar of Jewish history," it did not mention that person by name. It was Jack Salzman, who was identified more fully by the *Irish Echo*. In that article, Robert Mac-donald went on record condemning the fact that some people had questioned the appropriateness of a Jewish scholar working on this exhibition. Macdonald even alluded to "the aura of anti-Semitism" surrounding this issue.[40] That, in turn, raised the ire of some people in the community. They felt they were being recklessly and inaccu-rately labeled as biased. Two of the most important documents re-lated to this dispute—the public statement released by the Concerned Irish after the meeting at Fitzpatrick's and *The Gaelic Gotham Report*, an exhaustive inquiry into the exhibition undertaken by the Council for Scholarly Evaluation of *Gaelic Gotham*—both dismissed the charge as "unsubstantiated." Marion Casey theorizes, "I think it came out of Robert Macdonald's head. I think he made it up. That's my personal opinion. Because it was never even whispered around."[41]

But there's another side to this. Jan Ramirez reports, "I received at least two phone calls from perhaps you'd call them professional Irish Americans, people that somehow make a profession out of their Irish-ness, questioning why a guy who's deputy director of programs at the Jewish Museum was a paid, scholarly advisor to this project. [But] Jack isn't a scholar of Jewish history." In fact, Salzman was a relative newcomer to the Jewish Museum, having been the longtime director of Columbia University's Center for American Culture Studies. In that capacity, he accrued a great deal of experience directing projects and programs related to race, gender, ethnicity, urbanization, and immigration. He was also very familiar with the terrains of public funding and the foundation world.

Those were the qualifications relevant to this exhibition; his own ethnicity should have been incidental. But an aggressive strain of identity politics seemed to kick in, and Ramirez notes that she was even questioned about her own ethnicity. It was an interesting, albeit troubling, experience for her: "I'm just an American mongrel," Ramirez recounts. "I have no ethnic identity. There's so much of everybody in me. And it was fascinating for me to be with Americans who define themselves first as being non-Americans."

Jack Salzman recalls, "The fact that I was at the Jewish Museum made it just too much for some people to tolerate, I think." He too was asked about his ethnicity. Salzman claims that during a meeting with a representative from an immigration society, he was asked "if you think it's appropriate that someone who's Jewish is leading.' And I said the obvious thing to him, that I was not an African-American, and that had I not done the work on an encyclopedia that I think is now the most important reference book on black Americans in this country, it would never have been published." An essentialist assumption that ethnicity was equivalent to expertise, and that others need not apply, was surfacing once again. "Step up and present your genetic certification," in other words. In the final analysis, Jan Ramirez felt it became an advantage that the majority of the project team was *not* Irish; "we didn't come to it with any preconceived notions." Bernadette McCauley reflects that being Irish American "doesn't make me an expert, you know. I think I know what I know from work that I've done. Now I have insights, possibly, but I also have some baggage."[42]

Finally, Robert Macdonald reports that one of his staff members called an Irish cultural group in New Jersey to borrow a maquette. His staffer reported to him that the man asked, "Why is a Jew involved? A Jewish historian?" The museum turned elsewhere for a similar loan. So when Macdonald leveled the charge of anti-Semitism, it was grounded in actual experiences. It was a peripheral issue, to be sure, but one that pushed the two sides further away from one another. Moreover, anti-Semitism was related to another accusation

Macdonald directed at the exhibition's critics, one that the MCNY's opponents really took umbrage at. As Macdonald now recalls this struggle, "The element of McCarthyism was involved in this, and also anti-Semitism, two of the plagues of the Irish in this country."

Brendan Fay signed a letter addressed to Robert Macdonald on December 9, 1995, representing a coalition of eight people. They made two requests: a copy of the exhibition script and a meeting with the director to discuss their hopes and concerns. It was straightforward, concise, and nonaccusatory.

Macdonald replied promptly. One passage in particular packs the power and surprise of a sucker punch: "The campaign of misinformation and efforts to have the project boycotted are similar to activities in the early 1950s designed to intimidate academicians, artists, and performers. It also echoes the recent attacks on the National Endowment for the Arts and the National Endowment for the Humanities by those who want to restrict intellectual freedom."[43] Macdonald didn't name the key name here. He didn't have to. Anyone could recognize the chilling allusion.

"I remember Joe McCarthy," Robert Macdonald discloses.

Tailgunner Joe. In a real sense, he represented the worst of the Irish, a drunk, sleazy guy who used anything, who stood up and said, "I have a list." Well, that's what they [the critics] were doing to *Gaelic Gotham*. "They're going to use leprechauns, they're going to do this, they're going to do that." So as an historian, and maybe because I'm Irish, I equated activities such as threatening performers—calling people and telling them not to be involved with this show—with McCarthyism.

It was a very peevish and controversial gambit on Macdonald's part. But Macdonald reports that a performer slated to perform in a related program at the MCNY was told he'd never work in the Irish community again if he cooperated with the museum. Rumors were circulating that such pressures were being applied pervasively.

The press release issued by the Concerned Irish condemned Macdonald's remark as "ethnic stereotyping." Angela Carter also wrote at the time, "[When museums] are using public funds then the public has the right to ask questions and not be compared to McCarthy." Brendan Fay complained that the director's language "added insult to injury." John McInerney remembers, "I could almost see what was going on in Macdonald's mind, him having an image of the simian-faced hordes charging up Fifth Avenue to attack the Big House."[44]

But Robert Macdonald's perspective was that this was war: "Grenades were being thrown around, the museum was under fierce attack. . . . It got my trustees' backs up; they got pissed." From his perspective, there had been threats, misrepresentations, untruths, intimidation, and ultimatums issuing from the other side. Macdonald claims that he never disparaged Marion Casey publicly. But reflecting back now, he characterizes her as "a young, inexperienced, and obviously overwrought individual" who eventually "went over the top." Macdonald witnessed what he calls "crazed floundering and lashing out," "personal[ly] vindictive" and "almost psychotic activities" from her and her followers.

Macdonald was also very troubled that certain members of the ad hoc group had put this matter in front of congressmen and had complained directly to Sheldon Hackney, whom Macdonald felt was under extreme pressure from the ongoing debates over the future of public funding for culture. He was keenly aware as well of how other controversies had played out: "Martin [Harwit]'s experience as far as a guide of what not to do was very instructive. . . . I think that [the lesson from] the experience of the *Enola Gay* is that when you're in a struggle that goes to meeting your obligations for the integrity of the institution, you have to play hard." (See chapter 6 for a discussion of the *Enola Gay* exhibit.)

And Macdonald did play hard. "[Critics can say,] 'See, he might not be too smart, and he kind of looks like a soft touch. He's a pudgy guy.' But you have to let them know there are certain things that aren't going to happen. Beyond this line, I can't go. I can maneuver to the right and the left. But if you back me up, the answer's 'no.'" Some of Macdonald's critics feel that *he* crossed a line when he sent copies of his correspondence with faculty members affiliated with Fordham University and New York University to the presidents of those schools.

According to Macdonald, he was "disappointed" that these "superiors" "would allow their institutions to be used in an anti-intellectual political campaign designed to threaten people who were involved in this exhibit." But given the sanctity of intellectual freedom on campus, what would Macdonald have university leaders do? Punish their faculty for holding views that made someone else uncomfortable? In a basic sense, Macdonald was matching what he perceived to be volleys of intimidation, stroke for stroke. That reeked of McCarthyism from the critics' vantage point. Nancy Curtin, a Fordham historian who became a primary spokesperson for the Council for Scholarly Evaluation of *Gaelic Gotham*, was delighted that her president wrote back to Macdonald, defending her rights to express her opinions.[45]

In retrospect, Robert Macdonald admits that he "was too hard-nosed" and that he overreacted. David Lackey concludes, "He did the right thing. He handled it wrong." Jan Ramirez suspects that "his emotions got the better of him." Ed O'Donnell observes, "From a media standpoint, his personality was a big problem. 'McCarthyism.' He probably shouldn't have said that. He allowed his anger over what was going on to speak, instead of [offering] a cooler, dispassionate response." But in his thirty-plus years in the museum world, nothing had upset Macdonald more. He recollects, "The anti-Semitism greatly disturbed me because it reflected my Uncle Joe and Aunt Mary Louise and people like that, and it brought back some of the more unpleasant memories of growing up."

He continues, "They got my goat. They got my Irish up." Macdonald feels that the "Irish character," like a hero of a Shakespearean tragedy, contains fatal flaws. In his words, "There's an underside to the Irish—my family, myself. It's a melancholy, it's a brooding, it's a narrow-mindedness. . . . I saw what has made the Irish so great, and what has through history sometimes pulled them back."

Museum personnel and the exhibition team did indeed feel backed against a wall in significant ways. Jan Ramirez notes that more effort went into *Gaelic Gotham* than any other MCNY project during the past ten years. Moreover, although the staff had eighteen or nineteen other projects in various stages of development at the same time, *Gaelic Gotham* consumed an inordinate amount of their energy because it seemed to be constantly hemorrhaging. "The controversy wreaked a small amount of havoc with our check list, because there were certain loans where a lot of legwork had been done to identify certain materials, and suddenly that material was not available to us. . . . [Moreover], under normal circumstances you wouldn't suddenly find that half the performers wouldn't perform."

The Ancient Order of Hibernians and the former grand marshals of the St. Patrick's Day parade refused to donate materials, for example. The Emerald Societies of the fire and sanitation departments cooperated; the police department balked. Bernadette McCauley saw this as an annoyance, but not a major obstacle. She argues, "Personally, I have no problem with people saying, 'No, I'm a friend of Marion Casey's. Those are my rosary beads.' That's the real world, and I would want my friends to do that for me. But short of the Rosetta Stone, what other object couldn't be used in the exhibit instead?" Cumulatively, however, massaging bruised egos, finding substitutions, and filling in blanks were headaches.

Some of the defections resulted from a letter Marion Casey sent to the people from whom she was borrowing material for *Gaelic Gotham.* In the letter she stated that her contract as guest curator was not being renewed, although she claimed not to understand the reasons. She continued, "Since I no longer have any role in 'Gaelic Gotham,' there is no way for me to guarantee the integrity of my original concept nor the manner in which objects borrowed from the Irish community will be used or interpreted." Since the original conditions under which the loans had been secured had changed, Casey felt it was the ethical thing to do.

She saw herself as providing a bridge between the museum and the ethnic community. She was well known, trusted. Casey functioned as a broker, a go-between. She explains, "If someone said, 'Marion is looking for "X" object for an exhibition,' 'Oh, yeah, we know her,' and then they give it." But when she was replaced, the new project team was not similarly positioned. Casey continues, "It immediately started people questioning, which the museum would like to see as me coordinating some conspiracy to stop stuff, but it's just the way the community works. Word-of-mouth. Who knows who. And it would happen in the Dominican [or in any other ethnic] community just as quickly."[46]

McCauley and O'Donnell both describe how diversionary some of the outside agitation became. Marion Casey raised the possibility of legal action against the MCNY. Bernadette McCauley recalls, "When all the [potential] legal stuff was going on, Marion would send things and then the museum would send things. And I thought, 'Oh no, not something else. Am I going to be deposed?' And I just started filing it and throwing it out. . . . I didn't want to get swept up into the rhetoric of it, and lose sight of what the task really was." Moreover, the project team was under the gun. The three main consultants did not begin working together until June 1995. The exhibition was slated to go up the following March. Their time frame was merely a fraction of the time usually required to produce a major show. Ed O'Donnell remembers that "the waters were poisoned," and "It was beat the clock: I was trying to do it with one hand tied behind my back on three hours of sleep, and with no time." The way Jan Ramirez sees it, with a few additional months, they could have probably made it "a cleaner, meaner machine."[47]

But the controversy also forced the planning process into the open in some unexpected ways, generating interesting, unintended consequences. Jane McNamara, the associate head of education and programs at the MCNY and a project team member, notes, "It brought in some people who might not traditionally be part of the kind of core Irish New York community that all knows each other. And the Annie Finnegan trunk belonged to a woman who was not even Irish, who probably wouldn't have known about the exhibit had we not been compelled to place ads in the Irish newspapers soliciting material." That trunk, containing the ephemera of the life of an Irish-born servant (1877–1948)—letters of reference, photographs, religious medals and mass cards, among other things—was anonymously lent by a woman who had found the trunk discarded on the street. To David Lackey, it became the highlight of the exhibition, embodying a certain spirit, "sort of the Ark of the Covenant," he notes. According to Jan Ramirez, "[Initially], a lot of doors hadn't been knocked on. And we were forced to knock on those doors. So there was good that came out of it, too. A lot of stress, but some good."[48]

One of the main reasons that Macdonald chose to take such a hard line in these matters was to insulate his staff from all the turmoil. He wanted to help them get their work done. If that meant becoming the lightning rod for critics, so be it. Ultimately he felt that the reputation of the museum was on the line. Should Macdonald capitulate to the demands of the critics, he felt, the MCNY's name could be permanently sullied. As Jan Ramirez characterizes these critics, "They wanted to hear *Gaelic Gotham* was in shambles. They wanted to know that they were critical to it going forward, and it turned out that they weren't. It just went forward."

∎

The ancient Celts held a pervasive belief in shape-shifting, one life form effortlessly changing into another: "A hawk to-day, a boar yesterday / Wonderful instability!"[49] An intriguing aspect to this controversy is the way *it* continually morphed into different forms. Although Ed O'Donnell feels that this was essentially "a tempest in a teapot," he quips that *Gaelic Gotham*'s critics "left no stone uncast." The way he sees it, "They pulled out all the stops to bring this thing down." First, they emphasized money, then credentials. Charges of bigotry also came to the fore. Each theme assumed center stage for a short while, only to be supplanted by other concerns. The critics had also turned their attention to the structure of the exhibition, and ultimately to the script. (Curiously, censorship was virtually never mentioned in this controversy, by either side.) From Brendan Fay's perspective, "This was not a group that was committed to resolution."

When community members compared Casey's original proposal with the spotty information they could glean from such sources as NEH documentation of discussions with Macdonald, they discovered another line of attack. In their estimation, *Gaelic Gotham* was being changed from an "interpretive" exhibition to a "chronological" one instead. As Brother Emmett Corry wrote to the *Irish Echo*, "The original exhibition was created as a beautiful, hand-made tapestry is woven, with the scholarship and skill of years of study about the Irish-American community's life, work and contributions to New York City. By pulling the thread on the tapestry Mr. Macdonald has unraveled the original design and he now wonders why the Irish-American community questions what he has done."[50] It was a passionate, flowery defense of Casey's creation. Furthermore, the first sentence was repeated verbatim in John O'Mahony's *New York Post* overview three months later—a small example of how critics successfully used the press in a partisan way.

But to those on the museum side, a great deal was left unspoken in such remarks. For example, Bernadette McCauley believes that "Marion misinterpreted the NEH's response. They didn't say, 'This is the greatest thing since sliced bread.' I think they said, 'Interesting exhibit. Okay. Here's some money.' You know, Marion's spin on it was that it was perfect. . . . But there wasn't a strong narrative." For Jack Salzman,

[What] was never said, and that struck me as inexcusable on the part of the academic as well as the Irish community, was the assumption that Marion's NEH proposal, and the way in which she conceived of the exhibit, was in fact a good proposal and a good exhibit. The fact that it was funded by NEH just doesn't mean very much, in terms of whether it was good or bad. I would have given it about a C. I think we brought it up to about a C+.

In particular, the organizers cite three major omissions from Casey's proposal: the Draft Riots of 1863, Irish gays and lesbians, and gender issues. Poor Irish immigrants were a major component of the crowds during the Draft Riots, fueled by anger toward Abraham Lincoln and the fear that if Negroes were to be freed, the two groups would be competing for the same jobs.[51] Irish gay and lesbian life, of course, has become much more visible because of the annual brouhaha over the St. Patrick's Day parade. And the feminist movement has obviously focused increased attention on the historical treatment of women. The centerpiece of Marion Casey's proposal for *Sweet Recollections of Home* presented the material artifacts of an era of strict gender segregation: the re-creation of an Irish American living room in the borough of Queens in the 1940s, evoking Casey's own personal background.

In Casey's words, "We were essentially arguing that ethnic identities formed there, at home, and from there you radiate out and meet the city. . . . work, social life, education." She was, therefore, focusing on both the public and private aspects of being Irish. The way Brother Emmett Corry perceived it, this was primarily an exhibition about the Irish family and its attempts to hold on to its Irish identity. But David Lackey counters, "I don't think that's cutting edge." Jack Salzman adds, "The proposal was a good beginning, but one that needed to be worked on and rethought. There was no willingness to really deal with ethnic and racial conflict in the exhibit. . . . A show that wants to deal primarily with the interior of the home, to show how the Irish lived domestically, just misses too many points."

As with every aspect of this exhibition, a member of the opposition held a contradictory viewpoint. Nancy Curtin accused the project team of demonstrating the same sort of shortcomings for which the team faulted Marion Casey: "Macdonald and his people wanted this very glossy, rose-colored glasses, romanticized view of Irish history. But that's exactly what we didn't want. We'd like to deconstruct how identity is formed." What this demonstrates is that different constituencies saw things quite differently. Opposing *Gaelic Gotham* didn't necessarily guarantee unanimity among the critics. Everybody measured everything against deeply rooted preconceived notions.

In a letter to the editor published in the *Wall Street Journal* after *Gaelic Gotham* opened, Marion Casey wrote, "the exhibition currently on view bears absolutely no resemblance to the proposal I wrote that secured NEH funding." She still sticks to that position: "It was a different exhibition entirely." It is the only point on which she is in agreement with Robert Macdonald. Frank Naughton concurs: he believes it had been "eviscerated." But Jack Salzman challenges these views. Not only does he not feel there was such a great deal of distance between the original proposal and the final outcome, he is certain that it was strengthened in the end: "It may have been a little less celebratory. But I think it changed for the better. And I think had it not, NEH would have been all over us."[52] Several people felt compelled to "grade" *Gaelic Gotham*. Recall that Salzman awarded it a C+. O'Donnell, a "solid B." But Nancy Curtin thought it merited only a D, "a generous D, perhaps."

Furthermore, people on the production end reject the perception that *Gaelic Gotham* started out as "interpretive," but changed into a "chronological" exhibition. Jan Ramirez argues from the perspective of someone who was totally immersed in the process:

> Originally, it was going to be thematically arranged, as opposed to chronologically arranged. But all exhibits are interpretive. . . . we sat down and began to chart the flow of people with the object base we had. . . . and tracking visitor comments in the building [we've learned] they are desperate for chronological grounding. They don't tend to get thematic exhibitions when time isn't somehow strongly pronged through your subject matter.

Realizing this, the museum asked for NEH approval and then "flowed the themes through a chronological walk."

This particular part of the critique seems odd if you trace the paper trail left behind by *Gaelic Gotham*. In a 1992 version of the proposal you'll discover eight time periods, along with four "constants":

FIG. 9. *Gaelic Gotham*, 1996. Installation photograph. Museum of the City of New York. Used by permission.

continuous emigration from Ireland to New York; continuous social and political ties to Ireland; Catholic religion; and distinctive Irish American culture. In a 1993 draft outline, Marion Casey defined six chronological periods from 1664 to 1992. The 1994 NEH application presented eight time periods and the four constants as organizing principles.

The exhibition, therefore, was never projected as either exclusively interpretive or chronological. It was always envisioned as some combination. David Lackey was puzzled by what seemed to him an arbitrary distinction. As a designer, he likens his job to playing three-dimensional chess, whereas Bernadette McCauley is struck by the theatrical aspects of plaiting different elements together. That's one of the reasons Macdonald hesitated to release the script before *Gaelic Gotham* opened: it was only one ingredient in a complex mix.[53] But Macdonald's "guardedness"—as his critics emphasized—was also due to the threat of legal action being brought by Casey, in which case the script could become a vital piece of the discovery process. He didn't wish to tip his hand prematurely.

Beginning around January 1996, the critics' strategy became centered on forcing the museum to allow scholars of the Irish American experience to inspect the script to determine if it met "standards of contemporary scholarly excellence." To that end, the Council for Scholarly Evaluation of *Gaelic Gotham* was formed. Frank Naughton was the only person whose membership straddled both this and the earlier ad hoc group. To people like Angela Carter, it was time to step back: "Our part was really in keeping a controversy going until the scholars got into it." For Brendan Fay, the demand to see the script "became like, Jesus, trying to get the lotto or the crown jewels." But Macdonald feels that critics overestimated its importance and failed to understand that the script is not the show. "An exhibition is made up of ideas, of things, of light, of music. It's a holistic thing," he argues. Jan Ramirez speaks remarkably similarly, comparing it to the script for a Broadway play. "It's missing the lights. It's missing the costumes. It's missing the music."[54]

Once again, the fate of the public exhibition of the *Enola Gay* weighed heavily on Robert Macdonald's mind. "Look what they did to Martin [Harwit]," he suggests. "What they would have done is taken excerpts from the script and say, 'Aha! We told you those bastards . . .'" This contrasts markedly with the position of Nancy Curtin, who argues that the Council for Scholarly Evaluation of *Gaelic Gotham* was simply offering to share its best advice by reading the script and making suggestions: "They could have provided the community groups with the script, and perhaps reassured them, and then the controversy would have been over with." But she seriously underestimates the depth of negative feelings this controversy had engendered. Macdonald was probably correct. If the script had become public it would have fired up emotions, not calmed them. Brendan Fay remarks quite candidly, "I think some people in the Irish community were saying, 'Well, by Jesus, we're going to watch every single move till the day the door closes. And God help you. We won't let you forget.'"

Over the next months, the council pleaded to see the script. Alternatively, it *invited* the MCNY to furnish the latest version. It even demanded a copy, right up to the exhibition's opening. But the group wasn't able to apply significant leverage, and no transcript was forthcoming. Moreover, a sense of confusion reigned after the meeting at Fitzpatrick's Hotel and its call for "immediate cancellation." When that was reported in the media, spokespeople moderated their position, urging community outreach and review in order to avert cancellation. The exact terms of the demands were therefore somewhat ambiguous. A good index of the mutual suspicion that was generated over this matter is a statement in *The Gaelic Gotham Report* that some people doubted a script existed—an absurd, fantastical notion.[55]

Each side continually rejected or deflected the other's overtures. Macdonald offered the Irish History Roundtable the use of the museum, well before the exhibition's opening, to hold a forum to air their concerns. Macdonald wished to videotape the proceedings and integrate them into the show. But the proposal was rejected out of hand. Brother Emmett Corry was dismayed because he felt Macdonald would be demeaningly using them as "specimens," and John McInerney felt it was a "stupid, insulting, and underhanded" gesture, much as scholar Frederick Crews rejected a somewhat similar suggestion related to the Freud show (see chapter 4). In both these instances, critics did not wish to become part of an exhibit they felt they knew too little about, and where they could not control the context. But Corry and others never voiced this concern directly to the museum. Nor did they attempt to negotiate different terms. They simply ignored the invitation.

Some of the community activists also resented the intervention of Irish consul general Donal Hamill to help broker a resolution. John McInerney "invited him into" the fray, hoping that the consul could add some weight to the critics' position, especially because initially there were plans to tour *Gaelic Gotham* in Ireland. Hamill met with community members on three occasions, and also accompanied three prominent Irish Americans to the museum to discuss matters with the project team. But McInerney reports that the consul was very embarrassed by the call for closure, and asked him to "turn the temperature down." Once again, the critics' hopes to summon influential support were dampened. Moreover, the idea of a "foreigner" stepping in to solve "our problems" seemed offensive to some, another example of an "elite men's club" manipulating the downtrodden. Marion Casey was especially put off. She reports that Consul Hamill told her she was an obstacle to *Gaelic Gotham* going forward: "Basically, I should surrender my rights to anything in the interests of the community. And I'm an American citizen! Who's he to be telling me that?"

Each side already had made up its mind about the other, so that conciliatory gestures were swiftly misconstrued. Macdonald and his staff likewise turned a cold shoulder to the Council for Scholarly Evaluation of *Gaelic Gotham*. The month before the March 13, 1996, opening date, the council submitted a proposed time line to the MCNY that would include evaluation of the script by a panel of scholars. It also contained the proviso that the museum should remain flexible about the opening. In an *Irish Echo* article, roundtable president Walter J. Walsh (Brother Emmett Corry's successor) characterized this as an "ultimatum." But as the article went on to state, Walsh "did not say what the consequences would be if Macdonald failed to comply."

Such outside demands plainly had a hollow ring. Macdonald reports, "My trustees roared with laughter. 'Who are these fools?'"[56] The museum would not drop everything to accede to them, so the council was forced to conduct its own inquiries without directly interacting with representatives from the MCNY. Ed O'Donnell's earlier observation bears repeating: the waters had been poisoned.

The MCNY refused to negotiate with people whom it felt did not necessarily represent the broader community and were primarily bent on avenging the wrongs allegedly committed against Marion Casey. One of the details of *Gaelic Gotham* that was self-consciously worked out was that the show's subtitle would read "'A' History of the Irish in New York," rather than "'The' History." This was *one* interpretation, not the only one. In fact, Marion Casey's original preferences may have appealed to some Irish Americans, but would probably not be as interesting to the so-called new immigrants who have arrived since 1980. Young, hip, better educated, and politically and socially more liberal than many of their predecessors, the new Irish don't necessarily settle in the traditional Irish neighborhoods, nor are they restricted to traditional immigrant jobs such as being construction workers or nannies. The nostalgia over previous generational milestones is not as salient for everyone. Marion Casey's living room would probably hold little interest for this group, for example.

Several members of the museum staff and the project team found fault with the demands for community input or control. To Jack Salzman, "Community is never holistic. And there is a difficult political game going on. Who do you believe? And to whom do you cater? And how many points of view can a show really represent?" For Jan Ramirez, the controversy opened the museum to listening to people who otherwise probably would not have been heard. Looking back, "The lesson we learned is that when an entity comes to you and claims to speak for a community, you better make sure you know if that's true." Ramirez feels that the more the museum probed, the more complex and diverse it found the Irish community to be.

Robert Macdonald rejected the call for community inclusion as somewhat bogus. He feels that the protests were "driven by a very small, unrepresentative group, who frankly make their living at being Irish. And somehow they must have felt that their livelihood was threatened because they couldn't control this exhibit. Did they represent the Irish community of New York? Hell, no!" In fact, except for Macdonald's charges of anti-Semitism and McCarthyism, nothing riled the critics as much as Macdonald's assertion that "*Gaelic Gotham* is not for the Irish but about the Irish." He still supports that view: "We don't do exhibits for people here. We don't do them against people. We do them *about* people."[57]

Angela Carter had written that when a museum mounts a show on ethnic history, it must earn "the trust of the people whose story is being told." Helena Mulkerns found Macdonald's statement "condescending": "The inference is that we're going to do something for *them*, and we're *us*." It confirmed Brother Emmett Corry's belief that the director was "arrogant": "The denigration of the Irish has been going on for a long time. It's not new. See, when we see a man like Mr. Macdonald continuing that process at another level. . . . Ha-ha! It's like, you know, 'Stay out. You're not welcome. We're going to talk about you but you're still not welcome to come in and look at stuff about yourself.' It's just a sad, sad commentary."[58]

But Kerby Miller, the historical consultant who resigned, breaks rank with his fellow critics on this issue. What happens when you push the idea of community input to the extreme? "If it were a show about the KKK," he posits, "would you want 'community' involvement? What about groups about which nice people don't approve? You're quickly forced into a position you can't defend." While Nancy Curtin believes that community groups do have some place in the process of making an exhibition, she too is somewhat cautious and skeptical:

They [community members] are carrying a lot of the identity myths with them. And the scholars' responsibility is to deconstruct those myths, how they developed, where they came from, and what purpose they serve. Some of the things the scholars might have to say about the Irish experience in New York would be things the Irish community might regard as negative."[59]

The Museum of the City of New York has a Fifth Avenue address and a direct view of Central Park. But while it's *on* Fifth Avenue, it's not exactly *Fifth Avenue*. Located a few blocks north of East 96th Street, it lies in the transitional zone between the Upper East Side and East Harlem. It is beyond the ken of many New Yorkers. And yet for many it is a place that connotes old wealth, over the years having become the attic for the paraphernalia of the gentry. To Angela Carter, for example, "It's like a private club."

Joseph Noble moved from the Metropolitan Museum of Art to the directorship of the MCNY in 1971. The first show he mounted was *Drug Scene.* The idea struck him when he was being interviewed for the top position by the board of trustees. It was a gamble, but they liked it: this was a way to be "with it" and to do something constructive for the city. Noble reassured the trustees, "If this bombs, I resign."[60] But the exhibition shattered attendance records. It also helped shatter people's expectations of this museum.

In 1974 Noble masterminded the exhibition *VD*. Those letters were emblazoned on a large sign above the entablature of the museum's entryway. Lauded by the *Village Voice* as a "participatory happening," this exhibition featured free venereal disease screenings and three sets of mannequin couples: male/female, male/male, and female/female. Noble wanted his audience to understand that the transmission of VD did not discriminate based on sexual preference. Each of the mannequins was named, the heterosexuals playfully christened John and Mary after Mayor Lindsay and his wife.[61] Once again, it helped offset perceptions that this is a stuffy institution.

But antiquated perceptions of the MCNY persist, despite the museum's continuing efforts to develop programming that is inclusionary, contemporary, and diverse. After all, its staff receive the same sort of education, read the same professional journals, magazines, and books, and attend many of the same conferences that the hippest, latest cultural theorists do. MCNY staffers don't just genuflect to the city's forebears or polish and display the extensive silver collection. But critics who assail the place almost ritually allude to that silver.

Once *Gaelic Gotham* opened, Helena Mulkerns wrote in a letter to the *Irish Echo* that

> It is a disappointment and a shame that such a great opportunity has been squandered, through the conservatism and patriarchal attitudes of a patrician institution unwilling to spend money or time on the Irish. Ironically, the whole process has been typical of the kind of ethnic power games the Irish emigrants and subsequently Irish Americans historically had to battle in New York.

Her sentiments were echoed when Marion Casey concluded that this was a "Fifth Avenue" or "Big House" interpretation of the Irish.[62] It was, in these views, another contemptible update of the Anglo-Protestant abuses that the grandparents and great-grandparents of many of today's Irish Americans once experienced, a replay of the time when "No Irish Need Apply."

Robert Macdonald refutes all these charges wholeheartedly. "That's bullshit," he declares. "All they had to do is get a list of our board members. Half are women. At least a third are Jewish, although I haven't looked. Three are African American. It's not true. Simple as that." Jan Ramirez agrees. "Patrician in its past? Absolutely! But it's totally not true today, not relevant in any way. Our board has one or two patrician people left on it, but it is by no means patrician. Our staff is not patrician. There is, of course, our silver collection. But [the accusation is] a cop out." While Bernadette McCauley acknowledges "all that silver," she also believes that the MCNY has made a sincere effort to shed its reputation as a tired old fossil bed: "Ethnic power games? What power was being generated? That's a lot of words. They sound meaningful, but I don't think they are."

Nevertheless, elitism was a powerful and perpetual theme. For example, when thirteen people (including Angela Carter and Emmett Corry) wrote a letter to the *Irish Times* condemning *Gaelic Gotham*, their rage and bitterness were palpable. Invoking the memory of "our abused Famine immigrants," they dismissively grumbled that

"Acceptance in the world of Manhattan's social elite is not assimilation it is recolonisation."[63] A certain group of them could not let go of the struggle. In particular, people associated with the Irish History Roundtable had grand expectations for this exhibition. They imagined that *Gaelic Gotham* would be a marvelous celebration, much as countless military veterans ached to see the *Enola Gay* on display to commemorate their brave contribution to ending World War II. Although the outcomes of these cultural battles were different, in both instances the opponents suffered an acute, sinking feeling that a grand opportunity for honoring something sacred was slipping away from them.

A deep sense of disappointment and regret permeates many of the critics' statements. To cite just two: an article coauthored by Helena Mulkerns in the *Irish Echo* began, "What should have been a major celebration of the 300-year history of the Irish in New York . . . has already boiled over into bitter division." Angela Carter lamented, "It would have just been an incredible celebration."[64] But their conception clashed with the project team's goals and Macdonald's statement that *Gaelic Gotham* was "about the Irish, not for the Irish." Jan Ramirez asks, "Do you want, ultimately, to put up a show where everybody comes in and feels good? I don't think so. If it had been a love fest, or a valentine to the Irish community, it wouldn't have been quite as effective." Ed O'Donnell argues, "We weren't here to engage in ethnic cheerleading—truck out the stars and the parade of accomplishments."

Even so, the people who remained so opposed to this exhibition felt they were being bilked out of something they deserved. In strikingly similar terms, both Marion Casey and Helena Mulkerns deplore the fact that the Irish, unlike other groups, were treated in a singularly shoddy manner. Mulkerns complains, "Because the Irish are Europeans, you can't talk about racism. But that's not exactly true, because it *is* racist. It's a lack of respect for another culture." Casey protests,

> The fact that the Irish are white, there's not that assumption that yes, we have to treat them with kid gloves, as you would with some of the other ethnic groups. The only exception with a white group is the Jews. . . . It's just a group that is treated a little more carefully, as are blacks, Native Americans, and, as a matter of fact, are gays and

lesbians. . . . But when it came to the Irish, it was just walk all over them.

Neither celebration nor serious consideration was apparent to either of these women.

Gaelic Gotham garnered few enthusiastic reviews. The most thorough of the newspaper and journal assessments appeared in *American Quarterly*. The author took both sides to task for their behavior prior to the opening. But the writer ultimately backed the MCNY as "vindicated" and "clearly . . . victorious" with an exhibition that had its share of shortcomings but its strong points as well.[65] Many others noted the enormous volume of material, but also its cobbled-together character. Some visitors objected to material that could be expected to generate a range of opinions, for example, the presentation of the Draft Riots, Margaret Sanger's birth control campaign, and the ILGO. Here's a sample of voices we've already heard from: "Adequate, but terribly diminished," Brendan Fay says regretfully. "A good exhibit has great taste to it, whether it's bitter or sweet. But you walk away and say 'Wow.'" Neither he nor Angela Carter had that response. "Incredible clutter. A mess," she adds. John McInerney laments, "When I walked in, it didn't really open its arms to me." Nancy Curtin notes that the exhibition was "Everything and nothing. Sort of like giving crumbs to the Irish."

Those responsible for seeing *Gaelic Gotham* to fruition are candid about the exhibition's shortcomings. Surely there were mistakes. Surely there were oversights. With the benefit of more time and resources, the show might have been sharper, with a more strongly developed narrative line. Nevertheless, the team feels satisfaction that they beat the odds and got it up.

A month after the opening, the Council for Scholarly Evaluation of *Gaelic Gotham* held a public forum at Columbia University, sponsored by the Seminar on Irish Studies. The MCNY was invited to participate, but did not. Two scholars who were unaffiliated with the group made the major presentations of the evening: Allen Feldman (an anthropologist) and John Kuo Wei Tchen (a professor of Asian/Pacific-American studies). Their comments were reprinted in *The Gaelic Gotham Report*. Interestingly, neither man has expertise in Irish American history, which had earlier been a litmus test applied to those participating on the MCNY's team. Instead, the commentators' past experiences with museums, public funding, and public history were duly noted as germane to their ability to evaluate this venture.

Feldman portrayed *Gaelic Gotham* as "a thrown together shanty town of an exhibit," and Tchen characterized it as "a hodgepodge."[66] The report subjected the exhibition to what is undoubtedly the most thoroughgoing examination any museum show has ever received, once it has been mounted. Among other points, Feldman faulted *Gaelic Gotham* for slighting the original culture of the Irish and for failing to offer a comparative analysis with other ethnic groups. But remember, the show's title was *A History of the Irish in New York*, so Feldman was clearly calling for a broader scope than the museum promised. Tchen felt that the Draft Riots were slighted, although they weren't even included in the original plans.

The two men seemed to be calling for the sort of in-depth analysis, pursuit of specialized topics, and provision of substantial social and cultural context that a catalogue typically provides. (No catalogue was issued for this exhibition.) Had many of their suggestions been enacted, they likely would have confounded the casual museum visitor. In fact, a reviewer for the *Irish Times* was extremely put off by the abstruse language these scholars used in *The Gaelic Gotham Report* to describe intergroup relations. When the man later saw the exhibition for himself, he described it as "excellent." Moreover, he threatened, with a hint of jest, "I think I'll have to de-Other that guy [Feldman] when I see him."[67]

One of the focal points of *The Gaelic Gotham Report* is a comprehensive analysis of *every* item in the show—all 478 objects. The results are reported in bar graphs, pie charts, and a table listing each entry. It spreads over eleven pages. John McInerney frankly observes, "I thought it was a little obsessive in the detailing of the faults. . . . There was a lot of anger mixed in with the scholarship. It sort of beat you across the head and shoulders."

These data provide the basis for two startling conclusions. First, the report claims that of the objects with descriptive labels, 40 percent had "errors of fact or interpretation." Moreover, 80 percent of the descriptions reportedly misunderstood an object's relevance, or its interpretation is considered "unrealized." Frank Naughton explains: "If there was historical inaccuracy, or if there was a lost opportunity for addressing the relevance of an artifact, it was considered an opportunity lost. It was considered a mistake made."[68]

This parallels Marion Casey's own conclusions regarding *Gaelic Gotham*. "They like to throw around that the exhibition was 'object rich,'" she observes. However, "most of [the objects] came from the museum's own collections. The majority were acquired through standard museum practices, which means they came out of the homes of wealthy people. They didn't come out of an ethnic community." But Casey's critique cuts even deeper than recognizing these sources. She faults the MCNY for not fully recognizing what it had in hand:

> They didn't know how to read objects as ethnic. Like a pair of shoes, for example. They classify it in their catalogue as "worn by Mister So-and-So at some ball on Christmas, 1886." In fact, there's no mention at all until you pull out a shoe [which she did when she surveyed the MCNY's collection earlier on] that you know an Irish shoemaker made that shoe. That's a way to get at the heart and soul of a community, and they didn't know how to do that.

All the trappings of an objective, quantitative analysis are present in *The Gaelic Gotham Report*. However, the report provides no explanation of the criteria used for this evaluation. Nor does it specify who conducted it, which could obviously influence the results.[69] Moreover, "unrealized" becomes a catchall category whose meaningfulness is somewhat questionable. It obviously allows for a great deal of subjective interpretation. And the sheer size of the task makes it unlikely that anyone would ever redo this investigation; its scope automatically confers a high degree of legitimacy.

Moreover, putting *any* endeavor under such scrutiny is bound to pick up errors. For example, in the report itself, *Keeping the Tradition Alive*—the small exhibition Marion Casey curated at the MCNY in 1991—is inaccurately dated on the first page of the chronology of events. On page 105, the word "principle" appears where "principal" is clearly called for. If you were motivated to do so, you could send a team of investigators combing through these pages and probably come up with scores of other "flaws." Do these trivial errors take away from the general thrust of the document? Not significantly. But mistakes are bound to appear, even though the report was vetted through the council of the roundtable and four or five experts in Irish

American history before it was published. On the one hand, the "expert testimony" called for *Gaelic Gotham* to display a breadth and depth that were unrealistic for a single museum exhibition. On the other, the report put it under the microscope and discovered a multitude of unsightly blemishes.

One additional point. The report discusses the Annie Finnegan trunk, a source of much speculation and innuendo among the people who contested *Gaelic Gotham*. For the most part, they dismissed the "discovery story" as so much bunk. Brother Emmett Corry: "The finding of that trunk was like a very interesting 'extrapolation,' if you follow what I'm saying. That was a trunk which was probably up in the attic of the one of the homes of a member of the board. It wasn't found on the street. No. I don't believe that at all." Indeed, Annie Finnegan worked for the family of Louis S. Auchincloss earlier in the century; Auchincloss is now the chairman of the board of trustees of the MCNY. Was its inclusion an attempt to beef up an ailing checklist via a shamelessly amateurish bit of in-house chicanery? Or do you accept the story repeated by Jan Ramirez and Jane McNamara that a non-Irish woman anonymously loaned the trunk after she'd noticed the MCNY's appeal for contributions to *Gaelic Gotham*?

Whichever version rings true to you, the "set-up" account is another small example of how alienated the community critics felt from this exhibition, and to what degree their speculation precluded them from actually checking things out. Rather than simply acknowledging this difference of opinion and its significance, the report clearly sided with the critics. It viewed the "anonymous" label suspiciously and pointed out the statistical improbability of "discovering such a rare working class icon." It is a partisan statement. While Frank Naughton claims that the purpose of the report was to disseminate the story of what happened "in as disinterested a way as we could make it," he also clearly declares, "I was just convinced that it was impossible to work out anything decent with Macdonald, and that he was thoroughly untrustworthy. So I became a partisan, and I still am." For his part, Macdonald dismisses the notion that Auchincloss himself supplied the trunk as "ludicrous," "comical," and ultimately, "tragic."[70]

As noted, many people privately believe that a clash of personalities mushroomed into something much larger in this case. Robert Macdonald and Marion Casey obviously both had a great deal invested in this struggle. Macdonald was defending his institution; Casey, her vision and her professional reputation. Neither agenda was easily compromised. But Ed O'Donnell recognizes something significant in how things evolved. "[Look at] the language used to describe how epic this exhibit was going to be," he suggests. "And then you have to ask, 'If, in fact, this exhibition of Irish-American history in New York was so vital, so crucial, so sensitive, so one-of-a-kind, so rare an opportunity, then why would Miss Casey have walked away from the project based on a couple of perhaps significant contractual issues?'"

In any work situation, relationships change. Institutional priorities shift. People frequently feel that they've been screwed. When Marion Casey decided to persist in pushing for conditions of employment that were clearly not forthcoming, she backed herself into a corner. Perhaps she saved face by her uncompromising stance. But she ended up totally abandoning a project that had clearly meant a great deal to her. She left it in the hands of others she and her allies certainly felt were unqualified. Different people, faced with the same situation, might have recognized that things weren't going to proceed as they'd planned, swallowed their pride, and carried on as best they could. As O'Donnell further observes, "Anybody who believed in the fate of this exhibit would have bitten the bullet and done the exhibit, to make sure that her hand was on the tiller."

That may be blaming the victim, which Frank Naughton was so loath to do. More likely, it's the reality of working with people, working with institutions. Robert Macdonald reflects, "It was disturbing to realize that people would go to such lengths to destroy something that they proposed, that they purported to love. Very Irish."

If there were a multitude of mistakes in the exhibition, if it had a slapdash character, without a distinctive point of view, if it "lacked soul" (as Marion Casey feared, and Helena Mulkerns later charged), if it attracted little outside financial support and was not as flashy as it might have been, these faults are all somewhat attributable to the critics who undermined—at the very least, hobbled—the reconstituted project team's efforts to produce a credible exhibition. O'Donnell argues, "This was a totally needless, self-destructive, unfortunately very Irish kind of event, if you know the story. Rather than overthrowing the British, they [the Irish] were slicing each other's throats. This was, unfortunately, an excellent example of just that."[71]

A number of the principal players in this dispute seemed to lose all sense of the proportion of these events. A short time after *Gaelic Gotham*, Robert Macdonald visited Kilmainham Gaol, a former Victorian prison that is now an evocative museum of the Irish Resistance. "There you're talking about life and death," he says. "*Gaelic Gotham* wasn't about life and death." Ed O'Donnell confides that he was rather shocked "[when some people] compared the tragedy of the museum to the tragedy of the famine. Unbelievable. Would anybody angry at a Jewish museum dare to say this is the equivalent, this harkens up memories of the Holocaust?" O'Donnell imagines that "As time goes by, people will realize that it was not the epic-shattering moment of ethnocultural history that it was portrayed to be. It was just an exhibition."

One of the factors that allowed a contractual dispute to blossom into a much larger struggle was the media. This was primarily a local, not a national story. While the ethnic press regularly aired the issue, it grabbed the attention of the mainstream press only a few notable times. Bernadette McCauley minimizes the importance of the ethnic press: "The *Irish Echo* is not press coverage. It's a certain constituency that has a mouthpiece." That may be, but the ethnic press can allow parochial matters to simmer for a long time.

Because the ethnic press is rooted in a particular constituency, it is unlikely that reporters shed their professional perspective at day's end and anonymously meld into some community. Rather, identity and community overlap to a greater extent than is the case for other journalists. Writers, editors, columnists are more apt to work, live, and play in the same spots as their readers. In other words, the lines between individual acquaintance, personal loyalty, and professional standards and ethics are subject to blurring.

One of the members of the ad hoc Irish American group cited "shenanigans" in the way the NEH handled this exhibition and the public inquiries into it. One has to wonder if the term isn't relevant to press handling of it as well. For example, the *Irish Echo* published a review of *Gaelic Gotham* that has an overall positive ring to it. Yes, the writer pointed out shortcomings. But he also remarked, "It held my attention for the better part of an afternoon." Three weeks later, the *Echo* published a letter to the editor from Helena Mulkerns, reiterating the entire controversy and blasting the final outcome. It is twice to three times the length of the original review. The fact that she published a major bylined article in the *Irish Echo* about *Gaelic Gotham* and then appeared in print as a member of the community via her own letter is highly unusual—as is what essentially amounts to double-reviewing a show.[72]

Mulkerns, who has been a regular contributor to the *Echo* for approximately six years, explains that as she covered this story, she began to feel deeply about what was going on. Her editor balked at running what Mulkerns intended as an article, but that he redefined as more appropriate to be a letter to the editor instead: "My editor felt he wanted a more nonjudgmental approach, and he didn't want me to report the story any more. He figured I was somewhat biased in my approach." That doesn't particularly bother Mulkerns: "If objective journalism requires journalists to not feel strongly about the subject, well that's fine. . . . It had become more than a straightforward reporting job."

Mulkerns's perspective did not go unchallenged. She reports "fighting" with people who called her to complain, "'What are you doing writing this? Who do you think you are?' One particular journalist who writes for the *Echo* called to attack me and tell me how I was uninformed, I was 'New Irish,' a 'wetback,' I had nothing to do with this, and I should mind my own business."[73] Moreover, Mulkerns was with the crowd at Fitzpatrick's Hotel a few months earlier for the meeting of the Concerned Irish. She characterizes this as her introduction to the conflict, and she denies supporting the call for closure. Mulkerns claims she simply didn't know enough at that point to take a stand. But Brendan Fay, for one, claims she *did* support the community call. Did Mulkerns thus help to make the news that she also reported? Wherever the truth lies in this matter, when a writer rapidly shifts from reporter to rank-and-file citizen, from news gatherer to partisan, it summons to mind the possibility of additional confirmation of Fay's earlier declaration, "Fucking ethics of journalism were crossed here!"

According to Ed O'Donnell, "Very dear friends of Miss Casey are on the staff at the *Irish Echo*, and wrote what can only be described as unbelievably biased reporting on the issue." He characterizes Helena Mulkerns as "their main water carrier for the very slanted, anti-museum coverage," and alleges that "she's a best pal of you-know-who," implying Marion Casey. For her part, Mulkerns characterizes her relationship with Casey as that of "contemporaries," not friends; she knew and respected Casey's work before the controversy over *Gaelic Gotham*. But O'Donnell suspects that whatever Mulkerns produced "was probably virtually cowritten" with Casey.

Questionable journalistic practices surfaced elsewhere, most notably in a *Wall Street Journal* review. It adopted the point of view of the community critics, without serious cross-examination. The author, John McGinnis, mistakenly characterized the exhibition as having "a simple chronology." He claimed that the MCNY "relegated much of the exhibit to the museum's basement hallways," which was clearly an exaggeration.[74] And he singled out examples of stereotyping that he felt were not adequately explored.

Ed O'Donnell provides some insight into how this review evolved:

> He [McGinnis] specifically asked me, "Do you have any leprechauns here?" I can find you the square foot of the carpet where I was standing when he said that. And I said, "Well, what do you mean by that?" Because, you know, that's one of the charges, that this is all just going to be "leprechauns and whiskey bottles." And he said, "No, no, no. I'm just curious. Do you have any leprechauns or shamrocks?"

O'Donnell showed him a record album cover (Dennis Day's 1961 *Shillelaghs and Shamrocks!*) and a shamrock-covered music box, "And lo and behold! That was one of the central laser points of his review."

The anxiety about perpetuating Irish stereotypes had been voiced by a playwright quoted in the article Mulkerns coauthored in the *Irish Echo*, published before the exhibition opened. By O'Donnell's account, the *Wall Street Journal* reviewer intentionally sought out whatever would confirm those expectations. For the record, the wall label describing *Shillelaghs and Shamrocks!* reads as follows: "Dennis Day sang in the glee club at Manhattan College and went on to perform for radio and television host Jack Benny. Benny profiled him as an Irish tenor from New York. The album cover reveals how cultural stereotypes about the Irish were successfully perpetuated and marketed."[75] To have ignored such cultural clichés in this exhibition would have been indefensible. But even the inclusion of a few such examples drew some people's fire and allowed some lazy journalists to settle for skimming the surface of their story rather than rooting around for the more complete and more accurate picture.

Gaelic Gotham had a relatively low profile with the general public. But the effects of the controversy are still felt. Brendan Fay has been called a hypocrite, a traitor, a turncoat. Some people will no longer talk to him, and he feels a distinct coldness in the interaction he has with others. One member of the Concerned Irish believes that Fay was co-opted by "the other side," that he negotiated a separate peace: "Once he got all his stuff [representing the ILGO] in there, Brendan was all for the exhibit finally. Like he'd gone 180 degrees. What a character. Brendan turned out to be something other than what he started out to be." On closer examination, Brendan Fay remained open to hearing both sides, and acted on principle, not solely on the basis of personal loyalty. He thus became difficult to pigeonhole. Furthermore, he voluntarily gave up an opportunity that he had very much looked forward to, an invitation to present the MCNY's annual lecture on gay and lesbian history. In the end, "I felt almost equally disheartened with my own community as I had been with the museum." However, "I did what I had to do," he reflects. "And when I go to bed my conscience feels okay."[76]

Angela Carter feels drained and embittered. She is furious that Marion Casey does not have the curatorship of *Gaelic Gotham* on her résumé, and that the community—her Irish community—"got no exhibition." As she sums up her experience, "It was very wearing. It really was most disruptive for an entire year. And it has changed how I feel about everything, really. I've withdrawn from all public events. I just no longer want to see most of the people who cooperated with the museum. So now, I just stay with the roundtable and my Irish language groups."

Carter and other critics of the show within the Irish American community clearly continue to nurse their anger against Robert Macdonald and the museum. Soon after *Gaelic Gotham* opened, Marion Casey fired off an angry response to *New York Newsday*'s review of the show. It was not printed. Nearly four months later, she wrote a detailed rebuttal and statement of clarification to *World of Hibernia* regarding its coverage of the exhibition. But she never sent that letter. Perhaps the most revealing insight into Marion Casey's feelings about the entire situation can be found in a set of notes she drafted to herself in February 1996. Her lingering questions and pervading speculation, her sense of puzzlement and injustice, crest in this doleful comparison:

> **Look what happened to Ed O'Donnell in 1995:** He finished his dissertation and got his Ph.D. from Columbia. He got an assistant professorship at Hunter College and the *Gaelic Gotham* job, in addition to his Big Onion walking tour business which is benefitting substantially from his association with MCNY.

> **Look what happened to Marion Casey in 1995:** She postponed completing her dissertation in order to develop *Gaelic Gotham* so was unable to get her Ph.D. from NYU. She passed up opportunities for work while MCNY first delayed the exhibition, then protracted her contract negotiations. She lost income and her health suffered while Macdonald smeared her reputation for more than twelve months.

At the end of 1997 Casey was still writing her dissertation.

Jan Ramirez and her colleagues at the MCNY gained a great deal of experience by mounting this exhibition. Their commitment to presenting ethnic history continues: in the fall of 1997 they launched preliminary planning for a show about Arab Americans. This time they are keenly aware of the diversity of ethnic communities, and intend to meet with a broad cross-section of Arab American scholars, activists, and businesspeople to get "the lay of the land." In Ramirez's words, "We want to find out where the bodies are buried" before they charge into this new territory.[77]

And Robert Macdonald? *Gaelic Gotham* is largely in the past for him. Mistakes may have been made, and miscalculations. But he has moved on. Macdonald believes that the MCNY emerged the winner in this struggle: "The museum actually benefited from the controversy, in developing a credibility among the leadership of New York, and in the country. It said, 'This is a museum that is not afraid to deal with issues that are controversial . . . and that we're also not afraid to stand behind what we do.'" For Macdonald, the MCNY's good name was on the line. That's why he acted so belligerently: "A museum doesn't work on money. The reputation of the institution is the fuel that drives it. It's the asset that can't be replaced."

For Irish Americans like Brother Emmett Corry, who are passionate advocates for their community, *Gaelic Gotham* is another chapter in the history of anti-Irish bigotry. Moreover, there are always new battles to fight, new strategies to devise, to heighten the public's awareness of Irish suffering. Young women now earnestly dance in tribute to the Great Famine at soccer games. Famine conferences are held, money is raised for memorials, and a coalition of congressmen is lobbying the U.S. Postal Service to issue a commemorative stamp—paralleling a similar grassroots effort that has collected over a million signatures supporting a stamp honoring the African Burial Ground.

A year after *Gaelic Gotham* closed, Brother Corry was deeply upset by reports of the pregame and halftime shows during a 1997 Stanford–Notre Dame football game. The Stanford University band blurred the line between parody and direct insult with a mock debate between the devil and a Catholic cardinal and a frivolous depiction of the Great Famine with a fictionalized character, "Seamus O'Hungry." He was said to represent "a sparse cultural heritage that consisted only of fighting and then starving."[78]

But if *Gaelic Gothic* highlighted anything, it was the enormous breadth of the Irish experience, which such a spoof reduced to caricature. And if the controversy over *Gaelic Gotham* illustrated anything, it was the highly contested nature of *any* ethnic group's history.

4

War of the Words

Psychoanalysis and Its Discontents

I took Freud's words as gospel until I was exposed to other gospels. Now that I'm a postmodernist, I see all theories as approximations of explaining what's going on, and I'm not terribly attached to any one theory.

—Sophie Freud

WE ALL KNOW the classic stereotype of the psychoanalyst: dispassionate, aloof, and largely mum, embodying the somber weightiness of the turn-of-the-century Central European milieu from which this treatment technique—and worldview—emerged. To this day, it's an image associated with conventional tweeds, heavily accented speech, and the authority of age. An agitated atmosphere of intrigue churns behind and beneath the public formality and unruffled demeanor of this therapeutic cosmos. But these emotional extremes have always been characteristic of the field.

The history of psychoanalysis is a chronicle of intense rivalries and bitter betrayals, of meteoric rises to fame and precipitous falls from grace. The names of the dissenters, the enemies, the apostates, and the casualties litter each epoch: Fleiss, Jung, Adler, and Rank early on; Fromm, Sullivan, and Horney somewhat later; Kohut and Masson more recently. Psychoanalysis has been targeted by intellectual and social movements since the 1960s: feminists have waged a protracted struggle against what they see as its pervasive paternalism, and gay liberationists challenged the dominant psychoanalytic view of homosexuality as illness, forcing its removal from the *Diagnostic and Statistical Manual of Psychiatric Disorders* in 1973. Mavericks like Thomas Szasz have dismissed mental illness as a myth, R. D.

Laing honored it as an alternative form of communication, while Erving Goffman and D. L. Rosenhan have focused on the insanity of place rather than persons. Psychiatry in general and psychoanalysis in particular have no shortage of critics.

Clearly, this is a chronic condition. A 1979 *Time* magazine cover story spotlighted "Psychiatry's Depression." Noting that psychoanalysis had lost its rather exclusive therapeutic franchise to the competition of some two hundred rival approaches, the accompanying story presented an ersatz diagnosis of the field: "Standard conflictual anxiety and maturational variations, complicated by acute depression. Identity crisis accompanied by compensatory delusions of grandeur and a declining ability to cope." Its prognosis? "Problematic." *Time* followed this up fourteen years later with a cover presenting a portrait of Freud "lobotomized"; crucial jigsaw-puzzle pieces were missing from the master's hollow brow. It posed the provocative question, "Is Freud Dead?" This was an obvious allusion to the infamous *Time* cover from 1966, raising the same suspicion about God. The lead quote asks, in the mock-martyr tone of an exasperated and underappreciated parent, "He invented psychoanalysis and revolutionized 20th century ideas about the life of the mind. And this is the thanks he gets?"[1]

Some struggles are over arcane matters. But nowadays conflicts over psychoanalysis break out publicly more and more frequently. The stakes have always been high: Freud, after all, is one of the primary authors of modernist thought. His writings have influenced not only how we conduct therapy, but how we analyze everything from literary texts to everyday interactions, and how we reflect on the basics of human nature. It is virtually impossible to divorce Freud from the major currents of the twentieth century. Yet a throng of revisionists has generated a large body of faultfinding commentary over the past three decades or so, critical of Freud's major principles, Freudian therapeutic techniques, the Freud "establishment," and even the life and personal conduct of the man himself.

Some post-Freudians have displaced sex and the Oedipus Complex as the cornerstone of their practice, substituting instead narcissism, the self, and parental failures to nurture. Others argue that Freud's precepts defy scientific confirmation, and they question the ethics and validity of his early case studies. Still others have tried to debunk the entire Freudian enterprise: Jeffrey Moussaieff Masson has accused Freud of a "failure of moral courage" when he abandoned his theory of parental abuse and endorsed the belief in children's unconscious fantasizing instead. For Masson, this consequential shift from external reality to inner monsters marked the end, not the birth, of psychoanalysis.[2] Revisionists now subject Freud the man *and* the institution of psychoanalysis to the same sort of in-depth scrutiny dictated by the theory itself. Through their close reconsiderations of the case studies and exhumation of long-buried documents, many of them have produced damning critiques.

A great deal of this debate has occurred behind the closed doors of training institutes or in the pages and thematic sessions of specialized journals and conferences. But some of the more popularly written publications have garnered considerable notice. In particular, two books by the journalist Janet Malcolm offer rare glimpses into a byzantine world to which few people are directly privy. Both originally appeared as essays in the *New Yorker* and were later published in book form. *Psychoanalysis: The Impossible Profession* (1981) presents the world of an orthodox Freudian analyst. "Aaron Green" candidly admitted that his work was relentlessly demanding, lonely, guilt-provoking, and "unhealthy": "Analysts keep having to pick away at the scab that the patient tries to form between himself and the analyst to cover his wound."[3] But beyond the stresses of the therapeutic encounter lay the machinations within professional analytic societies. These are portrayed as places where jousting constantly opens up wounds, sites of passionate rivalries crosscut with unresolved transferences. Constituencies are inclined to be swept along with messianic figures or to resist them (the man of the moment was Heinz Kohut). The psychologist Morris Eagle laments, "What a field! There are loyalties organized around a charismatic figure. It reminds me of my old Stalinist days. It's the same fucking thing."[4]

Malcolm's second book on psychoanalysis, *In the Freud Archives* (1984), achieved much more notoriety. Here she turned her sights on the highest levels of the psychoanalytic establishment. The Sigmund Freud Archives is a nonprofit foundation that has collected and controlled a vast array of Freud letters, manuscripts, and memorabilia since around 1950. Until the time Malcolm wrote about it, the Archives was under the direction of Dr. Kurt Eissler, in close consultation with Freud's daughter Anna. Since its inception, the Archives has been funneling material to the Library of Congress (LOC), which

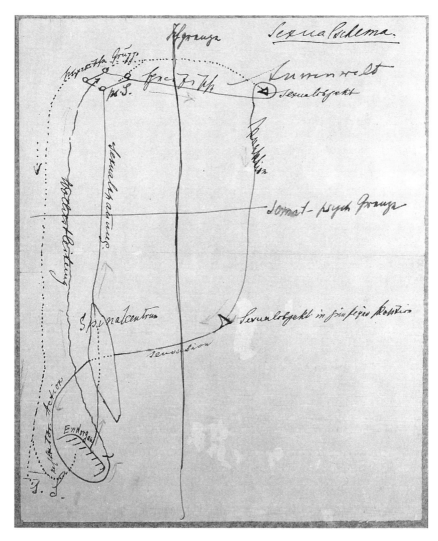

FIG. 10. Sigmund Freud, *Sexualschema*, 1894 (part of *Manuskript G*). A. W.
Freud et al., by arrangement with Mark Paterson and Associates. Photo courtesy of the Library of Congress.

has become the world's largest repository of Freud material. But in many cases Eissler honored donor requests to restrict documents, or he imposed such editorial control as director. In some instances the access of scholars has been prohibited until 2102. In such cases, Eissler and his associates have claimed that they were protecting the identity of Freud's former patients. But many critics charged that they have been covering up vital information and unfairly limiting a full examination of the psychoanalytic enterprise, warts and all.

Most readers undoubtedly remember Malcolm's book for its depiction of the colorful young analyst Jeffrey Masson. Masson became the projects director of the archives and was given unprecedented access to documents. By all accounts, he was being groomed to become Eissler's successor. But the relationship unraveled after Masson revealed his doubts about Freud's "discovery" of the unconscious to a *New York Times* reporter and attributed Freud's decision to discredit his patients' reports of sexual abuse as a strategic move to make his ideas more palatable to his colleagues and to the public. For Masson, Freud's "finding" was politic, not supported by the data. After Masson was removed from his position, he brashly told the same *Times* reporter that because of the significance of Freud's falsification, "They would have to recall every patient since 1901. It would be like the Pinto."[5]

Moreover, Malcolm presented two statements that Masson allegedly made to her that later became the basis for a protracted legal battle between the two. Masson reportedly had big plans for Anna Freud's house in London upon her death (her father had died there in 1939): he envisioned it as "a place of sex, women, fun." Masson was quoted as characterizing himself as "an intellectual gigolo."[6]

But while those remarks have achieved a measure of renown, Malcolm's book has a larger significance. It clearly exposed the pitched nature of the battle between Freud's critics and his defenders. As Eissler characterized the struggle, "The people who write against Freud are motivated by a desire for revenge. . . . Every time I read one of these 'revelations,' I think the bottom has been reached." Malcolm's book also introduced a man who would become a key player in the debate over the exhibition *Sigmund Freud: Conflict and Culture,* initially scheduled to open in May 1996 at the Library of Congress. That man is Peter J. Swales, an independent historian and Freud scholar, who told Malcolm, "What I'm doing, in a sense, is declaring war on a whole profession—psychoanalysis."[7] Malcolm unwittingly captured the opening volleys in what would break out more than a decade later as a feverish and very public quarrel.

Peter J. Swales has been dubbed the "bad boy" of psychoanalysis. It's a term he devilishly embraces. A self-described "performance artist" and autodidact, a man whose formal education in his native England did not extend beyond high school, and a guy who once worked for several years as a general business assistant for the Rolling Stones, Swales has carved out a distinctive niche for himself in the otherwise insular and professionalized world of Freud scholarship.

He fell into it, rather by accident. Swales became involved in book publishing in New York City around 1972. He discovered a European monograph edition of Freud's cocaine papers and successfully negotiated the North American publication rights. It was a totally new venture for Swales, and it sent him on a personal quest to uncover knowledge about Freud that has dominated his life. In his words, "I knew I'd found my gig." "Research is my narcotic," he declares.[8]

Swales has garnered a reputation for tracking down people, disclosing identities, and unearthing documents relevant to the early history of psychoanalysis that have consistently eluded other investigators. Conducting what he calls rigorous "social archaeology," Swales doggedly follows his hunches, regardless of how scandalous or unflattering his conclusions may be. Swales is most widely known for arguing that Sigmund Freud was "bonking his wife's sister": he alleges that Freud had an affair with his sister-in-law Minna, got her pregnant, and arranged for her to have an abortion.[9]

Not everyone buys his tale, of course. Swales boasts that Janet Malcolm referred to this particular piece of work as "an intellectual tour de force." But in truth her sentiments were more mixed than Swales admits: "The whole thing is immensely satisfying to contemplate as a piece of intellectual work; there are no loose ends, all the pieces fit, the joints are elegant. But it's all wrong. It's like a Van Meegeren forgery of Vermeer, in which all the pieces fit, too, but from which the soul of the original is entirely, almost absurdly, missing."[10]

Swales has ruffled a lot of feathers in the psychoanalytic world. Unbeholden to any one intellectual system (he adamantly asserts his independence of thought and his personal sovereignty, tracing his theoretical roots to the Scottish skeptics) he feels free to scrutinize Freud and his precepts in a manner that many of Freud's followers have been chary to attempt. He blasts psychoanalysts for their "incontinent interpretation of everything" and faults them for failing to recognize the real Freud: "Okay, they'll grant that he made six babies with his wife, but beyond that, Freud is chaste, puritanical, all these things, by their account. And I, on the other hand, am ready to recognize him on the basis of the texts in front of me, a guy who's by no means sexually disinterested." Swales tags himself "the only true Freudian." The way he presents it, Swales is unafraid to recognize the deviousness, dishonesty, and manipulativeness of his own character, and then confront the same features in the personage of Freud. He proclaims that he alone refuses to exempt Freud from the imputation of sexual interests and cunning motives.[11]

Swales had butted heads with the Archives long before the Library of Congress's announcement of the 1996 exhibition. Janet Malcolm reported that in 1979 Swales "was chafing under the restrictions of the Archives" in obtaining materials for his research at the LOC. He eventually met with Eissler, who helped Swales obtain two small grants from a foundation closely associated to the Archives. Swales was even invited to a 1980 brunch at Eissler's apartment, where he felt that he was "infiltrating the sanctum sanctorum, the holy of holies," but also reflected that "Their material shouldn't even be bloody locked up. I thought I could break the Freud Archives' monopoly on material."[12] Because of Swales's subsequent claims in papers and lectures and his publicly belligerent stance toward institutions that he believed were inhibiting free inquiry by tightly regulating access to their collections, his relationship with the Archives and the LOC was marked by mutual suspicion and antagonism.

Sigmund Freud: Conflict and Culture was the idea of Dr. Harold Blum, Eissler's successor as executive director of the Archives. Blum conceived of this as an exhibition to explore Freud's legacy, his enormous impact on various aspects of twentieth-century culture. It would consist of three major sections: "Historical/Biographical"; "From the Conscious to the Unconscious" (exploring major concepts and case studies); and "From the Psyche to Civilization" (theories of society, cultural impact, and "contested legacies"). Freud's manuscripts, correspondence, photographs, some of his antiquities, his consulting

FIG. 11. Freud's couch. From the collection of the Freud Museum, London.
Photograph courtesy of the Library of Congress. Used by permission.

couch from the Freud Museum in London, and even home movies
would be included. Examples of popular culture that demonstrate
Freud's influence would also be highlighted, from sensationalistic
comic book covers published in the 1950s, to clips from movies (including film classics such as *Compulsion, The Three Faces of Eve, Psycho,
Marnie,* and *Vertigo,* to *Bill and Ted's Excellent Adventure*) and television shows (including *The Dick Van Dyke Show, The Flintstones,* and
The Simpsons). James Billington, the Librarian of Congress, proudly
announced that this would be "a coming-out party for our collection." The American Psychoanalytic Association crowed that it was
expected to be one of the most widely attended exhibitions the LOC
ever mounted.[13]

Harold Blum is a Freud enthusiast. He is eager to emphasize how
much Freud's ideas have permeated and shaped contemporary thinking. He believes that Freudian insights offer the most compelling model of the human mind, are invaluable for treating individual problems, and provide the key to understanding pressing social

issues such as racism. Not surprisingly, Blum peppers his speech with concepts like "rationalization," "the return of the repressed," "resistance," and "projection." These are the tools of his trade, after all. He delights in pointing out that one of the early articles in the *New York Times* reporting the controversy that developed over this show mistakenly referred to "the Fraud critics" rather than "the Freud critics."[14] This slip, or parapraxis, confirms for Blum one of Freud's dynamic principles.

Blum claims that the goal of the exhibit is to educate the public about Freud—*sans* deception, *sans* proselytizing, *sans* partisanship. His purpose is to "be factual, accurate, and to present Freud as he was: not bowdlerized, not diluted, and not altered." But additional motives were apparent in his extemporaneous opening remarks at the International Psychoanalytical Congress in San Francisco in 1995, where he announced the LOC's acceptance of his exhibition proposal:

> Ladies and gentlemen, colleagues and friends, it's a great pleasure to address you at a time when psychoanalysis is so challenged and when we have so much Freud-denigration and throughout the world the devaluation of psychoanalysis. . . . In size and scope it will exceed any exhibition of Freud ever held anywhere in the world, and it's under the virtual sponsorship of the United States government. Freud's portrait will hang in the great rotunda of the Library of Congress where so many of our presidents' portraits have also been placed.[15]

This points to the exhibition being self-consciously conceived to prop up and promote a positive view of Freud, in light of an increasing chorus of criticism. It is becoming a commonplace that psychoanalysis is under a dual assault. Pharmaceutical breakthroughs shift the focus from the unconscious to brain circuitry and blood chemistry. Precise dosing replaces the "talking cure." Managed health care favors brief behavioral adjustments—mental fine-tuning, as it were—over protracted and costly psychological overhauls. In psychoanalytical terms, the glee over having Freud join the pantheon of American presidents hinted at an unresolved transference.

Swales and Blum are obvious adversaries, pulling the reputational body of Freud in contrary directions in a Solomonic drama. Had it just been the two of them opposing one another, it might look like a classic *folie à deux*. But others jumped—or were dragged—into the fray. One of the most important of these was Frederick Crews, a professor emeritus of English at the University of California-Berkeley. A distinguished literary critic, Crews became interested in Freudian theory as an interpretive tool in the 1960s. At the time, "The Freudian take on things just seemed to me intuitively right . . . [so] I rolled up my sleeves and started applying it." His influential study of Nathaniel Hawthorne, *The Sins of the Fathers: Hawthorne's Psychological Themes* (1966), was the major result.[16]

But it was a brief intellectual interlude. As he admits, "I gradually developed cold feet about the whole thing. . . . I had to decide what my ultimate loyalty was. Was it to this system of thought, or was it to the empirical point of view? And you know, I chose the latter." By 1970 he had ceased teaching Freudian methods of interpretation to students, and by 1980 he was "openly opposing" the whole psychoanalytic system of thought. His essay of that year, "Analysis Terminable," presented his new position. "I took a serious wrong turn in the 1960s," he states forthrightly. In fact, when his book on Hawthorne was reissued in 1989, he appended an essay explaining what theoretical mistakes he believes he made earlier and stating that he had rejected psychoanalysis "root and branch."[17]

Crews had been refining his new position in articles spanning fifteen years. His thoughts crystallized in two lengthy pieces published in the *New York Review of Books* in 1993 and 1994. The first blasted psychoanalysis as a pseudoscience and a shell game; the second linked it to the so-called recovered memory movement, a crusade whose faulty logic and excesses repel Crews. At the time, Crews's critiques seemed to be the talk of everyone who counted themselves among that rarified category called "intellectual."

In a basic respect, both Crews and Blum could probably agree that psychoanalysis was going through rough times, and an exhibition appearing at a venerable institution could give it a boost. But whereas Blum put a positive spin on things, Crews wished to lay bare this insidious objective: "The motive behind the exhibition was to polish up the tarnished image of a business that's heading into Chapter 11."[18]

Swales, Blum, and Crews: each man had his own vested interests, a reputation to defend, and the legacy of past experiences that colored his perceptions and shaped his expectations. *Sigmund Freud:*

Conflict and Culture provided the next battlefield for what was a protracted war between forces that were already well acquainted with one another. As was the case with both *Harlem on My Mind* and the ill-fated slavery exhibition at the LOC, the major participants had a history of significant struggles that antedated the Freud exhibition and helped cast this dispute in a certain way. Just as someone like John Henrik Clarke played a role in the 1969 struggle over black representation at the Metropolitan Museum of Art and then entered the debate in the early 1990s when the definition and management of the African Burial Ground were being decided, Peter J. Swales and Frederick Crews had likewise defined their enemies and had been on the attack for a long time. While this dispute might have appeared relatively new to the general public, it had been brewing steadily. The LOC exhibition simply provided a new opportunity to stage maneuvers.

Opponents in cultural struggles commonly become entwined in what Michel Foucault pithily characterizes as *"perpetual spirals of power and pleasure."*[19] That is, actors in these dramas derive satisfaction from exercising authority as well as from challenging or evading it. The Institute of Contemporary Art's director Patrick Murphy recalls observing with some alarm during the Robert Mapplethorpe controversy in 1989-90 "The almost vain delight of the art world about being on the front pages of the *New York Times*, instead of being in the Arts and Leisure section. Out of the ghetto and into the news."[20] Adversaries sustain an odd symbiosis. Each is the other's *raison d'être.* They are coupled in an obsessive dance that usually neither one can stop.

The combatants over the Freud exhibition, more so than in any other museum-centered controversy, illustrate Foucault's concept of such collusive struggles. They were well acquainted, aware of one another's foibles, and determined warriors for what each embraced as a just cause. These parties loathe one another. Yet they can't leave one another alone. Every epithet that they hurled—or that the media produced—was countered by its precise antonym. Accusations of "Freudian loyalists" or the "Freudian faithful" were answered with accusations of "defectors." True believers or keepers of the Freud shrine were contrasted with anti-Freudians. Labels such as fundamentalists, old-line, orthodox, cultlike, or whitewashers were rebutted with the overused tag of basher, and such labels as Freud idolator extraordinaire, neo-Freudophobe, doctrinaire, detractor. The rhetoric escalated considerably as the dispute unfolded: charges of being apologists, members of a sclerotic Freud establishment, or intellectual lowlife were answered with charges of acting like ayatollahs, thought police, or "Nazis hunting down 'Freudian Jews.'" At times it sounded like a psychoanalytic version of "doing the dozens." Peter Swales rolled his anger and resentments into a neologism, a single word that sounds something like a schoolyard taunt and captures the zest and sense of engagement this struggle engendered: "psucko-analysis."[21]

The story unfolded this way: the Library of Congress announced *Sigmund Freud: Conflict and Culture* in June 1994. It would open in Washington, D.C., in May 1996 and then travel to sites in the United States and Europe. Michael S. Roth, a historian affiliated with the Getty Research Institute for the History of Art and the Humanities, was appointed guest curator. Peter J. Swales firmly believes that this exhibition was the response of the "ultra Freudians" to Crews's bruising articles in the *New York Review of Books*.

Roth reached out to people with interest and knowledge in this field. When Roth contacted Peter Swales, Swales recalls, "I thought to myself, 'Well, this is really weird. Who is this guy? He wouldn't be doing this if he knew anything about me, because I'm much too controversial in terms of the people, the guiding spirits behind this exhibition. He can't know very much about modern Freud studies if he's coming to me for advice and information.'" But rather than steering clear, Roth relates that he was advised by Marvin Krantz, the historical specialist in the manuscript division at the LOC, to talk with Swales right away.

Swales was initially helpful, but was flabbergasted that Roth was unfamiliar with the work of the revisionist scholars whom Swales most highly esteems. He was also upset at the roster of exhibition advisers, catalogue contributors, and proposed participants in an associated conference. To Swales, the deck was completely stacked, jammed with pro-Freudian enthusiasts. Crews concurs: "There were no dissenters at all. The whole thing was an inside job." Furthermore, Swales regarded Roth as unqualified to be in charge, way out of his league: "this guy doesn't know how the land lies. He doesn't know the field. . . . privately, to myself, I had no respect. . . . I was talking to an ignoramus."

Roth felt "palpable" hostility and resentment from certain people. That may be partially explained by the fact that Swales believed Roth was being held hostage by his superiors, psychoanalysts manipulating arrangements for the exhibition behind the scenes. But Roth rejects that as an absurdity: "I don't even know who 'my superiors' would be. Nobody gives me orders," he states bluntly.[22]

Meanwhile, Frederick Crews was also vexed over what he was hearing about the proposed exhibition. He expressed his concerns in a letter written to the LOC manuscript division in June 1995. The need to avoid perpetuating what Crews characterizes as the "'immaculate conception' account of Freud's key discoveries" was paramount in his mind. Pointing to Ernest Jones's standard biography of Freud, Crews was worried that the same version of "fictionalized history" would be repeated. Specifically, Crews rejects the legend of Freud as "a Promethean individual who seizes knowledge for the benefit of mankind through a private effort of genius . . . through a kind of ascetic self-discipline, facing the horrible facts of unconscious sexual and aggressive wishes, and breaking through a repression which had been in place for millennia." Such heroic models do not generally stand up to scrutiny today. This view of Freud certainly doesn't, in light of a sizable body of revisionist writings. Crews closed his letter "wishing you good fortune in a delicate task."[23] The LOC's response was a polite brush-off.

Swales also wrote to the LOC. In his letter, he used a word that was subsequently bandied about by both sides: censorship. From Swales's perspective, the Freud Archives and the "Freud establishment" regularly engage in de facto censorship by restricting access to important materials and strictly regulating the ideological configuration of conferences. As he states, "they'll silence you to death."[24] But Swales's primary strategy was to draft another letter to the LOC and solicit people to sign on with him in support.

After vetting it with a few associates, Swales tapped in to a network of people he has remained in touch with since a Freud conference in Toronto in 1990, when he met a number of "commonly-spirited" colleagues. It was a group with whom he was already regularly sharing material. A meticulous archivist, Swales amassed a dossier related to the Freud exhibition of over three hundred pages: letters, news articles, press releases, published and unpublished letters to the editor, and Internet notices, in several languages.

Within weeks, Swales had gathered forty-two signatories. That number eventually grew to fifty, representing eleven countries: primarily university-affiliated M.D.'s and Ph.D.'s, including such noted Freud scholars as Mikkel Borch-Jacobsen, Frank Cioffi, Adolf Grünbaum, Morris Eagle, Paul Roazen, and Frank J. Sulloway. This was an ephemeral and eclectic collection of individuals, not a monolithic group. In this instance, concern about the perceived scope and philosophical "tilt" of the exhibition outweighed their doctrinal differences. (Says Swales, "There was no love lost among many of us petitioners.")[25] Oliver Sacks, Gloria Steinem, and Sophie Freud, a professor emerita of social work and a granddaughter of Freud, also signed on. Because their names were more recognizable than most of the other signatories, the press frequently singled them out as "representing" the group.

Swales characterizes the petition as "innocent" and "innocuous." A reading of the document largely confirms his interpretation. Two points are paramount. First, the signatories expressed concern that "the full spectrum of informed opinion about the status of Freud's contribution to intellectual history" be presented. Second, they proposed that Henry Cohen, an LOC legislative attorney, be appointed to the planning committee; he could therefore act as a liaison to these concerned outsiders. The letter was sent to James Hutson, the chief officer of the manuscript division, on July 31, 1995.[26] The fact that the petitioners never received what they felt was an adequate reply made certain of them feel angry, suspicious, and frustrated, and helped guarantee that what followed would be fought out largely within the media's glare. This was one of the last moments that cool heads or accurate characterizations prevailed.

Swales stated in a letter to the signatories that his message to the general public was "caveat emptor—to [let them] select what they want off a complete menu. (Consumer protection!)." He went on to explain that to suggest that one of *them* be appointed to the planning committee "could reek of an attempted putsch."[27] The military imagery was fitting; a war mentality soon prevailed. This was just *before* the petition was dispatched. Not only that, Swales was already speaking with a reporter. Once the media stepped in, things quickly intensified.

Roth wrote to Swales two weeks after the petition was sent to the LOC, with an open and conciliatory tone. He asked for a list of addresses of the signatories so that he could solicit their views. And indeed, Roth dispatched dozens of copies of a "Dear Scholar" letter a few weeks later, promising to incorporate dissident voices so that a partisan exhibition would not result. But others were reacting more feverishly. For example, one therapist wrote to James Billington that "The psychiatric world is rife with rumors." He continued, "it might not be going too far to say that it would be as if a group of die-hard Stalinists were to use The Library to promulgate the ideas of Marx and Lenin unchallenged." An academic psychologist wrote to Roth to complain that "All I see is party-line propaganda." The enduring viability of Cold War imagery—several years after the Cold War— was evident when another signatory complained that the exhibition proposal reminded him of "retouched portraits of [the] Stalinist era, with undesirable figures eliminated."[28] Roth was both amazed and depressed by such overreactions: "Stalin murdered like 50 million people, and maybe I had made a mistake. I really thought this was the kind of inflation that was characteristic of the stupidity in this field."

Channels of communication remained open, despite this rancor. It might have continued to be a case of delicate negotiation and compromise, but the press became a factor. Henceforward, each article seemed to ratchet the anxiety level, the hysteria level, and the pitch of the rhetoric a notch higher. The first such episode centered on an article in the November–December issue of *Lingua Franca*, a small-circulation magazine highlighting academic issues. "Fissures at an Exhibition" allowed the points of view of the major figures to be expressed: Roth, Blum, Swales, and Crews. But its relatively balanced viewpoint was undercut at the very beginning: a banner headline declared, "The Sigmund Freud exhibit at the Library of Congress won't open for nearly a year—but its critics are already trying to close it down."[29]

That allegation was seriously at odds with most of the text and with the language of the August petition. Moreover, it pegged the petitioners as trying to limit expression rather than seeking to enlarge its scope. The major bit of support for the article's opening allegation was a quote by Swales that "the whole project should be aborted."[30] That certainly can be read as betraying a strong belief that the exhibition was ill-conceived and should not be allowed to develop further. But one cannot extrapolate from that individual statement that the critics actively sought to shut the show down. According to Swales,

"We were definitely asking for balance, no question about it. . . . I've got no wish to see Sigmund Freud silenced. . . . He's the goose that laid the golden eggs for all these many signatories of the petition." Michael S. Roth rebukes *Lingua Franca* as a "paparazzi version of academic life." Rather than viewing this article as merely fanning the flames of controversy, he believes "it lit the match."

It didn't take long before the story burst onto the pages of major dailies. The catalyst for a wave of stories was a decision that transformed this from a clash of philosophical perspectives into An Event. In early December the LOC abruptly announced it was postponing the exhibit because of a budget shortfall. But many people had the nagging suspicion that this was a smokescreen, a pretense to avoid working through the objections that critics were raising. According to Frederick Crews, the announcement "came as just as much of a surprise to me and to people like Peter as it did to the psychoanalysts out there. But their immediate response was to say 'Aha! The enemies of Freud have succeeded in stopping the show. So this must have been their aim all along. They are censors.'"

The Associated Press picked up the story. So did the *Washington Post*, the *New York Times*, *Newsweek*, the *New Republic*, the *Philadelphia Inquirer*, the *Daily Telegraph* (London), *Deutsche Presse-Agentur*, *Die Presse*, and others. The *Philadelphia Inquirer*, for example, trumpeted its coverage with the accusation of "censorship." It's a form of packaging that general audiences can understand, even if they can't comprehend the complexities of the issues. It denotes action, not simply talk. And sure enough, the reporter elicited such charges from both Roth *and* Swales, lobbing similar criticisms across the page.[31] But what really riled Swales and other critics was one of the articles appearing in the *New York Times*. The pull quote declared, "The never-ending backlash against Freud confirms the potency of his theories."[32] Furthermore, a passage in the text tacitly accepted the validity of the Oedipus complex and the concept of resistance, viewing the critics as enacting the psychoanalytically inevitable conflict between the generations.

Crews was outraged that his critique could be reduced to the "mischievous antics of little Oedipal bastards who want to thumb their noses at Father Freud." Swales makes the general observation that "the media is [sic] vulgar. And simplistic . . . you only got to work for the Rolling Stones for six weeks to learn that one." What Swales

FIG. 12. Stuffed Freud doll, Freud Toy™ by the Toy
Works, Middle Falls, New York. From the author's
collection. Photograph by Bart Dellarmi.

felt was an oversimplification of the issues and a journalistic dismissal of the critics as immature tricksters triggered a forceful, specific reaction:

> Journalists are called hacks because they're not their own masters.
> They're not sovereigns unto themselves. They do what the person
> who gets in the cab tells them. That means to say, a journalist will
> write about everything pretending to know everything, but in fact
> knowing nothing, or a little bit more than nothing. And this is what
> prostitutes do. They'll go to bed virtually with anyone who pays
> them money enough to do that.

In a flourish of grandiosity in which he equates promiscuity with
evil and sexual fidelity with good, Swales observes that the "world of
the media is a world of fucking prostitutes. They are not faithfully

married to anything they write about. Unlike a guy like me, who by now for virtually a quarter of a century has devoted himself to Freud studies. I am a very faithful spouse of the field of Freud studies." This is a prime example of the ideological tenor of much of the discourse that followed the LOC's decision to postpone the Freud exhibition. It became so acrimonious that it turned many people off.

For some, becoming a signatory was basically a one-shot deal. For others, their involvement and the ensuing repercussions were somewhat more significant. For still others, such as Swales and Crews, this was the call to battle in an inevitable war. For example, Morris Eagle, a professor at the Derner Institute of Advanced Psychological Studies at Adelphi University and the president of the Division of Psychoanalysis of the American Psychological Association (APA), was not sure how comfortable he felt with some of "the bedfellows" when he signed the petition to the LOC. But for him it was a matter of conscience that reflected his Old Left background and triggered personal memories of another era: "I went back to remembering the days of McCarthy, where your decision to sign or not to sign a document was dependent on who else signed it, rather than the content. And I thought, 'Screw this. I'm not going to be a coward, and I'm not going to be intimidated. I agree with the content, and therefore I'll sign it.'" He was completely taken by surprise when the petition was misrepresented and criticism hailed down on him.

Morris Eagle feels that many professionals had knee-jerk, negative reactions to this public stand. When he confronted their criticisms, he discovered that most of them had not read the document. They instead accepted the press's version of the situation or got caught up in hysterical gossip. To some, he'd become "a demon, a monster." He was harangued over his decision to sign; he felt beleaguered, depressed, somewhat isolated. But he could also strike back. At an APA convention, tiring of constituents questioning how he could have signed on, he finally exploded with "Why don't you impeach me?" Eagle was particularly disturbed when he received a letter from Harold Blum's wife, a member of the APA division that Eagle headed at the time. She demanded that he withdraw his signature, and as he colorfully recalls, "I responded in a very restrained manner, but nevertheless, the message was clear. As we used to say back in Brooklyn, 'Go take a flying fuck to the moon.'"

Eagle has devoted his career to Freud studies, but he is not as emotionally invested in battling "the other side" as are people like Swales and Crews. He steadfastly believed that an exhibition should occur, a partisan show being better than no show. For him, "The welfare of the republic is not at stake here." Furthermore, he dismissed Swales's charge that the LOC would provide a federal imprimatur for psychoanalysis. "What's the big crime?" Eagle asks. But his harshest criticism is for the media, which he blames for generating and magnifying the controversy. He considers the media irresponsible for alleging that the critics wanted to derail the exhibition, or that their demands amounted to censorship.

Eagle was particularly angered after he spent hours on an Internet exchange with a *New York Times* critic, clarifying what had occurred. But when the critic's article appeared, "It was as if I'd never spoken with him. He had some other ax to grind. I don't understand this. There's like a deep corruption of the spirit and the intellect. . . . My feeling is that people have boring lives, and anything that will generate excitement, they won't let go of." Morris Eagle will never read a newspaper article again without feeling deeply suspicious about it. He feels that the desire for "pizazz" always trumps an attempt at "getting the facts straight."

Sophie Freud signed on late. Her decision turned on her recognition of names of others whom she respected. Like Morris Eagle, she too encountered enmity: "Some members of the family were angry at me. They saw it as a hostile act against our grandfather, who didn't deserve our hostility." It also provided the opportunity for her to be singled out as a prominent example: if Freud's own granddaughter was opposed, then something must really be amiss. But she has no regrets. Her involvement in the affair was limited: "It's not uppermost in my mind. What do I care one way or another?" In fact, she became more exercised over the *Enola Gay* exhibition than this one.[33]

Sophie Freud doesn't suspect the curator of having bad intentions. "But I did think that it might have happened that there was a very one-sided view of the Freudian legacy. And that it deserved to be broadened and expanded." But she was not drawn into the maelstrom of the ongoing, bitter struggle. In essence, she rejects the polarized perceptions that took center stage: "I think that there is no history that is not fictionalized. Everyone looks at history with his or her own perspective. I do not see history as a series of immovable facts. So I think it's silly of Mr. Crews to see that as an unusual situation."

Oliver Sacks—not renowned as a Freud scholar or Freud critic—was unprepared to find himself in the media spotlight. He later withdrew his name from Swales's letter, as did at least one other signatory. As time went on, this became more of a Manichean battle between good and evil, lightness and dark. Swales wrote to Sacks, "No doubt . . . Freudian fundamentalists everywhere are ecstatic at having won back your soul from the grips of Satan." Sacks replied, "I think this quiet voice in the middle has been almost drowned by the shrillness of polemic on both sides."[34] The attention of most people—even those who had reason enough to be professionally or personally concerned—was not captured for long. Increasingly the discussion was pulled toward the ideological extremes.

Both sides dug in their heels. On the Freud Archives home page, Harold Blum self-confidently claimed, "the Freud Exhibit was designed directly through original documents, scientific papers, and personal correspondence *without any deviation* from historical accuracy. . . . This [proposed] presentation of dissent and resistance to Freud's ideas did not satisfy the small group of vociferous and polemical critics determined to halt the Exhibit."[35] Blum alludes to a variety of historiography that few contemporary practitioners believe is possible in general, and that the Freud revisionists have revealed to be specious in this domain specifically. Morris Eagle, in a lengthy, impassioned overview written to his constituents, correctly noted that a siege mentality had colonized the psychoanalytic world, marked by "the tendency to react defensively or to overreact, to close ranks, to dichotomize between supposed friends and enemies, and to become more rigid and parochial in the face of criticisms and challenges."[36] But that's exactly how people act during war.

In his own manner Swales, like Blum, wrapped himself in virtue. (A newspaper headline about the dispute trumpeting "Clash of the Super Egos" seemed particularly apt.) Swales characterized psychoanalysts in the following way to a colleague: "They consistently lie about the facts, demonstrate a total disregard of the truth, slander the fifty petitioners—and try to menace and blacken them." In the "Dear Scholar" letter accompanying the dossier he'd assembled about the exhibition and the controversy (at that moment totaling just under two hundred pages), he described "a true-life Pirandelloesque moral-ity play with us guys & gals always maintaining the moral high-ground through thick & thin (and in spite of my own occasional boor-ishness) while our ignorant and vulgar opponents . . ."[37] A suggestion of grandiosity surfaced here, unquestionably. There was likely a little twinkle in Swales's eye as well.

In the philosophical slugfest that followed, one term in particular teed off those who were critics of the exhibition and critics of Freud. That term was "Freud basher." Morris Eagle finds it "extraordinarily inaccurate" and "truly disgusting": "The fact that people walk around calling others Freud bashers is a terrible commentary on the psychoanalytic establishment. It's one of those terms that reveals more about the accusers than the accused." For Sophie Freud, "To make this a body of belief that is either accepted or bashed, the whole thing is so absurd that I can view it with some amusement, I must admit." For Peter Swales, "It's *them* [the opposition] who've put the debate on that level."

But Frederick Crews had gleefully embraced the label in *The Memory Wars*, in his "Afterword: Confessions of a Freud Basher." In much the same fashion that some gay people opt to refer to them-selves as "queer" and some blacks banter with one another using "nigger," Crews turned an insult into a badge of honor:

> There's no such thing as an objective use of this term. A Freud basher is someone who suffers from a psychological syndrome; he has a compulsive need to kick Freud. And to use the term at all is to presuppose that there's not much the matter with Freud. In other words, the problem is entirely in the person who's doing the kick-ing. It's a shorthand way of circumventing questions of whether or not Freud actually discovered anything.[38]

Crews, who along with others has been accused of launching ad hominem attacks against Freud, can ably turn the tables on those who attack him.[39]

Crews and Swales swiftly moved to the front ranks, leaving many of their associates behind. An acrimonious battle was fought out by them and a few others in private exchanges of letters and in letters to the editor published in such venues as the *New York Times, Times Liter-ary Supplement* (London), *Tikkun,* the *Chronicle of Higher Education, Partisan Review,* and the newsletter of the Association for the Advancement of Philosophy and Psychiatry. Virtually every major article sparked a response, either of clarification or counteraccusation. The press continued to simplify matters or present conjecture as fact. For example, Paul Goldberger reported in the *New York Times* that the LOC was considering rescheduling the exhibition in 2000. He then conclusively stated that this was "a delay so long it gave the anti-Freud forces the clear sense that they had brought the library to its knees."[40] Goldberger cited no supporting evidence for this belief. Moreover, he smeared the exhibition's critics as "anti-Freud." Amazingly, he claimed clarity in a situation where ambiguity and speculation reigned. It confirmed the worst suspicions of Swales and Crews, who both firmly believe—also without furnishing corroboration—that the *New York Times* is under the sway of psychoanalysis, that it is "an absolute hotbed of Freudianism," that behind the scenes it is run by "instructions from the couch."

James Billington consistently claimed that the show was postponed, not canceled. He continually suggested inadequate funding as the reason. But rumors persisted that he had made the decision in order to head off conflict. There were, of course, the inevitable references to the *Enola Gay* exhibition. (Perhaps the most amusing moment of this entire episode was when Frederick Crews quipped, "This has become the Enola *Peter* Gay," referring to the psychoanalytically trained Yale historian whom he and Swales view as a member of "the opposition.")[41] The LOC's decision little more than two weeks later in December to abruptly cancel John Michael Vlach's exhibit on plantation life lent credence to the perception that the LOC was an institution cowering in the face of controversy.

Michael S. Roth had no privileged information about why the LOC shelved the exhibition beyond the financial reasons stated. But as a cultural historian keenly interested in how external pressures have made cultural administrators more "prudent," he suspects that "postponing the Freud show seemed like a way of being careful. . . . As a historian looking at the fate of exhibitions in this period, I think there are a lot of factors one would use to contextualize these decisions." Morris Eagle, in his own particular way, endorses the wimp theory of organizational behavior:

> It's likely that Billington shit in his pants when he received the letter. And then the people who signed the letter are accused of censor-

ship. He's not accused of cowardice, political cowardice. If I say to you, "I disagree with what you're doing," and you collapse in fear, what are you going to do? Turn around and tell me I intimidated you, or I tried to censor what you were doing? Talk about projection, externalizing one's own lack of guts.

In fact, the article in the *Washington Post* announcing the postponement strongly pointed to extra-financial considerations entering into the LOC's decision. Furthermore, Peter Swales claims that the *Post* reporter told him privately, in advance of writing and publishing his article, that LOC officials had informed him during his research that the petition prompted the postponement. When the reporter solicited Swales's reaction, it appeared to be independent confirmation of the rumor. This reporter seemed to be smudging the line between reporting the news and fabricating the news.[42]

Here's how LOC officials respond. The public affairs officer Jill Brett voluntarily shoulders the responsibility for the confusion about the exhibition's fate. In her efforts to get the word out, "I feel I failed miserably. In spite of great effort." Brett recalls that she showed Billington the *Lingua Franca* article, and he responded, "'So what. Big deal.' He's an academic himself." She continues, "I can attest absolutely, adamantly, that there was no intellectual component in his decision. None. We had passed the 'drop dead date,' and we were *way* behind in the money." The "drop dead date," Irene (Burnham) Chambers (Head of the Interpretive Programs Office) explains, is the date when the LOC must decide whether any exhibition can go forward. The decision is based on whether the LOC has sufficient funds for the show and whether any publications must be ready to appear simultaneously. In her recollection, postponements are not that unusual. She can think of four or five over the past seven years. The funds were simply not coming together for the Freud show, according to both Brett and Chambers.

Jill Brett continues:

I tried to convey that the best I could to Marc Fisher [the *Washington Post* reporter]. I tried to convey it in every way I could when his article was picked up. Of course, it was just red meat to people in that quiet Christmas season. I mean, I've never had calls from more obscure journals, from farther away in the world. . . . I've dealt with a lot of controversies, but I've never felt so incapable of bringing them to some sort of order and conclusion.

Brett also believes that since the *Washington Post* reported that the LOC had *shelved* the exhibition, people thought it had been canceled, not postponed. Furthermore, she admits to one additional error in judgment: "We should have said, 'we have to decide on a date right this minute,' instead of saying 'sometime in the future,' because it looked like we weren't serious. But we *were* serious. We should have had a date certain, even if we had to change it."[43] In the final analysis, a combination of poor communication, a somewhat ambiguous newspaper article that developed a life of its own, and a very, very determined opponent pointed this controversy in a particular direction.

Aggressively, excessively, and with occasional bits of his distinctively irrepressible humor thrown in, Peter Swales sustained the struggle. Janet Malcolm reported that in 1981 Swales wrote Jeffrey Masson a forty-five-page, single-spaced typewritten letter, detailing how he felt Masson had wronged him. She observed, "astonishingly, Swales's screed is unfailingly interesting. In Henry James's phrase, Swales 'is one of the people on whom nothing is lost,' and, like a James character, he takes things very far."[44] Swales never matched that herculean effort from 1981 during this dispute, but he in fact issued a number of lengthy, dense harangues. In so doing, he revealed a much more complex set of concerns and a much more ideological perspective than his direct and rather innocuous petition to the LOC represented. Swales does indeed takes things very far.

For one thing, the issue of Freud's advocates and the LOC cautiously husbanding archival materials has frustrated Swales and other researchers who don't qualify as being part of "the inner circle." Harold Blum reports that the bulk of the documents are now derestricted, 90 to 95 percent of them. But a secret stash of *anything* generates speculation and intrigue. A treasure trove could indeed await. Or unencumbered admittance to the Freud collection could prove to be a letdown, like Geraldo Rivera's much-hyped unlocking of Al Capone's near-empty vault. Blum states categorically that it is "absolute nonsense that we're hiding something scandalous." While that may be for future investigators to determine, even Crews concedes that Blum has speeded things along. So although Swales brings a certain substantiated history of rejection into this struggle, the past may indeed be the past in this respect. Swales may be clinging to a moot issue.

Possibly Swales's most memorable statement during this dispute was "the Freudians charge us with trying to pull a condom over their dildo of an exhibition."[45] He is drolly alluding, of course, to the numerous instances in which "censorship" was used to describe events. Swales employed the term to condemn psychoanalysts; he also denied that *he* would engage in such repressive behavior. Each party could readily spot this conduct in whatever their opponents did, yet vehemently denied that they themselves engaged in it. But Sophie Freud believes that "Censorship is a little bit of a paranoid word here. I'm not really sure it fits this situation." Frederick Crews also dismisses the notion. To him, it was a way for the organizers to cry wolf, in order to mobilize sympathy and support to guarantee that the show would proceed as planned, without any input from "the outside."

Crews was concerned far more about the fact that members of the American Psychoanalytic Association established the Task Force to Monitor Freud Exhibit. An Internet message from the coalition stated, "We are still recommending that APsA members use their contacts with academics to encourage them to write in support of the exhibition going ahead at the earliest possible moment. They should write using their academic titles and institutional letterheads. Letters from analysts are also welcome, but are viewed as inherently biased."[46] Crews interpreted this as sneaky, "In other words, to give no hint to the Library of Congress officials that they were representing psychoanalysis, rather that they were just representing academic objectivity. I regard that as rather sleazy, but I don't see any censorship issue here at all."

From Swales's perspective, if his good faith effort to petition the LOC could be framed by Michael S. Roth as "a minor attempt at censorship" and the LOC's postponement could be characterized by Harold Blum as "a submission to censorship . . . sabotage by a group of extremists," then wouldn't it only be fair to view the task force as exerting "undue influence"?[47] But from Roth's perspective, the attempt to stop an exhibition from taking place in the planning stages, because one might fear that it might not say what you want it to say, is a form of censorship. I think it's perfectly appropriate to criticize an exhibition or a play or a novel, once it's out. That's not censorship, that's criticism. . . . [But] I think it's completely bogus to claim that one is not involved in the censorship game because you think the person should redo the project.

Freud supporters, Freud critics, and the press all eagerly used "censorship." In the final analysis, it was useful as a weapon or to transmit a streamlined message, but it bore somewhat limited explanatory power.

Swales objected to both the intellectual and financial sponsorship of *Sigmund Freud: Conflict and Culture*. An earlier controversy over an exhibition the LOC hosted already had raised eyebrows about the institution allowing itself to be used as a "billboard for hire" for questionable political ends. The LOC presented *Against Hitler: German Resistance to National Socialism, 1933-1945* in July 1994. The exhibit was financed and organized by the Bonn government. Critics argued that it exaggerated the scope of indigenous resistance to Nazism during the war and touted postwar German democracy as a natural progression from those roots. A scathing article in the *Washington Post* described the diplomatic maneuvering to locate a Washington, D.C., venue as high-pressured and "feverish," charges that Billington and the German ambassador strongly denied. But observers suspected that this was a way for the Bonn government to polish up its image in the wake of the successes of the Holocaust Memorial Museum in Washington and *Schindler's List*, as well as to counterbalance D-Day celebrations and numerous contemporary neo-Nazi incidents in Germany. Those who opposed the exhibition felt it was seriously flawed, essentially public relations cloaked as history.[48]

Whatever the truth in this matter, the debate left a lingering scent of political complicity in the air. One of Swales's primary objections to the Freud show was obviously the question of sponsorship. Financial support was pledged by the Mary S. Sigourney Award Trust, the Dana Foundation, the American Psychoanalytic Foundation, Hoffman-La Roche, private individuals, and several Austrian sources: the Austrian Cultural Institute, the Department of Cultural Affairs, and the city of Vienna. Moreover, once the controversy broke out, the psychoanalytic community mobilized to assist in fund raising.[49]

For Swales, these constituencies had a great deal to gain by revitalizing Freud. (As Swales was diligent to point out, the paterfamilias is good for tourism and national identity: Freud's portrait graces Austria's fifty-schilling note.) As noted, Swales argues that the show was the direct response to Crews's widely read critiques in the *New York Review of Books* and articles in the popular media such as the "Is Freud Dead?" article in *Time*. Bottom line, he viewed it as an issue of survival for the psychiatric establishment: "the response of those people to the perceived threat, and it was a real enough threat to their industry, to their livelihoods, to their bread and butter, was hysterical and even psychotic."

But Swales, a resident alien who relishes citing the U.S. Constitution with immense authority to citizens who may have forgotten its exact wording from their high school government classes, accused the sponsors of this show of being "profoundly unAmerican" and of "seeking to . . . throw a private party in a federal institution with funds from the tax-paying public (ardent anti-Freudians among them)."[50] Swales echoed the arguments of some congressmen who see themselves as fiscal watchdogs when they rail against government support of the arts via funds from the National Endowment for the Arts. In those instances, artists are likewise blamed for indulging themselves and their exclusive cadres of supporters while feeding at the public trough (ardent gay activists, feminists, performance artists, experimental filmmakers—and yes, taxpayers all—among them).

Something about the above quotes is worth noting. They were a small part of a passionately argued, five-and-a-half-page, single-spaced, typewritten letter sent to a reporter, by which Swales hoped to get his point(s) across. Moreover, he copied it to Michael Roth, the LOC, Henry Cohen, and the fifty petitioners, guaranteeing that the major players would be kept up to speed, and that there could be no doubts about what Peter J. Swales thought. That was seldom a problem. Swales insists that his point of view be expressed—intensely and repeatedly.

Swales told a reporter, "Most people know me as a gentleman of perfect civility. It's only when people start lying, cheating, defrauding, that I become a polemicist and start calling a spade a spade."[51] As a self-described champion of truth, academic standards, freedom of inquiry, and other noble principles, Swales felt compelled to take up the mantle of a crusader when he believed that these precepts were under assault. If not him, then who? But off with the gloves. And let there be no verbal restraints. Morris Eagle reflects, "What would Fred Crews do if he didn't have this ax to grind? If he didn't have a group that he was constantly attacking? What would Peter Swales do? He wouldn't get invited anywhere." In other words, each man had a rogue reputation to preserve, just as the prestige (and commercial viability) of psychoanalysis was on the line too.

"In truth," Swales wrote to Oliver Sacks, "the Library of Congress has allowed itself to be bamboozled and usurped by a special interest group of Freudian propagandists." It was up to Swales to come to the rescue: "it's being held hostage here by a very marginal kind of group, an extremist group."[52] If that interpretation didn't sway folks, Swales invoked the threat of a fraud being perpetrated on the American people: without proper consideration of the revisionists, the exhibition was fundamentally flawed, a hoax. His assumption was that if the exhibition did not include some of the revisionists, their ideas could not possibly be given a fair hearing. (And this *was* an assumption, since the exhibition was barraged with criticism from the earliest stages, that is, *before* plans had become solidified.) Dipping further into his arsenal, Swales inveighed against a "federal imprimatur" being placed on Freud's life and work.

"Bamboozled," "co opted," "caved in," "complicitous," "fraudulent," "censored," "consumer protection." These terms were all muttered repeatedly during this controversy. Throughout this struggle, Peter J. Swales acted as if he alone understood how great the stakes were. But while he claimed to be acting on behalf of others, a strain of paternalism permeated Swales's approach. If you fear that people will be "force fed" a particular point of view by an exhibition, you're assuming that they don't digest what they've consumed by means of their idiosyncratic mixes of personal history, racial, religious, gender, and geographic biases, and countless other factors. You're assuming that they swallow things whole. In other words, worrying about someone else's reaction means that you believe that you know what it's going to be in advance.

Harold Blum makes an important point: the critics acted "as if ideas will have magical power over people." Not trusting adults to interpret ideas on their own reveals a basic lack of confidence in anyone's abilities—except your own, of course. Swales's behavior, and that of a few others, hardened over time. That led them to act in a more and more inflexibly ideological manner. It exasperated Michael S. Roth as the struggle dragged out; he was stuck in the middle and it seemed that everyone around him was shouting, but no one was really listening.

Less than three months after its surprise announcement that it was postponing *Sigmund Freud: Conflict and Culture*, a LOC press release in late February 1996 reported that the show was going to be realized. The American Psychoanalytic Association crowed about the success of its efforts on the exhibition's behalf, citing the mobilizing of grass-roots lobbying efforts, a letter of concern sent by its president (in concert with the head of the American Psychiatric Association) to Billington soon after the announcement of the postponement, and a meeting that had been held between LOC officials and representatives of the psychoanalytic community.[53] New funders were brought aboard, including Discovery Communications and some individuals.

The exhibition opened in Washington, D.C., in October 1998 and was scheduled to travel to New York and Vienna. There are also possible sites in Los Angeles, South America, and Israel (should all these venues successfully develop, the fees they will pay will become the major source of funds). New York City's Jewish Museum signed on. Its director, Joan Rosenbaum, was amazingly unconcerned about the controversy. Paramount for her was how the exhibition would bring authentic historical documents to life, not arguments over the minutiae of Freud's life and theories. Rosenbaum says of such practicalities, "It seemed like a pretty straightforward show, frankly. . . . What is the visitor experiencing? What kind of environment is it?"[54]

The exhibition retained its original character, although changes were incorporated, partially because there was over a year of additional planning time. Morris Eagle attended a strategy session and was listed as a member of the review panel. In the end, the three sections of the exhibition became "Formative Years," "The Individual: Therapy and Theory," and "From the Individual to Society." The topic of "contested legacies" was raised throughout, instead of being limited to a separate division. The introductory panels acknowledged the controversy over this show, while the curatorial voice asked about Freud, "Was he a scientist, a writer, a genius, or a fake?" In line with other contemporary exhibitions, visitors could buy a variety of souvenirs: posters, coffee mugs, T-shirts, journals, and even a wind-up Freud pillow that plays the tune "Memories" ($26).

There was also the opportunity to include new people in the catalogue and broaden its perspective; in certain instances, the postponement allowed people to participate whose schedules had originally forced them to decline the offer. But Roth's proposal that the exhibition's critics be represented in a videotape was emphatically rejected by Crews. He claimed it was "a lousy idea" that would ghettoize "the crazies and the dissenters." "We don't want to be in a cage," he declared.

The controversy confirmed each side's most serious misgivings about the other: their authoritarianism, irrationality, insatiable appetites for power, censorious inclinations, and self-serving motives. Each side was able to tally up its own slate of injuries, construct its own narratives of victimization and outrage, and add to the combatants' traditions of mutual animosity. Moreover, this dispute generated a great deal of posturing and grandstanding. Peter Swales is candid about this point, and about his contribution to the temper of the proceedings: "I'm an historian, but I also happen to be a polemicist. And as a polemicist I want my opponents to show their true colors, to reveal themselves to the general public in all their stupidity and their pathos, and their bathos, with a 'bah.' I want that. I don't want to censor them. Come on. You know, I want to hold them responsible for what they say."[55] Clearly, Swales has a great deal invested in insuring that the duel continues. In fact, Roth claims, "when I was trying to come up with strategies for including him [Swales] and his views, he said he gets a lot more out of being excluded than he does being included. . . . and that's the shell game."

As the struggle evolved, Crews charged Roth with lying and libeling him; Swales vented over-the-top cries of foul over minor edits of letters to the editor from him or from his cronies, and blasted one editor who dropped Swales's middle initial. In some respects, this struggle gradually devolved into discharges of enormous bluster over trifling matters.[56]

The way Harold Blum sees it, people coming from outside an exhibition team should not dictate to a curator, just as others shouldn't dictate to a professor what should be taught in a classroom. In his view, neither university provosts nor museum directors should be subject to undue influence; they must assert their autonomy. But the issue of who's inside and who's outside, how they've gotten there and how their positions are maintained, was very much at issue here.

The issue of balance became a pivotal one too. Blum's position was that if you try to balance perspectives, the danger is that you'll skirt controversy. If you try to please everyone so that they can see their own viewpoint, you lose some of the sparkle, dull some of the sharp outlines. It was a perspective endorsed by Peter Gay as well, who declared, "the dogma of 'fifty-fifty equal time' is anathema to the curatorial process."[57] But keep in mind, both Blum and Gay were on the inside, and would be giving up something should the quest for greater inclusion be successful.

For Crews, on the contrary, incorporating additional viewpoints would be a boon:

> Balance in the abstract is not an ideal. Should Hitler and Himmler and Eichmann get equal time in an exhibition about the Holocaust? Obviously not. If you have an exhibit about a total disaster you don't want to portray it as anything but a total disaster. The nature of the material determines how balanced it should be. In the case of Freud, we have a figure of tremendous controversy. People of good will take different views of this man. So let's make the exhibit as open to intellectually respectable differences of opinion as possible.

From his perspective, a plurality of viewpoints and the contrasts they could engender would sharpen matters, not dull them. The problem is that as appealing as this might sound in the abstract, good will is commonly the first thing to be abandoned in such emotionally charged instances. "I'm completely lacking in respect for Freud," Crews pronounced in *Memory Wars*.[58] With such declarations, conversations can quickly grind to a halt.

Crews formulated a constructive alternative to all this wrangling: the publication of his edited volume *Unauthorized Freud* was timed to coincide with the opening of the Freud exhibition. A compilation of scholarly and critical writings about Freud since about 1970, it presents an alternative voice to the one developed in the exhibition. It's a reasonable and valuable response. Unfortunately, exhibitions have an immediacy and accessibility for those who experience them that books do not. Books require much more individual effort to be understood. So while Crews's volume informs and extends the debate, it will undoubtedly appeal to a more specialized and considerably smaller audience than *Sigmund Freud: Conflict and Culture* will reach. (But note: The books edited by Crews and by Roth were both offered for sale at the exhibition.)

Reflecting on what he and the planning committee had accomplished—with the exhibition near completion, but still with considerable time before it was scheduled to open—Michael S. Roth noted,

> This show will not give psychoanalysis a blessing. It's not about that. It's about how Freud put his finger on certain problems that we still think are really important. Whether or not he had the right ideas about how to deal with them, eruptions of sex and violence continue to haunt us, as a culture and as individuals, and that's what Freud underlined. . . . Maybe he gave us bad tools to deal with them, but that attention to certain things that preoccupied him has preoccupied us too. And that doesn't give him a seal of approval. It just shows a significant historical figure.

The finished product largely confirmed Roth's statement. Freud was neither glorified, nor was he needlessly trashed. The bulk of the exhibition was matter-of-fact, while certain parts challenged visitors to critically assess the man and his work. The discussion of Freud's famous case of Dora faulted him for not recognizing the transference between patient and analyst earlier than he did: "Rather than interpreting what these hysterical symptoms meant to Dora, Freud gave them the significance that his theory of the sexual roots of hysteria required." On the recorded audio tour featuring Michael Roth, he acknowledged that Freud "influenced his patients unduly" and that "repression is a vexed concept." The curatorial perspective raised questions, leaving it to spectators to draw their own conclusions: "What makes an analyst's interpretation true? On what basis should it be confirmed or rejected? The issue of how to judge analytic interpretations has remained controversial, from Freud's time to our own."

Moreover, the exhibition design featured a running commentary of quotations from a wide variety of thinkers about Freud and his work, wrapped around the top border of the display cases. This offered a dynamic form of "balance," where visitors could select from a menu of choices and construct different narratives. The informed viewer would discover few surprises; the exhibition was more a

primer than a theoretical breakthrough. It would be easy to find fault
with the show, should you be inclined to do so; disappointments
were inevitable with a subject this vast. For example, my favorite
popular culture reference, when Doris Day takes Rock Hudson to a
strip club featuring Sigrid Freud, the "Id" Girl, in *Lover Come Back*
(1961) was overlooked. But the initial fears that this would be an un-
bridled tribute were unfounded.

For the LOC associate librarian, Winston Tabb, this controversy,
as well as the one over *Back of the Big House,* helped clarify the LOC's
mission in regard to mounting exhibitions. The LOC is a library that
does exhibitions; it is not a museum per se. The public may not generally draw that distinction, but it is an important one nonetheless.
Tabb therefore asserts that issues of balance and distinctive curatorial
points of view are not as relevant here as they might be in other venues. For the most part, the LOC organizes displays to showcase its
collections. "We want to get more people to know about and come
and use the Library's collections," Tabb argues. What is the measure
of success to him? "Do more scholars come in and write more books
and more articles based upon the material they find here?"[59] He
views the LOC's role as facilitation, not pontification.

That prods us to return to one of the opening issues. *Is* Freud
dead? Given the intensity of the debate around this exhibition, certainly not. Curiously, it's the one point of consensus among all the
major players. For Harold Blum and Peter Gay, Freud remains the
fountainhead. For Sophie Freud, Morris Eagle, and many other teachers, researchers, and practitioners, Freud's theories have a secure
place alongside other philosophies and psychologies of human behavior. Nevertheless, refinement of his key principles is deemed necessary and possible. Michael S. Roth believes that Freud remains an
important historical figure, although he hesitates to predict what we
might think of his ideas twenty-five years into the future.

Even Freud's shrillest dissenters acknowledge his continuing viability, albeit with serious reservations. According to Frederick Crews,

> You can be scientifically dead in the sense that your work is not pro-
> ducing any fruitful concepts that are leading to exciting research.
> You can be dead in the sense that people have discovered that your
> propositions contradict each other, or that they have no operational
> meaning. In these ways, the Freudian system is most definitely

dead. But as a popularity contest, Freud is not dead at all. Freud is thriving in many ways.

Let's give Peter J. Swales the last word. Why not? Spend a little time with him, and you'll understand it's a tactical position he struggles for with great gusto: "Either Freud is on a life support mechanism, and they're desperate that somebody like me or Fred Crews is going to pull the plug. Or Freud did in fact die many years ago, but they're hiding the death certificate in the Sigmund Freud Archives, restricting it till 2102!"

5

A Matter of Perspective

Revisionist History and *The West as America*

> The West is dead!
> You may lose a sweetheart,
> But you won't forget her.
> —Charles M. Russell, *Good Medicine:*
> *Memories of the Real West*

THE SETTLEMENT OF the West is an American foundation myth. Its archetypal characters are recognized worldwide. While the majority of the mines gouged into the Rockies have long been played out, and vast stretches of the Great Plains have proven impervious to sustained cultivation, the West remains a seemingly inexhaustible resource for scholars and artists. Musicians, filmmakers, writers, painters, even dancers continue to find inspiration in this terrain, which is as much physical as it is psychological, as much tangible as it is symbolic. The late John Wayne pops up in more cultural spaces today than most live members of the Screen Actors Guild do, while the pop musician Paula Cole dwells on her disappointed dreams of love and plaintively wonders, "where have all the cowboys gone?"

When the National Museum of American Art (NMAA), a branch of the Smithsonian Institution, mounted *The West as America: Reinterpreting Images of the Frontier, 1820–1920* in 1991, it was venturing into disputed territory. "Reinterpreting" is the key word here. Many others have already staked their claims in these parts. Often they don't cotton to newcomers, nor to their faddish ideas.

Redefining the genre of the western—especially its incarnation on the big screen—has been going on for some time, of course. In particular, several films from the Vietnam War era significantly altered our expectations of these stories. Sam Peckinpah's controversial film *The Wild Bunch* (1969) is most remembered for its orgy of blood. Arthur Penn's *Little Big Man* (1970) highlighted the life and times of 121-year-old Jack Crabb, a white man raised as a Cheyenne (simply called "the Human Beings"). Genocide of the American Indian was easily equated with genocide of the Vietnamese. The heroes of Robert Altman's *McCabe and Mrs. Miller* (1971) were an opportunistic gambler and a madam, whose get-rich-quick schemes intersected in the town of Presbyterian Church.

These movies all focus on characters living on society's margins. They share a strong anti-authoritarian sense. They challenged the public to reexamine how Americans conducted themselves in the past, in light of what was occurring in Southeast Asia at the time these movies were released. They reflected the zeitgeist just as they helped to define it. (Keep in mind that these movies were all produced in the same tumultuous era as *Harlem on My Mind*.)

No sooner does someone sound the death knell for the western than it is revitalized. The current cycle began in 1992 with Clint Eastwood's highly acclaimed movie *Unforgiven*, merely a year after *The West as America* appeared in Washington, D.C. It is suffused with post-Vietnam, post-Watergate cynicism and skepticism that congeal into a "postmodernist sensibility." What was once the sort of story clearly etched in black and white now blurs into multiple shades of grey.

Look beyond all its Marxist, feminist, and antiracist sentiments, and you'll discover the film's most radical innovation: the character of W. W. Beauchamp. Beauchamp is a writer. Dime novels, high adventure, that sort of thing. As such, he is more a myth maker than a passive recorder of events. Beauchamp *manufactures* the Wild West as much as he records it. He magnifies and embellishes incidents to generate more exciting tales and bigger revenues. A running gag is the mispronunciation of his grandiloquently entitled adventure story *The Duke of Death* as *The Duck of Death*.

Beauchamp's allegiance to his subjects rapidly shifts to take advantage of breaking opportunities. Strawberry Alice's girls may peddle their bodies, but Beauchamp sells his integrity. For cheap. Moreover, he's a wimp, as a telltale puddle of piss betrays him in a moment of fear. Beauchamp's inclusion guarantees that this movie displays a degree of reflexivity that earlier westerns never did. Combined with its pervasive ambiguity, arbitrariness, and deconstruction of "heroism," *Unforgiven* breathed new life into the genre. Black westerns (*Posse*), female-dominated westerns (Sharon Stone in *The Quick and the Dead*), and cross-dressing westerns (*The Ballad of Little Jo*) have followed. But whereas *Unforgiven* garnered critical acclaim and numerous awards, including Oscars for best picture, best director, and best supporting actor, *The West as America* was loudly condemned.

Timing, as we know, can be critical to the reception of art and culture. For one thing, this exhibition appeared at the same moment that the New West was becoming a buzz phrase. Sun Belt cities were booming, as were vast stretches of the Pacific coast. Suburban developments were hungrily gobbling up land, wealthy investors were becoming gentlemen ranchers, cattle were being tracked by computer chips embedded in their ears, while locals and tourists alike could sip Cowboy Cappuccino in places like Buffalo, Wyoming. But many parts of the West were also steadily dying, bypassed outposts for whom prosperity was an elusive possibility.

There is no "West" today; there are many. Prosperous pockets exist, bolstered in many instances by a surge of newcomers. But there are also the rural poor, casualties of the boom and bust in commodities like oil, coal, and gypsum; increasing economies of scale in ranching and farming; or simply the sheer harshness of much of this land. Linger over Richard Avedon's haunting photographs of drifters, miners, oil field workers, carnies, truck drivers, and waitresses on the pages of *In the American West* (1985), for example, and you'll discover the unadorned, unromanticized West of the late 1970s and early 1980s. Once you've viewed image after image of wind-dried, suncreased, blood-stained, oil-smeared, and coal dust–encrusted faces and bodies, you'll never again be able to hear the names of towns like Wildhorse, Golden, and Aurora, Colorado, or Sweetwater, Texas, and summon up fanciful images of life there. On the other hand, Chloride, Nevada, and Deadwood, South Dakota, obtain increased resonance. In many cases, Avedon's characters are likely the disappointed and diminishing descendants of nineteenth-century pioneers who pushed ever westward in search of a promising new life.

Such visual evidence provides a small clue to why Frank Popper and Deborah Popper, Rutgers University professors of urban studies and geography, respectively, in 1987 proposed returning large parts of the Great Plains back to nature. Their vision: create an immense "buffalo commons," the prairie analog to Camilo José Vergara's proposal for Detroit to become a postindustrial historical ruin.[1] Both concepts entail recognizing attempts at human settlement that have failed. The Poppers' proposal is dramatic but not very politic; it is unlikely to be enacted in the foreseeable future. However, it makes clear that one hundred years after Frederick Turner's influential essay declared the frontier to be closed, it may be opening up once again. Residents steadily die off or leave. Collectively, they may put the lie to the indomitable American spirit that until recently successfully staked its claims across an enormous swath of North American territory and, until recently, prevailed in every major military conflict in which the United States has participated.

An identity crisis exists in today's West, a complex amalgam of people and vested interests. Conflicts between naturalists and large corporations, for instance, echo many of the classic battles between Europeans and Indians, Americans and Mexicans, free rangers and ranchers, that have played out in different times in this region. Environmental disasters such as the *Exxon Valdez* accident in 1989 highlight the difficulties of balancing economic development against destruction of the environment. "The West" no longer offers a simple model of American values and aspirations.

Over the past few years, the so-called new historians of the American West have reframed how we view this region. They focus on previously overlooked topics such as gender and race, as well as the degrees of power apportioned to different groups based on these differences. They chronicle failure, not merely success. They reject ethnocentrism in favor of adopting the points of view of those pushed off the land and left out of the historical record. Their accounts of the arrival of European Americans include the cultural, political, and ecological costs incurred—plus the body counts. Scholars such as Patricia Nelson Limerick, Daniel Worster, Peggy Pascoe, Richard White, Richard Slotkin, and others have produced a body of work that demands careful attention, whether you embrace or reject their perspectives. As one observer sees it, "They are blazing a pioneer's trail toward an altered view of the moral status of America itself   [reflecting] the willingness of the 60's generation to find the invisible worm eating away at the once blushing rose of the American self-image."[2]

Preparations for the quincentennial of Columbus's arrival in the Americas also spurred intense scrutiny of American history and the American character. In 1991 Cristobal Colon, a direct descendant of Columbus, was chosen grand marshal of Pasadena's annual Tournament of Roses parade. But the decision was blasted by a city councilman who complained that this present-day nobleman was "a symbol of greed, slavery, rape, and genocide." Columbus Day celebrations generated protests in many American cities in 1992. In Boston, for example, American Indians petitioned to be included in the annual parade. They presented their case via a flyer picturing Columbus and an Indian, which posed the question, "Which one is the savage?" While an Indian representative insisted that "What Columbus did was worse than the Holocaust," the parade grand marshal in working-class East Boston countered, "We're Italian-Americans, and they've taken all our heroes away from us."[3] As has become customary in such disputes, invocation of the Holocaust elevates one side's claims to a particular level of significance. The other side, however, feels unjustly attacked: its power and influence challenged, its identity pummeled.

This politicized revisionist urge impacted the scholarly and museum world as well. In the spring of 1991 Vernon Bellecourt, a founder of the American Indian Movement, threw a pint of his own blood onto the sail of a ship's replica in the exhibition *First Encounters* at the Science Museum in St. Paul, Minnesota.[4] Kirkpatrick Sales's *Conquest of Paradise* (1991) is merely one example of the many books that recast Columbus from discoverer to invader, explorer to exploiter, the initiator of a bloody human conquest, as well as what has become a centuries-long ecocidal disaster. *The Buried Mirror: Reflections on Spain and the New World*, a five-hour television miniseries broadcast in 1992 and developed with support from the Smithsonian, viewed the quincentenary from the perspective of Spanish culture, narrated by the novelist Carlos Fuentes. Taken together, these examples complemented the objectives of the curator and essay writers for *The West as America*: to critically reexamine received wisdom about American history, intergroup relations, and the American character, squeezing new insights from very familiar material.

One final factor bears noting: the Persian Gulf War, which broke out not long after the termination of the Cold War, was, in a basic respect, an "emotionally cool" conflict: its high-tech nature mimicked a child's video game, although thousands of people lost their lives off-screen when "smart bombs" found their targets. Media coverage was markedly different than it had been during the protracted Vietnam conflict, which then featured scores and scores of American body bags or massacred Vietnamese women and children on what seemed to be a daily basis. The bombing of Iraq began on January 17, 1991. Military operations ended on February 28. Victory celebrations in cities like Chicago, Washington, D.C., and New York spilled into June of that year. In other words, these activities virtually coincided with *The West as America*, which ran from March 15 to July 7, 1991.

Operation Desert Storm produced an unforeseen climatic shift, providing a chilly reception for the exhibition. Americans were swept up in a patriotic fervor. The Iraqi leader Saddam Hussein was the indisputable tyrant, his face embossed on toilet paper, "voodoo dolls," and even condoms. Desert Storm trading cards were issued. T-shirts bore such logos as "These Colors Don't Run" (featuring the U.S. flag), "Bush Sinks One of His Famous Putts" (the President knocking the head of Hussein into a hole), and "Public Enemy Number One" (Hussein's face in the center of a target). America was good. It was strong. And it was on the side of all that was right once again. It was an inopportune moment to be raising prickly questions about American history or the American character.

As President Bush adroitly observed, the remarkable brevity of the conflict, the extremely small number of U.S. casualties, and the clarity of the mission finally, *finally*, "kicked the Vietnam syndrome once and for all."[5] Americans had reason to feel pride and strength again. The U.S. Ordnance Museum in Aberdeen, Maryland, put weapons from the war on display, adding to a "mile of tanks" where visitors could touch the real thing, "the steel monsters." Kids collected pennies to subsidize the June commemoration in New York, much as children pitched in to support the war effort during World War II. In an important respect, the victory parade that never took place after Vietnam, and thus never brought a sense of closure to that tragic chapter of American history, finally occurred. (Veterans representing past U.S. wars participated in these celebrations nearly two decades later.) These public celebrations therefore served an important compensatory purpose. One observer noted the creation of a "moral community" during this time. New York's ticker-tape parade became "a communal bath" washing over the millions—yes, millions—estimated to be in attendance.[6]

Besides these general contextual factors, significant changes have been influencing museum shows and memorialization projects pertaining to the West. A bill proposing to commemorate the Indians who lost their lives in the infamous battle with General George Custer failed in Congress at the end of 1990. The idea was deemed "politically correct" and "revisionist." "All it is is a bill of appeasement," complained one critic.[7] But it successfully passed in 1991, the same year that *The West as America* went up.

The legislation mandated a significant name change, from Custer Battlefield to the Little Bighorn Battlefield National Monument. It also authorized a new monument to be built at the southern Montana site. A memorial to the Seventh Cavalry casualties of the 1876 battle already exists. Proposals for the new Indian monument included a three-hundred-foot tower, which would have dwarfed the existing twelve-foot obelisk, or—in a brash gesture—demolishing Mount Rushmore and carting the rubble to this site. In the end, a relatively unobtrusive grass-covered berm won the design competition, but wrangling over its placement continues. The importance of renaming the site—foregrounding the experiences of those who have been overlooked previously—and the push and pull of opposing factions parallel the struggle over the African Burial Ground (formerly the "Negros Burying Ground") in Manhattan in the early 1990s.

Moreover, a number of contemporary art exhibitions have presented Indian drawings of their own experiences. Concepts such as "resistance" and "autonomy" commonly accompany such presentations, and they typically include commentary by contemporary Indian artists. This approach challenges the customary perspective of the European observer and offers a multiplicity of voices. It is increasingly winning favor in the museum world.

The West as America at the National Museum of American Art consisted of six sections: "Prelude to Expansion: Repainting the Past"; "Picturing Progress in the Era of Westward Expansion"; "Inventing 'the Indian'"; "Settlement and Development: Claiming the West"; "'The Kiss of Enterprise': The Western Landscape as Symbol and Resource"; and "Doing the 'Old America': The Image of the American West, 1880-1920." It included paintings, sculpture, photographs, and prints—lots of them. Various individuals, ranging from mature scholars to a doctoral candidate in art history, wrote the essays accompanying each section. This exhibition demonstrates how the NMAA is an incubator of talent: at least three of the contributors to the catalogue held predoctoral fellowships there. In every case but one, the show's contributors also wrote the wall labels for their particular part. For an exhibition that drew the accusation that it exercised an authoritarian voice, it was remarkably democratic in the manner it was assembled.

William H. Truettner's concept for this show was straightforward. As a curator of painting and sculpture at the NMAA, he wanted to reevaluate the large body of western art produced during the nineteenth and early twentieth centuries. The art historical scholarship related to these works had become stale. The artists were generally thought to be passive reporters of the "real thing"; the art itself long considered heroic, authentic, documentary representations of our collective tradition. But Bill Truettner sensed another, untold story here. Spurred by the insights of revisionist history, as well as being stimulated by deconstructivist interpretive approaches that had become influential in art history (as they had in other academic disciplines), Truettner wished to open up a new dialogue.

He and his colleagues felt that this art had never received the thorough analysis that it deserved. They wished to contextualize the artists and the art, explore the works' rhetorical strategies, and uncover their ideological bent. Moreover, Truettner and his colleagues sought to untangle both the conscious and the unconscious motivations of the creators and closely examine the relationships between artist, patron, and various publics. In other words, by stripping away the deposits of myth that have accumulated over time, they hoped to enlarge our understanding of this genre.

The main thrust of the exhibition was summarized by the NMAA's director, Elizabeth Broun, in the foreword to the catalogue: "precisely because art possesses the power to persuade, it is a masterful mediator between the alarming facts of history and the loudly proclaimed ideals of progress." In this view, western art glossed over many of the more troubling consequences of the march of European Americans across the continent. Those costs included the displacement of native peoples, suppression of their cultures, and exploitation of natural resources. Art was not the *cause* of these abuses, of course. But it nourished expansionist doctrines such as Manifest Destiny, giving them credence and support.[8] One point was steadily driven home: visitors to the show should take nothing of what they saw at face value.

Truettner tentatively named the show *The Promised Land*. But the exhibition contributor Alex Nemerov convinced him that most people would miss his ironic intent, and expect this to be the latest in a long series of laudatory exhibitions of western "masterpieces" mounted over the years. That title was therefore dropped. As Truettner and Nemerov later pointedly wrote in defense of their venture, they rejected "a Romantic theory of transcendent artistic creation that is as old as the hills and just about as inert."[9]

Controversy broke out immediately. At the bottom of page 1 of the comment book accompanying *The West as America,* no less a public figure than the historian and Librarian Emeritus of Congress Daniel Boorstin offered a biting, dismissive critique. "A perverse, historically inaccurate destructive exhibit! No credit to the Smithsonian!" he boldly charged. Boorstin's reflections set off a spirited debate, argued in what grew to be a set of four large books where visitors recorded their reactions.

Comment books may be a commonplace in museums today, but they were a new feature in 1991. Betsy Broun can't swear to it, but she believes that the NMAA may have inaugurated the idea in American museums.[10] She recalls that they included a comment book to get feedback regarding an audio tour during the show *Masterworks of Louis Comfort Tiffany* in their Renwick Gallery in 1989. After that, NMAA officials routinely included them in their exhibitions.

American Art (a journal published by the NMAA) concluded that 509 of 735 comments recorded during *The West as America* were "specifically positive about some aspect of the show."[11] Indeed, words such as "courageous," "honest," "challenging," "thought-provoking," and "instructive" appear in the books. They seem to have surfaced more frequently as the run of the show continued. Many contributors were remarkably thoughtful, such as the person who wrote this in book 4: "There's an old proverb in Spanish: 'En este mundo traidor, nada es verdad y nada es mentira; todo es segun el color de[l] cristal con que se miraba [*sic*]' which in English means, 'In this sad world, nothing is true and nothing is false; everything is according to the color of the glass through which one looks.'" There was a great deal of forthright criticism as well, which sometimes seemed seared into the pages. Reminiscent of a major complaint about *Harlem on My Mind*, visitors griped about "A little too much sociology and hindsight," or "I resent a distorted sociological lecture in an art exhibit." One person even stamped the word "BULLSHIT" in red ink.

But like an open microphone at a public forum, the books also elicited the inanities of people who merely wished to heard: "Detroit Pistons Rule!!" "Stacy Loves Sean," and the ubiquitous "Kilroy was here!" Moreover, the opportunity to leave their mark aroused simple-minded slogans of multiculturalism, musings that could make people of a variety of political persuasions wince. "Where are more Blacks! We were here 1st." "Mandingo Warrior." In at least two instances, cartoonists left *their* interpretations of the West. In one scenario, "Indians With Attitudes"—Native Americans dressed in a pastiche of traditional and hip-hop styles—declare, "Yo Cowboys Ya Better Chill Out!" "If You Think Its a Joke Watch the Gun Smoke!" But beyond these fatuous entries, comment books surely have never become as consequential as they were for *The West as America*.

The show's shortcomings were also bandied about in the media. Newspaper and magazine articles bore such clever titles as "Time to Circle the Wagons," "Shootout at the PC Corral," "How the West Was Spun," and "Westward Hokum." It was clear that this was an extremely savory story.[12] *Time*: "Its tone is prosecutorial . . . pushes too far." *New York*: "a carping tone that can get on your nerves." The *San Francisco Chronicle*: "a schoolmarmy tone that seems to get on everyone's nerves."[13] Eventually the debate reached Capitol Hill.

Ken Ringle of the *Washington Post* was one of the first critics to weigh in, and he raised practically every criticism that others subsequently developed and refined. *The West as America* was "the Smithsonian Institution's first politically correct art exhibit." It was cynical. It dwelt on victimization. It was a waste of your tax dollars. The "aging radicals" who masterminded the exhibition "insist Karl Marx was the real driver of all those covered wagons." And finally, the curators should have left well enough alone: "They're uncomfortable with the sense of wonder that's in many of these paintings."[14] For Ringle, this exhibition was a serious misfire.

But the unquestioned sense of wonder is exactly what Truettner and his associates wished to puncture in their presentation of this material. They set out to demystify a body of work, not to unreflexively laud it. Alex Nemerov fundamentally questions Ringle's authority: "The show elicited these colorful, would-be art historical prattlings on the part of people with, to my knowledge, no background in the history of art, or in art historical methodologies." Ringle may have been a strategically placed journalist—a local pundit, even—but he was sadly behind the times in theoretical sophistication: "His paradigm for a cultural endeavor was roughly that which he learned as a graduate of the University of Virginia in the early '60s," notes Nemerov. "It was a broad, apolitical, humanist endeavor. And anything other than that constituted this brazen affront. . . . rather a sort of petrified notion of cultural discourse."[15]

Martin F. Nolan, writing in the *Boston Globe*, developed an argument similar to Ringle's. He characterized most of the show's entries as beautiful and concluded that "Like most works of art, they blessedly need no captions."[16] But Julie Schimmel, another exhibition contributor, emphatically dismisses such theoretical know-nothingism:

> Bullshit. That kind of criticism to me comes out of earlier schools of criticism such as the work of Clement Greenberg, where there is only intuitive experience. And words are really sort of excess baggage. . . . I think works of art may speak without explanation to a small, elite group of painters, artists, and art historians, but in general I think they absolutely need explanatory text.

Alex Nemerov likewise rejects this stance as "the silence of the ineffable."

> Lurking within the criticism of this show is a kind of anti-visual bias. When literature is the topic, I think it's fair to want to try to interpret it from many different points of view. But I think there is a sense that art is what it is. So with realist painting especially, there's a sense of "Hey, what's there to say?" And any analysis at all is construed as this ridiculous reading into the work.

Thus the visitor's comment "If you believe that the authors [*sic*] message can be seen in these paintings then you're ready to see Christ in the billboard ads for spaghetti."[17]

What about the charge, then, that *The West as America* was "politically correct"? Asked to define the term, Alex Nemerov remarks, "I think what it means is subjecting the work of the past to the standards of contemporary morality. And judging it with a kind of withering, a holier-than-thou scorn." Is such a characterization pertinent to this exhibition? He continues,

> I think in some ways it was, yes. I think that the exhibition was motivated by a lot of anger towards the way art had been shown and presented in books and in other museum exhibitions. . . . I think in reacting against the extraordinarily tepid and uninteresting ways the work had been presented, we reacted strongly enough to warrant that p.c. label, which never should have characterized the whole show, but it aptly characterized parts of it.

Julie Schimmel, who authored the section "Inventing 'the Indian,'" has a mixed response. In her view, the show was "politically correct in an admirable way. It deconstructed images of the American West." She characterizes it as "extremely worthwhile," "a real breakthrough." But she denies that it was encumbered by the sort of heavy-handed terminology that is frequently coupled with a politically correct perspective: "I don't know jargon. If I had known it, maybe I would have put it in."[18]

But the politically correct designation particularly infuriates Elizabeth Johns, whose section on the settlement and development pictures of artists like George Caleb Bingham emphasized the self-promotion and reassurance projected in such works. She explains,

> Politically correct means to me that people are being accused of having empathy with minorities . . . [and that] it is not rooted in a moral commitment, but rather it is simply fashionable, and clearly calculated to win a reputation or to make money. You can imagine what I was doing in the '60s, and it makes me furious for someone to interpret my own stand, which has been consistent in my life since then, as motivated by something that has nothing to do with my moral principles. . . . It's cynicism at its most extreme.[19]

Were the curators a bunch of old radicals, spouting what Charles Krauthammer described as "half-baked Marxist meanness"? Were they guilty of presenting "Socialist claptrap," or of having a "Marxist ax to grind," as some contributors to the comment books suggested? What about other visitors, who drew parallels between what they saw and read on the museum's walls and propaganda from the USSR, East Germany, the American New Left, or even the notorious 1937 Nazi exhibition of "Degenerate Art," where "the viewers were instructed how to properly condemn the artists, the art, and the subject of the art"? To a person, the curators dispute these associations.[20]

Elizabeth Johns: "I'm an aging moderate. I have been involved personally in a number of radical causes, sometimes at great personal cost. But I don't identify that as my stance as a scholar. It's my stance as a person." Alex Nemerov, still a graduate student at the time *The West as America* was mounted: "I'm young. And I'm not a radical really. The ideas in that show are hardly the most 'out there.' So, 'no' on both counts." Julie Schimmel reflects, "I have become more radical as I have aged. I'm probably now twice as radical as I was at the point of that exhibition." Joni Kinsey, who assembled the artists' biographies for the catalogue, observes how changing academic fashions render mundane some ideas that were once considered extreme: "Post-structuralist and deconstructionist theory have in some ways made what I was doing even as little as ten years ago much less radical than it seemed at the time."[21]

Bill Truettner, a soft-spoken, diffident man, prefers to explain himself through his writing rather than by speaking. His demeanor belies the fiendishness attributed to him, and he drolly dismisses this charge:

> Some woman wrote to me from Chicago, and she said, "You must be very young and have long hair." And I mean, she just painted this perfect description of a '60s hippie. So I wrote back to her and I said, "I am a grandfather. I have gray hair. I mow my lawn every Saturday." And you know, among my academic colleagues, I'm very mainstream. I'm not at all on the fringe. For museums, I'm a little more on the fringe, but hardly a radical.[22]

Yet despite the appearance of consensus on this matter, internal divisions eventually developed among the contributors. The divisions opened up along gender lines. According to Elizabeth Johns,

> Several of the contributors felt that Bill Truettner paid particular homage to the theoretical slant of Alex Nemerov. From my point of view, I could see that by the end of the project, it was very much a collaboration between the two of them. Some of the rest of us were fairly left alone. . . . It rather fell apart toward the end, when the give-and-take was moved into the hands of only the curator and his favorite contributor.

Moreover, Julie Schimmel complains, "Afterwards, there was a lecture trail or a symposium trail. And the only two people that were ever chosen to represent the exhibition were Alex Nemerov and Bill Truettner. None of the women who had contributed to the show were ever represented in these dialogues. And that was very irritating."

This was not merely carping about favoritism and inclusion. For Elizabeth Johns, the exhibition *did* adopt a radical stance, which many critics discerned as well. But while this put her off, her critique was from the vantage point of a seasoned academic insider. She felt that the tenor of the show's commentary turned more sharply radical as it progressed from beginning to end, pulling visitors' experiences away from the more moderate position Johns feels she mapped out in her catalogue essay:

> It is, shall we say, power wielding in academe today to take an extraordinarily tough neo-Marxist stance that everything in the past was governed by market forces and callousness, and we extinguished the Indians, and there were no people who moved westward with anything but a ridiculous idealism, etc. My read of this after thirty years in academia is that it comes from a group of people who substitute this very hard political take on the past for any action on the political scene today. It is macho, even though there are women who do this, but I identify it almost completely with armchair horsemen.

Johns argues for a contextualization approach, rather than superimposing interpretations on artworks based on academic fads and fashions.[23]

The wall labels raised people's hackles the most. These mini-interpretations are typically a relatively minor feature of exhibitions. They often provide little more than basic identifying information. Yet they commanded center stage in the controversy over *The West as America*.

There is a built-in problem with wall labels, of course. In the expansive space of a catalogue essay, authors may erect elaborate theoretical structures and buttress them with layer upon layer of supporting evidence. But a catalogue is typically geared toward a more selective, certainly a more specialized audience. A member of the general public tends to purchase a catalogue to enjoy the reproductions of a favorite artist's work, rather than to keep current with the latest scholarship. Journalists and politicians seldom have the time to digest an exhibition catalogue, nor do they have the inclination.

For the most part, the catalogue to *The West as America* is a well-reasoned look at western art. It considers new ideas and introduces some new themes, yet a reader would note many similarities with other such contemporary texts on a variety of topics. The only essay that is flavored with theoretical language is the final one, by Alex Nemerov. Sure, you'll find terms such as repression, sublimation, overdetermination, intertextuality, and discourse. But several of these concepts have entered general dialogue as a result of the widespread understanding of basic Freudian doctrines. While theoretical heavy hitters such as Michel Foucault and Roland Barthes are cited in the notes section, they don't crowd the text itself. Nemerov may take more imaginative leaps than his colleagues, pursuing both an ideological and a formalist art criticism, but his essay is not the sort of dense postmodernist tract that can be penetrated only by a select few true believers.[24] Especially to a reader looking it over a few years after its publication, the catalogue seems tame.

Wall labels, on the other hand, are the sound bites of the museum world. They aim for maximum impact with an economy of terms. The subtleties of a fully developed essay are necessarily dropped. Wall labels are for everyman and everywoman. They should be condensed, concentrated, concise. But in the case of *The West as America* they turned out to be "blunt instruments," in the words of NMAA director Broun.

Betsy Broun reviewed all the labels before the show opened, and found nothing wrong with them. As curator, Bill Truettner had reviewed them too. Reconsidering things now, both feel they miscalculated. And both feel contrite.

Broun reflects,

I thought they were fine. But I realize now that I was reading them from the perspective of an academic. I was not listening with the inner ear of someone who might come in off the street with a general background. They were heavy-handed. Many of the labels used jargon that sounds fine in a graduate seminar. But just sounds out of sync [in a museum].

Bill Truettner wonders, "What were we thinking?" He understands that "When you nuance your argument, critics manage not to face the issues that you're trying to talk about. And if you don't nuance it, then you just set yourself up to be knocked down. And we really did set ourselves up, I think."[25] A classic case, then, of "Damned if you do, damned if you don't."

Truettner recalls a pivotal moment when the "pitch" of the labels was perfected: "Alex [Nemerov] and I kept looking at each other and saying, 'Nobody's going to get this.' And so we cranked up the labels more than we should, because we didn't think other people were going to understand the issues in this." For his part, Nemerov recalls a specific influence: "I had in my mind the work of Barbara Kruger, particularly her very confrontational, politically charged art of the late '80s and early '90s. That could not help but get the attention of the beholder, and was very much on my mind when I wrote my labels." He describes how this influence seeped into a particular example:

> The [Eanger Irving] Couse painting [*The Captive*, 1892] concerned gender issues. And I think to experiment with a Krugeresque mode of label writing, and to concern oneself with questions of violence to women and racist fears of miscegenation, which that picture very explicitly concerns on both counts, was not something one could do happily in the halls of "the nation's attic."[26]

If hyperbole prevailed, it was in part because the curators' expectations were so high for this show. By arguing that all art has a political basis, they were fashioning an alternative to the typical art exhibition. Truettner, who frankly admits that he was "pretty innocent and pretty dumb" in this instance, did not anticipate the antipathy expressed from the first few pages onward in the comment books. "Do you hate the United States?" one woman began. "If you insist on

FIG. 13. Eanger Irving Couse, *The Captive*, 1892. Oil on canvas. Phoenix Art Museum. Gift of Mr. and Mrs. Read Mullan and others by exchange. Used by permission.

imposing your sophmoric [*sic*] bias (Marxist-deconstructionist) on the public please have the basic decency to allow for *other* explanations. Beautiful art, but your interpretations ruin it for me." Her remarks were promptly followed by another person's dismissal: "An exhibit of *revisionist* bull jive, made by anemic, analytical academics who shed no blood, sweat, or tears in the frontier of the West!" Just as race, religious affiliation, or military service were the litmus tests that conferred legitimacy on combatants in other controversies, the writer here was claiming that personal experience in "taming the West" should be the primary qualification for examining this material. (But were that true, we'd be at a theoretical dead end; few, if any, people bearing that qualification survive today.)

Joni Kinsey's reaction demonstrates the degree to which the curators erred: "The labels did come down a bit hard. They didn't pose questions or interpretations that would allow sensitive viewers to consider them as possibilities and make up their own minds. It was heavy-handed. I actually had the same reaction, and I was one of the choir they didn't have to preach to." A writer in the comment book was much less tactful: "What a crock of shit! . . . Don't force your pc views down my independently thinking throat!"[27]

The Yale professor Alan Trachtenberg offered perhaps the most thorough critique of the exhibition. Truettner and his colleagues took his lengthy assessment seriously because it was refreshingly free of the rancor that suffused so much of the rest of the commentary. Trachtenberg argued that they had substituted the "hermeneutics of suspicion" for a "stubborn filiopiety" in their approach to this material. In other words, they had replaced an unreflective reverence with a pervasive impulse to debunk. He faulted the exhibition in two major respects. First, "Too often the curators simply repudiated official art, instead of reaching beyond it to a positive alternative vision." Trachtenberg was therefore asking that attention be paid to work produced by others—sometimes literally "Other," such as Indians, blacks, and Hispanics—as well as by people actually living and working in the Old West. In a sense, his remarks foreshadowed exhibitions like ones on Indian drawings in ledger books, which have followed in subsequent years. However, Trachtenberg was proposing a significantly different agenda than the organizers had in mind. They primarily wished to subject some familiar works to a sweeping review.

Trachtenberg detected a second, related deficiency: after the smoke cleared, this was another instance of putting elite culture under the microscope and coming up with a monocausal, constrictive explanation. Trachtenberg argued, "By a strange twist of intention, they tended to replicate—through reversal—the very beliefs and attitudes they wanted to repudiate. Their demythologizing process led to a simplistic, negative version of the West, a remythologizing of the subject in much the same way, only now as the locus of all that is wrong with America." Sure enough, a visitor offered the same critique in comment book 1: "[A] serious flaw in the exhibit:

railroading one polemical line over all the art at hand. Not unlike what the commentators themselves are accusing others of." Truettner in particular was chastened by these appraisals. In later writing, he underscored the importance of carefully steering between the Scylla of aestheticism and the Charybdis of historicism. Drifting too close toward either side poses its own distinctive dangers. Truettner thereafter advocated navigating a middle course. As he now realizes, "we did bang it flat for a lot of people."[28]

The battle over *The West as America* defies easy classification as a struggle between elitists and populists. Populists—Truettner and his colleagues, for example—reject artistic genius and focus instead on the process, content, and context of artistic production. Elitists uphold the transcendent view of artistic virtuosity and extol artworks as apolitical and universal. In this instance, many members of the general public rejected the newer, populist criticism, even though it was designed to draw them into the dialogue. Some were put off by the language. Others were simply reluctant to relinquish tried-and-true notions. By aligning themselves this way, the public may unintentionally support an elitist critical establishment that for the most part couldn't care less about its opinions.

A month or so after *The West as America* opened, both Bill Truettner and Betsy Broun decided that some of the wall labels needed to be changed. "You can blame me for that," Broun declares. She felt that the curators needed to reword the labels in order to connect more directly to people's lived experience, using language that was at the same time more understandable and less assertive. "You could almost feel the metaphoric finger waggling in many of those labels," she reflects, even though neither she, Truettner, nor anyone else had foreseen a problem. Broun's goal was to "take the edge off" some of the texts, not to change their meaning or fundamentally alter the show's architecture. It was simply intended to be a fine-tuning, to "present the same ideas in a much more persuasive and pleasant way."[29]

In all, about ten of the fifty-five labels were modified. Alex Nemerov rewrote one in his section about a Charles Russell painting (*Carson's Men*, 1913), where he linked three men to the Crucifixion. In the retelling, phrases such as "white exploration" that was "glorious and just" were dropped, as was the reference to "a turn-of-the-century culture convinced of the righteousness of imperialism." "That was not a much-loved label," Nemerov recalls, even though his discussion in this instance represented a more traditional art historical search for affinities, rather than postmodernist flights of fancy.[30] (One notation in the comment book read, "Kit Carson as Christ, you're kidding, right?" Another mockingly suggested taking things to even more absurd interpretive heights: "He missed the Exxon logo disguised as a teepee in the one where the artist was connected to the Indian via the triangles.") Its replacement offered an expanded argument, citing precise details.

Bill Truettner drafted most of the rewrites, which then passed through Betsy Broun's office. In a number of instances, the new version cited specific examples or added descriptive material. This grounded a premise in evidence and made it concrete, rather than merely asserting it or assuming that visitors would automatically know enough to fill in the blanks themselves. Terse statements were expanded. References to "whiteness," or race were largely (although not completely) deleted. For example, a text regarding depictions of Indians underwent two significant alterations. "[R]ows of rectilinear frames, each containing a domesticated 'savage' Indian, provided a dramatic demonstration of white power and control," became "Rows of rectilinear frames, each containing a domesticated 'savage' Indian, also served a political purpose." The passage "One of the most insidious aspects of white privilege historically has been its unquestioned claim to be standing at world center" was dropped in its entirety. A reference to "visual conceit" and social distance replaced it.

Changes were evident as early as the lead text panel. The original version read:

> Images leading from Christopher Columbus to Kit Carson show westward expansion as an heroic experience.
>
> These images appear realistic but are carefully staged fictions.
>
> They persuaded nineteenth-century Americans that westward expansion was inevitable and just. They also justified the conflict and hardship of nation building
>
> Images don't always mean what they seem to say.

The new version retained the boldness of this venture. But it presented a broader rationalization for the exhibition, clarifying what the curators were responding to:

> Images from Christopher Columbus to Kit Carson show the discovery and settlement of the West as a heroic undertaking.
>
> Nineteenth-century artists and the public believed that these images represented a faithful account of civilization advancing westward. Grand compositions filled with light, color, and factual detail persuaded viewers that western scenes were literally true.
>
> A more recent approach argues that these images are carefully staged fictions, constructed from both supposition and fact. Their role was to justify the hardship and conflict of nation building.
>
> This exhibition advocates the latter view. It assumes that all history is unconsciously edited by those who make it. Western scenes, therefore, extolled progress but rarely noted damaging social and environmental change. Looking beneath the surface of these images gives us a better understanding of why national problems created during the era of westward expansion still affect us today.

By emphasizing that "all history is unconsciously edited," Truettner stopped short of declaring that calculated, heavy-handed motives guided the production of this art work. Yet by stating up front that his goal for this exhibition was to dig deeply into this material, he made it clear that the contributors intended to ferret out multiple tiers of meaning that had been overlooked previously.

In at least two instances, new labels presented evidence and opposing arguments and then asked viewers to choose their position. "Is [Frederic] Remington's *Fight for the Water Hole* simply a transcription of a frontier event, or does it borrow its imagery—a group of outnumbered whites desperately defending against the 'strike' of a racial enemy—from the urban world [of immigrants and labor conflict, c. 1903] where Remington lived?"[31] Or consider the modified discussion of Charles Russell's *For Supremacy*, (1895): "As in Remington's *The Scalp*, the warriors in Russell's painting gesture wildly—mouths open, bodies leaning elastically, weapons (or a scalp) slung back or overhead. Compare their attitudes to the cowboys' stoic calm in Remington's *Fight for the Water Hole* or Russell's *Caught in a Circle*." Both of

FIG. 14. Frederic Remington, *Fight for the Water Hole*, 1903. Oil on canvas. Museum of Fine Arts, Houston; the Hogg Brothers Collection, gift of Miss Ima Hogg. Used by permission.

these descriptions are much more accommodating to viewers and shift the final authority back to them.

Truettner and Broun intended these changes to be a responsible reply to the complaints of critics and the general public. They were an admission that the original presentation was deficient in certain respects, and that misunderstandings could be modulated. But their conciliatory gesture backfired. It was interpreted as backpedaling rather than refining. A visitor wrote, "I was here while a young man was walking around *changing* the captions! Talk about giving in! The show *is* the show, whatever it is. How about keeping the old captions with a line through them!" To Broun and Truettner's dismay, some articles in the press echoed these sentiments.[32]

As Bill Truettner reflects, "I didn't see that as losing face. We wanted to communicate more effectively, but by then, rewriting labels became a political issue. It was like that's an admission that you guys did it wrong. And we were sort of caught every way we turned." He continues, "God knows, I would have gone back and rewritten a lot more labels if we could. I wrote one about *Storming of the Teocalli by Cortez and His Troops* [Emanuel Leutze, 1848], which now I wish I could take back. I think I rewrote that label in my sleep for about the next year or so." Arguing that artists invoked historical conquests to lend support to nineteenth-century battles against Mexico and the Indians, critics found fault with Truettner's interpretation. The Spanish conquistadors were shown brutalizing their opponents, not as morally triumphant. Many felt that the contributors failed to look closely enough at the work, that they were instead obstructed by their ideological blinders.

Betsy Broun was similarly flummoxed:

> My attempts to respond to criticism with meaningful change were simply regarded by the other camp as a sort of lily-livered retreat in the face of opposition. It seemed to reinforce the idea that we didn't have confidence in our first presentation. So now I know you're probably better off to stand your ground. If you have something you're willing to defend in terms of ideas, you're better off defending it. I thought that since it was still early in the presentation, we could make it a stronger show for those who came [to visit] after. But all we did was add another layer of controversy.

Because *The West as America* became controversial almost immediately, virtually everything related to it was framed in those terms. For example, the Denver Art Museum and the Saint Louis Art Museum were listed in the catalogue as venues for the show after it left Washington, D.C. But those plans disintegrated. Critics smugly speculated that the show had become too problematic; it wouldn't play beyond the Beltway. In other words, it was not worth the risk. Yet in the end, financial problems and other banalities intruded *before* the exhibition opened at the NMAA. The show grew to be very large, with many large pieces. It would have had to be scaled back to fit into other museums, and the curators were loath to fiddle with the design. Moreover, the costs of hosting the exhibition exceeded original estimates, so that it became a more expensive enterprise than originally budgeted. That too spoiled its chances to be seen elsewhere.

The price tag also became an issue when critics and politicians attacked the show as a misuse of taxpayers' money. Senator Ted Stevens (R-Alaska), who admitted he had not seen the exhibition, led the attack at an Appropriations Committee hearing in mid-May. Significantly, Stevens also found fault with a documentary about the *Exxon Valdez* disaster, once screened by the Smithsonian, as well as the aforementioned television series *The Buried Mirror*, subsidized with Smithsonian money. His censure of the museum was likely part retaliation, part "the politics of diversion," drawing attention away from unflattering aspects of his own domain.[33] Stevens found allies in Senators Slade Gorton (R-Washington) and Alan Simpson (R-Wyoming), both of whom made public statements condemning the show. In the end, nothing happened beyond minor political grandstanding and bluster.

The National Museum of American Art, which dates back to 1829, was the first federal art collection in the United States. It is one of the galaxy of museums administered by the Smithsonian Institution, focusing exclusively on American art. But in this instance, none of the direct costs of the exhibition came from federal funds. An NMAA board member provided a grant. The bulk of the money came from Smithsonian trust assets, money that is generated through revenue-producing activities. Of course, it was developed and presented in a federal facility, which means that salaries and other costs were federally subsidized. But calls for congressional oversight nullify the deference normally accorded scholarly, scientific, or medical authorities whenever tax dollars are involved—that is, until an elected official becomes riled and decides to tug on the strings of appropriations.

The fact that this was occurring at a branch of the Smithsonian simply fueled the outrage. For Alex Nemerov, "The Smithsonian is the sacred place of Judy Garland's shoes and so on. It's not the place to mess with the icons of American history. I think people felt that their money, their taxpayers' dollars, was going to support this anti-American hooey, which was actually not true." And as Betsy Broun explains,

> Because we are the Smithsonian, it's anticipated that somehow ideas presented here have been ordained to be true. And so I think a lot of the public didn't come here expecting to find themselves thrown in the middle of a debate about history. It was a learning experience for us to understand how much our audiences expect us to deliver some neatly packaged truth they can truly believe in.

Sure enough, one visitor remarked, "The curators . . . took a small truth and made it into THE TRUTH."

The West as America jolted those members of the public who endorse the image of museums as places of refinement and inspiration, repositories of truth and beauty, or sanctuaries from the real world, detached from the politics of the moment. It threw new light on images and ideas that have been an important part of people's identities for generations.

As noted, some folks simply don't want to relinquish cherished myths. In fact, none of us is completely comfortable with that prospect. One of the most heartfelt entries in the comment books highlights how a scholarly enterprise cannot dislodge strongly held beliefs, regardless of the seamlessness of its arguments, without prompting an outcry:

> I will always imagine myself as a pioneer or a railroad man settling the West. These pictures are wonderful. The propaganda in them does not destroy my dream—the reality of the West is not available to us or to the curator of this exhibit. . . . I'm happy with the myth. I cried like a baby at *Dances With Wolves*. I loved it. I know the scholars and curators would have poopooed my red eyes.

The man attached an addendum, establishing his ancestry and hammering down his right to his position: "My Great Grandfather was a sheriff in Kansas in 1874!" Psychologically, emotionally, and ideologically speaking, he would not be moved.

But were others spurred to change their positions? In the museum world, for instance? B. Byron Price, at the time the executive director of the National Cowboy Hall of Fame and Western Heritage Center in Oklahoma City, represents an important perspective. The Cowboy Hall of Fame loaned about half a dozen works to the exhibition. As a hub for western art and culture, the Cowboy Hall of Fame was vitally concerned with a show of this magnitude, appearing in such a central American institution and presenting major new scholarship. In one article, Price acknowledged that the show was "a watershed," but also responded rather defensively: "If the art condemned in this exhibit is indeed flawed by racism, gender bias, and imperialism, then it follows that the museums exhibiting such works without caveats or as unbiased historical narrative, must also be guilty of promoting these concepts. Should these same institutions

FIG. 15. *Charles Schreyvogel Painting on the Roof of His Apartment Building in Hoboken, New Jersey*, 1903. National Cowboy Hall of Fame and Western Heritage Center, Oklahoma City, Oklahoma. Used by permission.

now don sack cloth and ashes, repent, and proclaim themselves museums of the western holocaust?"[34]

Price, who has become the executive director of the Buffalo Bill Historical Center in Cody, Wyoming, assesses matters differently now. A type of analysis that was considered to be "out there" not very long ago has become much more the norm. *The West as America* has pulled scholarship toward much broader concerns, compelling investigators to consider the multiple layers of meaning, and how they were fabricated, in western art. The thorough scholar can no longer be content with seeing these images as unmediated documentaries of real events.

A photograph that became a leitmotif of the exhibition delightfully captures in pictorial form what the essayists were arguing in their written contributions. *Charles Schreyvogel Painting on the Roof of*

His Apartment Building in Hoboken, New Jersey (1903) shows the renowned artist at his easel, set among the chimneys and ventilating stacks of his urban home. His subject? A model decked out in western garb, kneeling and aiming a pistol. The two face down one another, both of them standing just across the Hudson from New York City. Thus was the Old West imagined and re-created for an eastern audience, transformed by the remove of years, many miles, and subsequent social needs and interests.

Price believes that *The West as America* forced a national debate about western art. And he feels that is a good thing: "It really elevated our game. It's really sharpened our skills. The curators came with very sharp swords, and were very well trained. And one had to get beyond the emotional aspects of 'You can't say that about *our* art,' and [instead] engage in meaningful discussion on the themes that were presented." That doesn't mean that Price agreed with all the interpretations presented in the show. But in the end, while some assertions were "far-fetched," the arguments could not be dismissed as "horsefeathers." To his mind, we can never look at Western art in the same ways ever again. He sees the direct effects of this exhibition in the heightened scrutiny given to issues such as diversity and gender in wall texts and essays, and in new types of exhibitions such as *Powerful Images: Persistent Voices,* assembled by Museums West, a consortium of ten institutions in the United States and Canada. *The West as America* was an eye-opener. But Price has gotten past his initial shock: "Perhaps the strident tones gave it its muscle. It gave the show its bite, and that's probably why we paid attention."[35]

That was exactly what some of the principals were after in this case. On reflection, Alex Nemerov observes,

> If we wrote kind of open-ended labels, let's say, labels that went something like "on the one hand this, but on the other hand that," we would risk losing the interest of a museum goer. And what would have happened was that museum goer would parade through our exhibition and read it as nothing more than a conventional narrative of westward expansion and settlement. And that, needless to say, would be a disaster for us.

This became a mission in Nemerov's eyes: "We wanted to write really forceful labels. We did thrust upon them, as it were, singular points of view. And the didacticism of the labels was there." But would he change his approach if he were to do it all again? "Probably not," he replies.

But Nemerov had no continuing stake in the museum. He did not have to directly take the heat and he was not responsible for mopping up any mess. The situation was different for Truettner and Broun. Truettner admits, "I was pretty scared. I didn't feel good. I was worried. You know, I usually swim about half a mile three times a week, and for a period of six months I was swimming a mile about four or five times a week." He never felt that his job was in jeopardy. Rather, it was the newness of the situation that was unsettling: "That was the first time the Smithsonian had been hit, and nobody quite knew what to make of it. There were threats to the budget. And we both [he and Broun] were worried that we had sort of done a disservice to our colleagues and made life a little more difficult for them." Broun, too, concedes that "it made a lot of people nervous" in Congress and in the Smithsonian hierarchy. But she also avows that Smithsonian officials never wavered in their support of her and the exhibition.

In retrospect, some of the contributors assign the primary responsibility for the controversy to the youngest of the group, Alex Nemerov. Julie Schimmel argues that the urge to deconstruct accepted doctrines and interpretations represents a generational impulse: "Sometimes it's a way of making a mark as a younger art historian. I don't mean that younger art historians are evil. But there's a certain force from which they shoot from their graduate programs." Elizabeth Johns argues similarly:

> From my point of view, the only somewhat overly glib reading of the past was by Alex Nemerov. And that's to be understood, because he was a young guy. It's a lot easier [at that stage of your life and career] to generalize somewhat outrageously about all of the West being settled by exploitative, thoughtless, ruthless people . . . if you've never known ambiguity in your own actions.

What may have appeared to be a united front of like-minded thinkers behind this show in fact turned out to be an ephemeral, loosely connected confederation of individuals—none of whom predicted that a show about a subject that most people thought was as arid as a dried-out cow pod would have ever triggered as spirited a debate as erupted over *The West as America*.

In the final analysis, what is the exhibition's legacy? Joni Kinsey believes that "What the show did very well was to demonstrate that both American art and American western art are more complicated and much more interesting than anybody ever thought they were." She raises the important issue of balance, which some reviewers and scores of viewers felt was pointedly lacking in this instance. But balance *was* being addressed, just not within the show. Rather, the team felt it was presenting a bold new alternative to traditional approaches:

> A lot of people were saying, "These are really glorious, wonderful, ecstatic, sublime kinds of paintings that say lots of great things about our country and its history. Why aren't you pointing that out?" I think the curators and the writers were giving the opposite point of view, saying, "Well yes, of course, but there's many other things going on, and in some cases that sense of wonder needs to be tempered with a bit more awareness of what actually did go on. And the agendas behind these paintings." I think it was an attempt to balance the score, and maybe it swung the pendulum a bit too far. But it was very much in response to a one-sided history that had preceded it.

Summing up, Kinsey believes that the organizers may have sabotaged themselves and their goals.

Only Betsy Broun appears unequivocal in her evaluation of the contretemps. While she admits that the museum made some mistakes and that its execution of its plans was not perfect, she places the experience squarely in the "plus" column: "It was a great, exciting period for us. It was one of the first times we really did manage to bridge that gap where we had a highly sophisticated set of academic ideas that were presented to a very, very broad public that got engaged with them. So I still look back on it as a kind of golden moment."

Bill Truettner is much more circumspect in his evaluation. He can state proudly, "We did sort of turn over the whole canon of western art, and we made people think differently about it, I guess." But that's not the entire story: "In the process, I think we left a lot of people dubious about ever trying to follow with exhibitions that were critical of the West. We scared a lot of people off, when we meant to set a new precedent."

Alex Nemerov echoes his mentor's sentiments:

It was both a spectacular failure and a spectacular success, both in ways we couldn't have imagined. It was a failure in the sense that the show was designed to open up discourse within museums, to encourage other museums to launch critical exhibitions about works of art. What it ended up doing, I'm afraid, is creating this atmosphere of self-censorship, wherein museums saw the horrors that could befall one if one presented a critical show, and consequently [they] became even more staid and conservative and resolutely uncontroversial in their exhibitions. The success, though, clearly has to do with the fact that we went into this show hoping to change the discourse about western art.

Elizabeth Johns focuses more exclusively on the impact on the NMAA itself: "I think the museum will never again be able to do anything with the unquestioned authority with which the curators put this exhibition on. I don't think that the museum has put on a bold show since. For at least a generation, no one in that museum will dare to do anything that even approaches revisionist history." Julie Schimmel concurs: "I think it made it more cautious. I *know* it made it more cautious." What Betsy Broun touts as a "golden moment," then, quickly lost its brilliance for other observers.

An interesting measure of how a museum recoups after battle is the saga of *Revisiting the White City: American Art at the 1893 World's Fair,* mounted at the National Museum of American Art in 1993. The idea was to re-create and critically evaluate the salon-style exhibition held a hundred years earlier. The larger story of how this late-twentieth-century exhibit evolved is especially engaging when recounted by Diane Dillon.

Like some of the contributors to *The West as America,* Dillon started working as a summer intern at the NMAA in 1988 while she was a graduate student in art history. Planning for *Revisiting the White City* was just beginning then. (Incidentally, the 1893 World's Fair [the Columbian Exposition] celebrated the four-hundredth anniversary of Columbus's arrival in the New World; this show was the NMAA's recognition of the five-hundredth anniversary, during a much more politically critical time.) Dillon proposed an organizing scheme for the exhibition that Smithsonian staffers accepted. She moved to Washington to work on every phase of the show: she attended all the meetings with the show's designers, researched individual works of

art, wrote wall labels, and traveled around the country to evaluate the
condition of works to be loaned. Dillon is the "deep throat"of this
tale, the ultimate insider.

Dillon claims that no one felt ill at ease with her ideas until the
controversy broke over *The West as America*. That struggle changed
everything:

> They were uncomfortable with the idea that paintings can have any
> kind of ideological force. After *The West as America,* they were eager
> to go back to this notion that these paintings could be transcendent
> signifiers, and they really wanted this show just to be celebratory,
> that this World's Fair was this great achievement for American art
> and architecture, a great sign of our cultural progress.

In other words, Dillon claims that the museum became excessively circumspect, terrified of going out on a theoretical limb:

> I had presented a much more complicated narrative about the ways
> that these paintings participated in the fair's larger discourses about
> race, gender inequality, and class tensions. And all of those things
> were verboten. They were especially concerned with any sense that
> these works somehow could be connected with the larger capitalist
> enterprise that was the World's Fair. The whole marketplace charac-
> ter of the event somehow tainted the purity of the art.[36]

Like her predecessors who worked on *The West as America*, Dillon
felt that her ideas were mainstream. She was not, she insists, proposing "some wacko theory." Moreover, she cites the Chicago Historical
Society's version of the same material, *Grand Illusions: Chicago's World
Fair of 1893.* Dillon argues, "They had no fear. They talked very up
front about the incredible racial tensions at the fair, the controversies
over representation of women's work, and the fair as a publicity machine. All these things the Smithsonian think just were not museum
issues."

After *The West as America,* NMAA officials decided to vet every
catalogue essay through every curator. That created what seemed like
an impossible situation to Dillon, with continuous demands for revisions. As a direct result, Dillon wrote five drafts of her catalogue
essay over eighteen months. She believed that the last version "was
going to fly." But Dillon was not able to reach an acceptable compromise with the curators, including Betsy Broun, who assumed more

control over the project as it progressed. Dillon was ordered to make changes she did not feel she could: "I decided I didn't want to publish something under my name that's so watered down it's actually historically misleading. And they said, 'Fine, we'll just do without it.'"[37]

Dillon says that after she was dismissed ("It's like you immediately become bad meat," she laments) Broun took the introductory sections of her essay and rewrote them, "dumbing them down." They became the wall texts in the exhibition, and accompanied a color plate section in the catalogue, substituting for the missing essay. Dillon was disappointed at how she was treated, as well as by the outcome of the show. "I thought the show was a skeleton of what it should have been," Dillon reflects. "It seemed completely hollowed out to me." She sums up her experiences in this way:

> I wouldn't have signed on if I didn't think it had the potential to be a critical show. But in the end, they weren't willing to do that, I think, for fear of any reactions from Capitol Hill or elsewhere. They just wanted something that would be safe, noncontroversial. They wanted to have pictures that people would like, that were honoring both the individual pictures and the fair as this celebratory event in American culture, which is a completely ahistoricist reading. And completely goes against 99.9 percent of the published scholarship.

How does Betsy Broun characterize her museum since it attracted such intense scrutiny? "People want to believe that somehow there's been a chilling effect. I do not feel that," she insists. Broun affirms that she has had terrific backing from the Smithsonian administration in support of the NMAA's programs. Nevertheless, Broun corroborates what Dillon reports about increased vetting: "We make sure that all of our catalogue manuscripts and all of our label copy is reviewed by an ad hoc committee that includes both academics and general public readers. We want to know that what we're saying makes sense and is said in a way that's persuasive to the man-on-the-street, as well as Professor Somebody." Gatekeeping, in other words, is taken more seriously than it once was.

Broun argues that Diane Dillon's essay "just never really was professional enough that we felt we could publish it," even though "she may prefer to interpret that as pulling punches." Broun does admit, however, that the catalogue they issued was weaker than it might have been, leaving important ground uncovered. In NMAA curator

Bill Truettner's estimation, *Revisiting the White City* was indeed "watered down," a "tragic sort of misfire." He feels that he now operates in a more restrictive working environment where "people are encouraged less to follow new ideas."[38]

Once such a perception has taken root, many ensuing experiences seem to confirm it. For example, the art historian Martin Berger submitted a manuscript on Thomas Eakins to *American Art*, the scholarly journal produced by the NMAA. The article focuses on the painting *Swimming* (1885), which features a group of nude men. Berger discusses industrialization, the creation of community, and masculinity. But the homosocial or possibly homoerotic themes in this work are barely addressed in his analysis. Eakins's sexual proclivities have been the subject of much speculation in recent years; tantalizing hints have come from his personal life and his work. Yet Berger's interests are hardly sensationalistic. However, he was surprised and dismayed when his manuscript was sent out to eight reviewers over approximately two years before it was eventually accepted for publication. Berger feels that the NMAA was playing it extremely safe in this instance, just as the exhibitions it now presents strike him as being conservative. He believes that the museum has been "trying to drain politics out of its shows."[39]

This example confirms Diane Dillon's worst fears. Remarking on her colleague's experience, Dillon feels this represents "the overcautiousness, the zealousness to make sure that any piece of writing published by the museum is not going to offend anyone." Moreover, Dillon rejects the NMAA's official rationalizations for now operating as it does: "The museum's excuse about being so cautious with catalogues is that they want them to be user-friendly, and accessible to the public, and noncontroversial, because they publish their more cutting-edge scholarship in the journal. But Martin's experience contradicts that claim. That's the free, scholarly voice, and the catalogues are the more conservative, mainstream publications." The perception, then, is that being the subject of intense public controversies changed the National Museum of American Art. The extent to which these claims are true is somewhat incidental, however. When perceptions become corroborated and shared, they become reality. Controversies have indeed affected people's assessment of this museum and its activities.

■

Elizabeth Johns reports an interesting experience that illustrates how the precise timing of *The West as America*'s debut, combined with the place where it appeared, contributed to setting off such a controversial response. She recalls, "After this uproar, I had occasion to visit a friend in Los Angeles. We went to the Gene Autry Western Heritage Museum, paid something like $6.50 or $8.50, and in the very first three rooms of the permanent exhibition found that the move westward was motivated by greed, involved genocide of virtually the entire Native American population, and most people who went were ne'er-do-wells from the East who wanted to make money." She continues, "Nobody complained. Nobody picketed. But a government-funded institution could not say even one-tenth of that without getting called on it."[40] This was most especially true for the National Museum of American Art, as a branch of the revered Smithsonian Institution, during a time of intense patriotic fervor, and when artists and museums were increasingly suspect as makers and presenters of offensive, blasphemous, obscene, and even anti-American work.

6

Battle Royal

The Final Mission of the *Enola Gay*

Art is supposed to take sides.
Should Picasso have given equal time
to the other side to balance *Guernica?*
—Jonathan Reynolds,
Stonewall Jackson's House

MANY OF THE same issues swirling about *The West as America* exploded three years later at another Smithsonian museum. That was when the National Air and Space Museum (NASM) made public its plans to exhibit the B-29 bomber *Enola Gay*, on the fiftieth anniversary of its bombing of Hiroshima, Japan. (The plane was named after Commander Paul W. Tibbetts, Jr.'s mother.)[1] The initial planning proposal was prepared in February 1991, just prior to the opening of *The West as America*. Its working title was *The Crossroads: The End of World War II, the Atomic Bomb and the Origins of the Cold War*. However, veterans had begun campaigning for display of the plane soon after Dr. Martin O. Harwit, a Cornell University astrophysicist, became the NASM's director in 1987. (The museum, which opened in 1976, is the most visited in the world.)

Harwit and members of his staff had held numerous discussions with veterans, military historians, academic historians, and others in anticipation of such an exhibition. He envisioned presenting a section of the plane alongside pictures of the damage it caused, artifacts from ground zero, plus documents and scholarship pertinent to the decision to use this new weapon. Harwit's first title was *From Guernica to Hiroshima—Bombing in World War II*, addressing the progressive escalation of bombing of civilian populations from 1937 to 1945.

FIG. 16. Commander Paul W. Tibbetts, Jr., and the *Enola Gay*, c. 1945. U.S. Air Force Photo Collection (USAF Neg. No. A-59468 C). Photograph courtesy of Stephen P. Aubin, Air Force Association.

Controversy eventually engulfed all the proposed elements, besides the plane itself. One can only imagine the firestorm of protest that could have been set off by such a title, paralleling fascist atrocities with American actions.

The work of the critic Tom Engelhardt provides a conceptual bridge between these two Smithsonian exhibitions. Engelhardt describes a "victory culture," a set of beliefs that dominated American thinking since colonial times. A central precept was that savages—be they Indians or the Japanese in their sneak attack on Pearl Harbor—continuously provoked conflicts that Americans felt compelled to respond to, typically with vanquishing force. This and related ideas, which remained strong through the 1950s, nurtured the baby boomers. They permeated popular culture: the new medium of television, toys and games, even children's bed sheets and wallpaper all symbolically captured and relived the frontier experience and the Old West. But Engelhardt argues that post–World War II America, entwined in an anxious Cold War, also experienced "triumphalist despair." By 1975—post-Vietnam and post-Watergate—the victory culture became antiquated.[2]

What was left in its wake? A society searching for a new identity. The public may temporarily settle on some replay of the past, such as the military strike against Saddam Hussein and the celebrations of his defeat held in 1991. But mostly there is a generational split between those who still cling to the victory culture and those who have adopted a critical, postmodernist sensibility toward the world.

Postmodernism is ascendant. It is fueled in part by the immense disenchantment of baby boomers, caused by the gap between their childhood heroes and the cataclysmic social, political, and military experiences of the 1960s and '70s. But proponents of the victory culture are not all dead. Not yet. They mobilized in 1989, for example, when the self-declared radical student "Dread" Scott Tyler placed an American flag on the floor as part of an art installation at the School of the Art Institute of Chicago. Veterans led the protests. For one thing, they repeatedly folded the flag and ceremoniously placed it on a shelf in the gallery. It was reinstated in each instance by the artist's supporters and gallery personnel. Opponents also staged two raucous street demonstrations, attracting thousands of angry people.

During the same period, a movement of zealous politicians and grassroots enthusiasts sought to amend the U.S. Constitution with an anti–flag desecration measure. These events demonstrated that patriotism could be as much a hot-button issue as gender, race, and religion, even though many people assume that it is a passé notion.[3]

Since the U.S. bombing of the Japanese cities of Hiroshima and Nagasaki in 1945, we have become a nation split between what one observer recently termed the "culture of consensus" and the "culture of dissent."[4] A Gallup poll released in the midst of the NASM controversy confirms this. The pollsters uncovered a clear generational divide: 57 percent of those under the age of fifty opposed the bomb, while 55 percent of those over the age of fifty said they would have dropped it. Moreover, 60 percent of the Americans surveyed did not know that Harry S. Truman was the president who ordered the nuclear bombing of Japan. And 49 percent felt they would have tried some other way to force the Japanese to surrender. These findings lend quantitative support to what we might suspect: this event, its urgency and its significance, has faded in the public's memory. What is a milestone in some people's lives blurs into near oblivion for many others.[5]

When Bill Truettner and Alex Nemerov reflected on their experiences as organizers of the earlier Smithsonian exhibit *The West as America*, they observed, "in a culturally diverse country it is no longer possible to present . . . an unproblematic version of 'our' America."[6] But that's exactly what many people long for. For example, the Illinois Veterans of Foreign Wars passed out a handbill during the protests against Scott Tyler's flag installation entitled "You Remember the REAL America." It nostalgically recalled an Old West sort of world where "men were men" and where the sense of entitlement by others was not epidemic. The handbill thus heralded a time before the empowerment movements of the 1950s, '60s, and '70s, which upended the status quo. It captured one generation's sense of loss of better, "simpler" times in the face of another generation's demands and preferences.

Whether generational conflict is literally one of age or of allegiance to a particular worldview, it was central to the wrangling over both *The West as America* and *The Crossroads*. Critics of *The Crossroads* frequently blamed the tumultuous 1960s as the source of everything troublesome today, including the so-called revisionist history re-flected in the exhibition. "New Left ideological ditchwater," screamed an editorial. "Karl Marx or Jane Fonda would have signed off on that . . . ," trumpeted an article.[7]

This battle was also shaped by America's postwar relationship with Japan. Massive American support helped rebuild Japan. Forty years after V-J Day, it had become an economic powerhouse. Such a power-house, in fact, that in the late 1980s and early 1990s, economically flush Japanese gobbled up Rockefeller Center, Columbia Pictures, MCA/Universal, the Seattle Mariners, and chunks of choice real es-tate in New York, Los Angeles, and other major U.S. cities. People nervously joked that families would be forced to start a new tradition in New York City, trekking to "Mitsubishi Center" at Christmas time to view the giant holiday tree. The Japanese also snared scores of masterpieces in an overheated art market, such as Van Gogh's *Portrait of Dr. Gachet* for a whopping $82.5 million in 1990. Japan represented an economic juggernaut—capable, it seemed, of superseding Ameri-can dominance in the world marketplace.

As competition and tensions increased between the countries, so did hate crimes and anti-Asian defamation. There was the frequently invoked 1982 murder of Vincent Chin by two white, unemployed auto workers in Detroit, who mistook him for Japanese. The incident became emblematic for American fears of being overtaken by this Asian behemoth. In 1990 Pat Choate published the conspiratorial book *Agents of Influence*, alleging that the Japanese spent hundreds of millions of dollars to favorably lobby American public opinion. In 1992 Senator Ernest Hollings (D-South Carolina) reacted angrily when Japanese leaders suggested that American workers were lazy and lacked a work ethic. He "joked" to factory workers in his home state that they "should draw a mushroom cloud and put under it: 'Made in America by lazy and illiterate Americans and tested in Japan.'"[8] For a few weeks afterwards, this triggered strong reactions, here and abroad.

In 1993 the movie *Rising Sun* sparked sharp criticism from Asian American groups. The *New York Times* reviewer Vincent Canby protested that "Not since Pearl Harbor has Japan-bashing been such big and popular business." In the movie, a murder mystery, Japanese businessmen appear to control everyone in Los Angeles: the mayor, police, professors, journalists, and even members of Congress. Two scenes in particular riled the ethnic critics. In one, a young Japanese playboy (and suspect in the case) audaciously samples sushi from the bare breasts of one nude Caucasian woman, and licks saki off another. In the second scene, a group of black homeboys surround some Japanese thugs in their car and vandalize it. A character played by Wesley Snipes observes the action and quips, "Rough neighborhoods may be America's last advantage." The Media Action Network for Asian-Americans feared that the movie could incite racial violence and demanded (unsuccessfully) that a disclaimer be included "asking audiences not to assume 'all Japanese people are trying to take over America.'"[9] Significantly, the opening scene is of a grainy video playing in a karaoke bar. The tune it accompanies? The cowboy classic "Don't Fence Me In."

Interestingly, the Japanese bubble had burst by the time *The Crossroads*—subsequently named *The Last Act: The Atomic Bomb and the End of World War II*—was being debated. Japanese corporate executives who had speculated wildly in the art market were stuck with inventories of grossly overpriced work, for example. In late December 1992, a joint *New York Times*/CBS News/Tokyo Broadcasting System poll revealed that Japanese confidence in their economic strength was slipping, just as Americans' confidence in their own was starting to rise.[10] Nevertheless, the perception of a contemporary Japanese threat lingered. An international relationship that had once been cordial and stable was now unsettled. These strains activated racist fears in both countries. They also helped shape the perceptions Americans and Japanese had of history as well.

The amount of commentary generated by this exhibition is unprecedented. The *Journal of American History* devoted approximately three-quarters of its space in one issue to this matter, reflecting the concerns of professional historians over exhibitions, history's many interpretations, and the increasingly public dialogue over how historians do their work.[11] Articles have appeared in anthologies about museums.[12] Books have been published: a collection of essays; a reproduction of the original exhibition script, along with an overview and criticism; and an exhaustive account by former NASM director Martin Harwit.[13] The Air Force Association (AFA), an independent, nonprofit lobbying and educational group that was in the forefront of critiquing the museum, compiled five substantial volumes of material. These included copies of news releases, letters, memos, reports, and news articles from around the country; script analyses; the first version of the script; a chronology of events; and other key records. Stacked up, they are bigger than the Manhattan telephone directory and the Manhattan yellow pages combined.

In major respects, this was the "next act" in the drama that commenced at the NMAA in 1991 with *The West as America*. In both instances, debates familiar among historians proved to be inflammatory when they were exposed to an atmosphere of impassioned public opinion. In both instances, the media stoked the fires. Politicians who had already censured cultural expressions found a new opportunity to grandstand here. The critics of *The Last Act*—military veterans and others—were more persistent in this episode than in any other museum controversy. They demonstrated *ganbaru*, a Japanese term for the sort of stick-to-itiveness personified by Shoichi Yokoi, a soldier who hid in the jungles of Guam for twenty-seven years after V-J Day, in essence privately carrying on the war.[14] They stubbornly embraced the standard narrative of the Good War; its atomic conclusion was a merciful end for *both* sides. In their retelling, the *Enola Gay* and the bomb were not weapons of war, but bearers of peace. It is a stance that forces its backers to replay the same brittle film loop over and over in their minds, and precludes them from even looking at any new versions.

Ken Ringle, whose reportage was central to the controversy over *The West as America*, devoted his attention to this story as well. Once again, his approach to these matters was duplicated by many others. In a lengthy page one story in the *Washington Post*, Ringle first introduces Grayford C. Payne, a local seventy-four-year-old survivor of the Bataan death march and five Japanese prison camps. Payne is close to tears at one point. Ringle follows that emotional personal testimony with the perspective of the forty-three-year-old co-curator of the Smithsonian exhibition, Michael Neufeld. This man's age automatically signals that his entire life has been lived post–World War II. His knowledge of the war is secondary, coming only from books. The implication: experience confers legitimacy. Case closed.[15]

Ringle's strategy and arguments are familiar: they recapitulate the approach of the acclaimed writer Paul Fussell in his essay "Thank God for the Atom Bomb" (1981). A twenty-one-year-old, war-weary lieutenant in 1945, Fussell belonged to a unit slated for the projected invasion of the Japanese home islands. He and his comrades cried when they heard that the atomic bombs had been dropped. Understandably, they shed tears of relief, tears of realization: they now had futures. These men were actually there; they'd experienced the danger, the anxiety, the muck, and the carnage up close.

Fussell's perspective can be condensed into several axioms. *Critics of the decision to use the bomb are too young to understand*. When he notes that one of his academic antagonists was ten years old in 1945, he does so to vaporize the man's credibility. *Critics are too distant from the action*. "In general," he says, "the principle is, the farther from the scene of horror, the easier the talk." Once again, either critics were youths at the time (maybe not even born yet) or they were in service, but deployed behind the front lines. *Fighting men are the salt of the earth*. Their perceptions are immediate, their memories not biased by elitist theorizing. "The testimony of experience," Fussell argues, "has tended to come from rough diamonds." *The purpose of history is to remember things* exactly *as they were*. Take a snapshot and preserve the moment. Don't interpret it, don't place it in context. "Understanding the past requires pretending that you don't know the present," Fussell argues.[16]

In Fussell's view, you're either pedigreed by ordeal, seasoned by experience, or you're not. Frankly, he doesn't wish to hear from the latter group. He cuts off the possibility of dialogue before it begins. To his mind, only one perspective is authentic. Yet his authoritarianism makes a reader wonder: what is Fussell so frightened of? If his account is indeed so substantial and unassailable, why not place it next to different narratives? Shouldn't it emerge the clear-cut victor? Fussell's arguments disguise a dread that this might not be such a black-and-white matter. Maybe there *are* additional arguments to explore.

The "new western history" is akin, for want of a better term, to revisionist interpretations of the decision to drop the atomic bomb in 1945. But there is an important distinction: historians have been closely reexamining the issue of the atomic bomb for a much longer time, their enterprise boosted each time documents are declassified or otherwise become available for study. Gar Alperovitz is commonly cited for initiating the revisionist approach. In books such as *Atomic Diplomacy, Hiroshima, and Potsdam: The Use of the Atomic Bomb and the*

American Confrontation with the Soviet Union (1965) and *The Decision to Use the Atomic Bomb and the Architecture of an American Myth* (1995), Alperovitz has argued that the American desire to gain political leverage over the Soviet Union, not just the urgency of ending the war and saving American lives, influenced Truman's decision to use the bomb.

Over the past thirty years, many others have followed this lead to explore other factors contributing to this momentous decision. It is important to note, however, that "revisionism" is a very tricky term here. Several observers during the *Last Act* controversy pointed out that for twenty years after the war's end, military leaders and civilians—including General Eisenhower, Herbert Hoover, and John Foster Dulles—voiced doubts about the bomb's necessity without being censured. Moreover, in 1970 Senator Barry Goldwater excluded the *Enola Gay* from his definition of "historic aircraft" that the NASM should display.[17] Today's "revisionists" could have been called mainstream once, if anyone bothered to label them at all, just as today's "traditionalists" might have been chastised in the past for *their* partial and partisan recall of certain events.

The Last Act included documents such as a top secret report from Henry L. Stimson, secretary of war to President Truman in April 1945, raising concerns about the postwar ramifications of the bomb's use (declassified in 1973), and a page from Truman's diary in July 1945, noting that the target of an atomic bomb should be soldiers, not women and children. According to the NASM's former director, Harwit, documents declassified as recently as 1993 were slated for display. NASM officials intended for such documents to establish the historical context of the bomb's use, rather than to arrogantly reinterpret the decision with the clarity of hindsight. Nevertheless, conservative commentators such as Thomas Sowell blasted "politically correct" "tenured guerrillas with pensions" acting as "Monday morning quarterbacks," while the AFA chief of media relations, Jack Giese, characterized the exhibition as "looking at 1945 military behavior with 1994 eyes."[18]

But Martin Harwit lobs those criticisms back at the show's critics. From his perspective, they were the ones whose perceptions were skewed by the passage of time: "The American Legion and the veterans really had been aroused only through the Air Force Association's attacks on us. And what they and the veterans were doing was to look with the sort of hindsight that looking at one's youth and seeing the golden moments produces." Furthermore, Harwit felt that inclusion of documents from the time would augment perceptions shaped not only by selective memory but by certain inherent limitations of access as well:

> Plus, they were looking at it from the point of view of information that was being made public. In wartime there's a hefty dose of propaganda, and a hefty dose of misinformation, because obviously you don't want any of your enemies to know what you're actually doing. And so what you read in the newspapers, and what you hear on the radio at that time, is very different from what is actually going on.[19]

Harwit didn't wish to deny the veterans' experiences. He sought to tell everyone as complete a story as possible, bolstered by the hard copy of that time.

The yield of all the years of postwar historical research was very much in evidence in the proposed script for *The Last Act*. Seven "Historical Controversies" reiterated the major themes of this scholarship:

"Would the Bomb Have Been Dropped on the Germans?"
"Did the United States Ignore the Japanese Peace Initiative?"
"Would the War Have Ended Sooner if the United States Had Guaranteed the Emperor's Position?"
"How Important Was the Soviet Factor in the 'Decision to Drop the Bomb'?"
"Was a Warning or Demonstration Possible?"
"Was the Invasion Inevitable if the Atomic Bomb Had Not Been Dropped?"
"Was the Decision to Drop the Bomb Justified?"[20]

In other words, these queries broached the possibility that racism, postwar diplomatic strategies, and inflated projections of casualty statistics factored into this event—along with the earnest desire to end the war with a minimum of additional American casualties.[21] Like the organizers of *The West as America*, these curators were increasing the complexity of their subject, not simplifying it. They weren't settling for stock explanations. But Donald C. Rehl, a retired B-29 pilot from Indiana who was one of the veterans who pressured the NASM to restore the *Enola Gay*, pleaded to director

Harwit in a letter, "Please tell me why there is a problem deciding in what historical context the *Enola Gay* should be displayed?" Two years later, seven members of the House of Representatives also strongly objected to the NASM's contextualizing approach, protesting in a letter to Smithsonian secretary I. Michael Heyman that this was "one of the most morally unambiguous events of the 20th century."[22] To honor that perspective would mean to nearly forgo examination.

In theory, two very different methods could be used in this exhibition. One would emphasize emotion. The goal? To feel the pain of U.S. servicemen, empathize or sympathize with them, and honor their bravery and sacrifice. The other would stress rational investigation, to figure out why people were in anguished situations in the first place. The goal here would be a deep understanding of why something occurred. The NASM aimed to activate both strategies. But in the end, Secretary Heyman deferred to the critics' demands: he chose to strip the exhibition of serious discourse. "The aircraft speaks for itself in this exhibit," he declared after an eviscerated display opened.[23]

Journalists besides Ken Ringle, such as Richard Grenier and Charles Krauthammer, launched similar critiques of both *The West as America* and *The Last Act*. Once again, headline writers outdid themselves to grab readers' attention. Military references prevailed: "Air and Space Exhibit Gets Flak Even before Takeoff," "Smithsonian's *Enola Gay* Exhibit in Cross Fire of Vets and Survivors," and "*Enola Gay* Stirs Nuclear Fallout at Smithsonian."[24] Writers could not resist using the word "bomb." Repeatedly.[25] And as NASM officials first reshaped and then drastically scaled back the venture because of intense criticism, articles characterized it as "torpedoed," its "mission aborted," its "wings clipped."[26]

But beyond such preciousness, some headlines betrayed deeper concerns. "An Indelicate Balance," in the *Tampa Tribune*, for example, signals a much-debated factor: vets, politicians, and others felt that these curators had stacked the presentation against the heroism of American fighting men, against the sincerity of the president, against America itself.[27] In particular, they were infuriated by this passage in the original script: "For most Americans this war was fundamentally different from the one waged against Germany and Italy—it was a

FIG. 17. Henry Payne, *Natural Born Killers* editorial cartoon, 1995. Reprinted by permission of United Features Syndicate, Inc.

war of vengeance. For most Japanese it was a war to defend their unique culture against Western imperialism."

On the face of it, it does seem as if the curators are skewing their presentation and sympathizing with the Japanese. But that is largely an illusion. The NASM director, Martin Harwit, sent the director of the Air Force Association a copy of the first draft of the script to elicit his response and input, but advised the AFA that the document was not intended for public scrutiny at this stage. Harwit feels it was a betrayal of confidence that the AFA published this fragment in its *Air Force Magazine*. What Harwit did not realize was that the AFA was leaked a copy of the script some two weeks *before*: "A lot of stuff leaked out of there," reports Stephen P. Aubin, the AFA's director of communications. "It was like [a] sieve, which suggested to us that there was a lot of disaffection among parts of the staff. And it would generally take a circuitous route. It might go from over there to some of our contacts in other places, which would eventually end up back to us. But we had a pretty steady paper flow throughout the process."[28]

The passage in the script appeared to imply that Americans were racist and spiteful, while the Japanese were honorably protecting themselves. Although the museum removed these words in later versions, the passage developed a robust afterlife: it was quoted over and over as representing the museum's viewpoint. Abstracting elements from their context is a proven ploy of ideologues. It certainly worked in this instance, effectively distorting the curators' intentions. But consider the excerpt in context:

> In 1931 the Japanese Army occupied Manchuria; six years later it invaded the rest of China. From 1937 to 1945, the Japanese Empire would be constantly at war.
>
> Japanese expansionism was marked by naked aggression and extreme brutality. The slaughter of tens of thousands of Chinese in Nanking in 1937 shocked the world. Atrocities by Japanese troops included brutal mistreatment of civilians, forced laborers and prisoners of war, and biological experiments on human victims.
>
> In December 1941, Japan attacked U.S. bases at Pearl Harbor, Hawaii, and launched other surprise assaults against Allied territories in the Pacific. Thus began a wider conflict marked by extreme bitterness. *For most Americans this war was fundamentally different from the one waged against Germany and Italy—it was a war of vengeance. For most Japanese, it was a war to defend their unique culture against Western imperialism.* As the war approached its end in 1945, it appeared to both sides that it was a fight to the finish. (Emphasis added)[29]

This makes it clear that curators were not glossing over Japanese offenses, nor were they excusing Japan's conduct. They were, however, seeking to understand the outlooks of both sides. Here's what "balance" meant to Tom Crouch, the chair of the aeronautics department at the NASM: "There were people who think it is fair to tell this story from 30,000 feet. And I think that's fine. But I don't think it's an honest telling of the story. You have to have the stuff on the ground, too."[30]

The issue of "balance" resonated in various ways throughout this debate. The phrases "war of vengeance" and "defending a unique culture" achieved mantra status in the media and among opponents to *The Last Act*. One other element did too. The *Wall Street Journal* roundly reproached the NASM's proposed presentation in a 1994 editorial. One part it condemned was the curatorial characterization of kamikaze pilots as "'youths, their bodies overflowing with life.' Of the youth and life of the Americans who fought and bled in the Pacific there is no mention." But Harwit recounts that this was a direct quote from a surviving Japanese pilot, not the curators speaking. Once again, the curators included it to represent the Japanese mindset, in order to convey the tenacity of their fighting.[31]

Ken Ringle quoted this editorial in his own feature in the *Washington Post*. He cited as well the *Journal*'s description of this passage as "oozing romanticism." Ringle's repetition of these (unsigned) sentiments gave them validation and amplified their resonance. They "confirmed" suspicions of bias. But Harwit emphasized that balance meant offsetting the size and gleam of the newly restored *Enola Gay* by presenting evidence of the human costs of the bombing. "To avoid the perception of cold, heartless militarism," he wrote, "we needed to infuse awareness that the bomb had caused damage and suffering."[32]

Some tiny objects to be loaned by museums in Hiroshima and Nagasaki upset the critics' equilibrium. Scorched clothing. A watch with hands forever frozen at the moment of the bomb's impact. A schoolgirl's lunch pail. (Its carbonized rice and peas survive; her corpse was never found.) Critics understood how these things would tug at the hearts of viewers and potentially distract them from fully embracing the heroism and necessity of this military exploit.[33]

A cover story in *American Journalism Review* turned the tables in this matter, thoroughly faulting the media's treatment of this story. In a basic respect, this critique rests on one of the central tenets of media criticism: the media prefer the drama of events over a close analysis of issues. Bitter controversy, angered and menacing politicians, appeals to old-time heroics by the AFA's publicity machine are simple to frame as stories. Digesting and summarizing thirty years or more of in-depth, nuanced critical history, on the other hand, is not only daunting, it is unrealistic when journalists are faced with incessant deadlines.

Journalists chose the path of least resistance. According to the authors Tony Capaccio and Uday Mohan, journalists largely accepted the exhibition critics at their word and failed to thoroughly check out their claims. That's how out-of-context statements persist and prevail. For all the alleged "liberal bias" in the media, the mainstream media were generally eager to take the patriotic high road in this

case. Moreover, a throng of specialized publications took the oppo-
nents' message directly to a number of interest groups. Articles ap-
peared in the *Officer*, the *World War II Times, Inside the Pentagon*, the
Retired Officer Magazine, and the AFA-sponsored *Air Force Magazine*.
The controversy was also reported by the *American Legion, Air Force
Times*, the *Jewish Veteran, Veteran's Voice, American Legion Auxiliary,
Tennessee VFW News*, and the *Sunflower Legionnaire. Air Classics* and
General Aviation News and Flyer picked it up, as did *Aviation History*. It
even became a *Popular Mechanics* cover story.

Not only did the replication of claims seem to automatically confirm them; it intensified people's anger and in some cases moved
them to vent directly to the Smithsonian. In fact, at one juncture the
museum was receiving over a hundred letters a week. The exhibition
co-curator Tom D. Crouch describes feeling "enervated" coming to
work each day to face fresh articles in the papers and magazines, and
the mounting stacks of irate correspondence. (Of the letters, he remembers, "Five percent were supporting us, and 95 percent were essentially calling for blood. Or abusive, at least abusive and angry.")
Capaccio and Mohan conclude, "The controversy was largely fueled
by media accounts that uncritically accepted the conventional ration-
ale for the bomb, ignored contrary historical evidence, and reinforced
the charge that the planned exhibit was a pro-Japanese, anti-American tract." Michael Neufeld sums matters up with more intensity:
"The entire media was acting like a lynch mob, with their cries for
blood."[34]

In the struggle over *The West as America*, Betsy Broun recalls, "We
were a little uncertain how far to go in defending ourselves, when to
answer back, when to let things go by. There was a camp in the museum and in the public affairs office at the Smithsonian that said, 'You
don't want to go to war with people who buy their ink by the barrel.'"
This, after all, was a new experience for National Museum of American Art staffers. Broun thinks differently now: "I have come to feel
that's not right. When errors appear in the press, you need to respond
immediately, frankly and freely . . . I think we were a little too inclined to huddle behind closed doors."

Martin Harwit too failed to mount an effective counterattack. Contributing to his reticence was a congressional investigation of the secretary of energy being conducted at about the same time *The Last Act* was
being debated, an inquiry that upbraided her for actively trying to cull

the favor of the press for her agency. That was very much on Harwit's mind. Moreover, "If we had spent even a fraction of what AFA did, Congress would have been down on me like a ton of bricks."

As Stephen Aubin remembers it, "We would keep waiting for the counterattack. Because we were hitting hard. We were hitting them right between the eyes. And you know what? It never came." Being a media professional, Aubin had certain expectations. But these opponents were mismatched:

> I think he [Harwit] could have given us a tougher fight. I think he still would have lost because basically I think the issues on his side were unwinnable. We had succeeded early on at defining the issue. And there was no way for him to undo the damage. But we were surprised, day in and day out. And we were very cautious, never cocky throughout this.

The AFA's definition of the issues kept the NASM on the defensive, continually blocking and dodging strong blows. An unnamed NASM official was quoted as saying, "We believed in rational discussion. We didn't want to get into a knife fight." But different ground rules applied here. As Michael Neufeld sees it, "This was a campaign. I mean, that's impossible to miss. And it was very skillfully handled. They [the AFA] did a tremendously good job of public relations, and we did a very poor job of public relations."[35]

One additional newspaper headline merits mention. It too betrays some deeper meanings. "History Upheld," crowed the *American Legion* in August 1995. This was seven months after the NASM had abandoned its exhibition plans after curators had developed five versions of its script. *The Last Act* was originally envisioned as a 5,500-square-foot exhibit, including the plane; photo documentation of the Pacific war, the bombing, and its aftermath; and discussions of the scientific, diplomatic, and human dimensions of these momentous events. But in the end it was reduced to a display of the *Enola Gay*'s fuselage, tail section, two engines, and a propeller; one video featuring crew members and Commander Paul W. Tibbets, Jr., and another documenting the restoration of the plane; photographs of the development of the B-29; and newspaper headlines the day after the bomb was dropped.

Who can fail to be moved by the words of one veteran who appealed to Representative Sidney Yates (D-Illinois)? He wrote,

> I have told the Smithsonian that it is my intention to see the *Enola Gay* proudly restored and displayed and that I intend, once again, to see Gen. Paul Tibbetts sit in the pilot's cockpit . . . Tibbetts and I are now [respectively 75 and] 73. We do not have much time and we deserve better than to have the Smithsonian take this occasion away from us.

Here is a man facing his mortality, longing for one final confirmation of his identity and self-worth. He was one of a group of vets Martin Harwit referred to as "only five old men," a self-characterization taken directly from one of the many letters this vet and the others addressed to the museum and to various officials. This same man lamented that from his vantage point, intellectuals "mock everything."[36]

Veterans demanded respect in this case. They cheered their victory when the exhibition was scaled back to the B-29 and little else. But their elation was tempered by the recognition that this was possibly their "last hurrah," or to borrow an image from *The West as America*, their "last stand." As Martin Harwit reflects, the Smithsonian's National Museum of American History displayed an atomic bomb casing on the fortieth anniversary, but no debate ensued. But fiftieth anniversaries are a bigger milestone and are much more symbolically weighted. Moreover, Harwit believes that many veterans were still in the workforce during that earlier anniversary and were now retired. They were in strong communication with one another. Various veterans' groups were meeting more frequently. Increased leisure time, camaraderie, and nostalgic reflection thus spawned powerful opposition: "I think having that much time, they were able to concentrate on the attack on the exhibition. At other times, they might have hardly read about it in the newspapers, and gone to work the next day."

"A vigorous watch by veterans forced the Smithsonian to answer to the people this time," the *VFW* boasted. But "The disturbing question remains: Who will safeguard the integrity of our history 10, 20, or 50 years from now?" This quote implies that history is an objective record of what happened, that it remains constant and is not to be modified. What results when that theory is put on display? The air force historian Richard Hallion dismissed the exhibition that opened on June 28, 1995, as nothing more than "a beer can with a label."[37]

■

FIG. 18. Photograph of three young Japanese Americans incarcerated at
Jerome, Arkansas, concentration camp during World War II. Japanese American National Museum (ID # 91.139.7), a gift of Masy A. Masuoka, O.D. Used
by permission.

Interestingly, another Smithsonian exhibition, highlighting the relo-
cation of Japanese Americans during World War II, might have been
controversial, yet it provoked only a limited outcry. *A More Perfect
Union,* mounted at the National Museum of American History in
1987 and curated by Tom Crouch, focused on America's "concentration camps," where over 120,000 Americans of Japanese descent were
detained during and after World War II. How to explain the different

reception? A presidential commission had addressed the issue. The redress movement had strong support in Congress, where hearings had been conducted. Influential officials such as Senator Daniel K. Inouye (D-Hawaii) were advocating open discussion of this instance of a sweeping violation of civil liberties. In the end, an official apology was issued and monetary reparations paid to surviving internees in 1988. The few critics of the exhibition who emerged were on the social and political fringe and were not backed up by significant national constituencies.[38] They had little public credibility and attracted faint notice.

Moreover, *A More Perfect Union* predated the redefinition of museums as contested sites. So while this exhibition bypassed American heroics—in fact, it directly confronted American frailties—it was not the lightning rod for criticism that *The Last Act* and so many other exhibitions in the 1990s have become. Had it debuted later, it might very possibly have proven to be more flammable. No one in a position of power showed any interest in defending *The Last Act*, however. No one stepped forward in its defense. In fact, it is difficult to imagine any positive political payoff from becoming an advocate of this exhibition.[39]

Some recent commentators repudiate the notion of "culture wars" as an extreme term, out of touch with most of the general public's reality. But this represents a type of revisionism too. Listen to some more of the columnist Thomas Sowell's diatribe, uttered in the heat of battle:

> It [*The Last Act*] is all of a piece with photographs of a cross immersed in urine, American flags placed on museum floors for people to walk on, and other examples of tax-subsidized "culture." . . . The curriculum, the museum, the movie screen, the art gallery, and even corporate philanthropy are all ideological battlefields—and in most of these institutions, only one side is battling. That is why they are winning."[40]

Granted, Sowell is a well-known commentator, not the man-on-the-street. Granted that as a black conservative he is an anomaly. But Sowell, like many other opinion leaders at the time, was explicitly adopting the language of battle. He and others frightened many people by doing so. If "culture wars" is a hyped-up, overblown, and alarmist concept, hold the partisans on both sides of the noisy cul-

tural conflicts of the late 1980s and 1990s responsible. To be historically accurate, and faithful to the temper of the times, we must dupli-
cate their terms and re-create this context of pronounced struggle.

Not only were some journalists poised to attack this exhibition. Certain politicians were too. For example, Alan Simpson (R-Wyoming),
one of the critics of *The West of America*, secured an inside track in this
controversy. In January 1995 he was named by Bob Dole (R-Kansas),
then the Senate majority leader, to the Smithsonian's governing board
of regents. And consider Representative Dick Armey (R-California),
an outspoken critic of the National Endowment for the Arts. In 1990
he paternalistically compared artist/beneficiaries of government
funding to his own college-aged daughter, declaring that both should
respect his decree "He who pays the bills, sets the standards."
Armey's was an extreme voice, in some respects shouting from the
wilderness when he said this in 1990. By 1995 he had become the
House majority leader.

Armey joined eighty other lawmakers to send a bipartisan letter
to the Smithsonian chairman, I. Michael Heyman, in January 1995,
calling for Martin Harwit's resignation—a week before the regents
were to decide the fate of the exhibit. Among his fellow signatories
were his longtime associate Representative Dana Rohrbacher (R-California), another outspoken foe of government support of the arts,
who once railed that "tax dollars were being 'flushed into the sewer
of fetishes, depravity, and pornography'"; Representative Bob Dor-
nan (R-California), who in 1990 denounced the artist Judy Chicago's
feminist installation *The Dinner Party* as "ceramic 3-D pornography";
and Representative Phil Crane (R-Illinois), who had perennially proposed to abolish the NEA. The "Republican Revolution" of 1994
brought all these men closer to the centers of power than they had
been when they launched their first cultural attacks. Their condemnation of *The Last Act* was simply "business as usual" for them.[41]

Moreover, Ted Stevens (R-Alaska), who was central to the political offensive against *The West as America*, went gunning for the Smithsonian once again as chairman of the Senate Rules and Administration Committee. The senator's credentials to lead the charge were
heralded in several news articles: a member of the Flying Tigers in
China during World War II, Stevens grilled Heyman and the NASM
curator Tom Crouch at a hearing after Harwit had resigned as NASM

director. The purpose of that inquiry was to create guidelines to prevent any future controversies before they erupted publicly. At an earlier session Stevens allowed veterans to testify about their war experiences and present their reactions to the proposed exhibition. (And note: Senator Jesse Helms [R-North Carolina], the most rabid congressional critic of the arts and culture during this era, sat on the same committee.) With its oversight of the Smithsonian, this committee was important: about 75 percent of the Smithsonian's operating budget comes from the federal government.[42]

Representative Sam Johnson (R-Texas), one of two members appointed by House speaker Newt Gingrich to the Smithsonian board of regents, became the point man in the congressional assault on the exhibition. Harwit is particularly critical of Johnson's conduct in this matter, charging that "Heyman had essentially become the lackey, if you want to call it that, on anything that Johnson objected to." Matters came to a boil when Representative Gerald B. Solomon (R-New York) threatened to zero out the Smithsonian's appropriation if the NASM didn't accommodate the wishes of the American Legion, which also emerged as an important critic of the exhibition. "The Smithsonian is getting on my nerves," he griped in a letter he sent to Harwit and copied to Heyman. Harwit concedes, "I'd been in Washington long enough to know that there was no way he could do that, but I think Heyman, who'd only been there four months, probably didn't want to risk it." The upshot? Harwit resigned three months later; he had been increasingly isolated from decision making in the Smithsonian and realized that he had "zero time" left. Moreover, Heyman apologized to Congress, admitting that the exhibition "was out of balance, hence appearing to be historically inaccurate."[43]

Thelma Golden, formerly a curator at the Whitney Museum of American Art, pinpoints a critical difference between working with visual art and working with material culture. This distinction governed the relationship between the NASM and various constituencies. "[I]n an art museum, you work relatively independently. I didn't have to go out and vet all my ideas about black masculinity with all the 'black masculinity experts,' for example [regarding *Black Male*, 1994]." She continues,

> But if you do a show about the *Enola Gay*, and you're a material culture museum, you can't just say, "This is my idea about the *Enola*

Gay." When things are in the public domain, you have to deal with the public domain. You've got people to answer to immediately. You don't own the material. I didn't have to go out and get the "Black Male Council" to say, "Things are fine, go ahead."

But to use Martin Harwit's term, the NASM had "stakeholders" to whom it had to answer. Plenty of them. One of the most important was the Air Force Association. By many definitions, the AFA launched a crusade against this exhibition, although both John T. Correll, the editor in chief of the AFA's *Air Force Magazine,* and Stephen Aubin, the AFA's director of communications, disclaim that perception. They each report that they started to hear rumblings about the proposed exhibition from veterans among their membership. Their initial interest was to check out what was happening and report on it to their constituents. That gradually led them to publish an extensive analysis of the script in *Air Force Magazine,* along with a number of follow-up analyses and articles—an unprecedented, microscopic examination of an exhibition *before* it was mounted. Eventually the AFA also launched an extensive lobbying campaign against the show. According to Steve Aubin, "We tried to work with them [NASM staff] . . . and warned them, 'You're basically slapping a lot of veterans in the face, and people are not going to take kindly to this.'"

Significantly, the NASM and the AFA are twin offspring of the same man. General H. H. "Hap" Arnold was pivotal to the founding of the AFA; he guaranteed that aircraft were conserved after World War II; and he successfully lobbied Congress to establish a Smithsonian branch dedicated to aviation history. The connections between the two enterprises are therefore manifold. The AFA's stake in the outcome of *The Last Act* can be simply put: an exhibition that confirmed the necessity of bombing Japan to end the war could fortify the AFA's lobbying clout in Congress.

On the other hand, an exhibition that raised serious questions about that decision and its aftermath could dampen Congressional enthusiasm for sustaining military appropriations, especially in a newly post–Cold War world. That would have serious financial consequences for the aerospace and defense industries, with which the AFA is closely allied. These are very real concerns for these parties: recent reports indicate that the air force has lost about six hundred pilots to commercial airlines over the past few years, because of the incentives the private sector can offer. Moreover, the air force has experienced a loss of about one-third of its personnel overall, and its allocations for equipment procurement have decreased at a rate of from 60 to 80 percent. So this was not merely a debate about the display of "stuff." It concerned money, power, and prestige as well. According to Martin Harwit, "I think they [the AFA] felt that we should be their shrine in Washington."[44] But this exhibition seriously contradicted a purely memorial impetus.

Some veterans took the idea of a crusade literally: they wished to wrench the *Enola Gay* from the NASM's control. Many vets were upset that the plane had remained in storage over the years and was allowed to deteriorate. To them, this signaled a profound lack of respect on the part of the Smithsonian. Moreover, many vets became extremely annoyed and impatient because of the amount of time it took to restore the plane. The grassroots cast this as an issue of betrayed trust. The professionals—who invested tens of thousands of hours to complete a historically accurate restoration, the most extensive ever tackled by the Smithsonian—insisted that the work had to be done correctly and the time budgeted in respect to concurrent projects. Some zealots were so angry at the NASM that they floated schemes to install the *Enola Gay* elsewhere in the country (e.g., at the Truman Presidential Library). Out of the hands of the infidels, she would be properly commemorated.[45]

Veterans' suspicions of the NASM thus predated the script. The AFA deepened them. Of all the groups that have opposed museum exhibitions, the AFA was the largest, the most politically and media savvy, and the most unrelenting in its campaign. With a membership that is 160,000 strong—but it is not, strictly speaking, a veterans' organization like the American Legion—the AFA has strength, influence, and resources. It is a significantly different type of opponent than the ad hoc coalitions of protesters that have temporarily mobilized against other shows. Lobbying is what the AFA does. It already had confederates in the media and government, and it exploited those contacts.

Martin Harwit primarily blames the AFA for the controversy around *The Last Act*. In his retelling, the AFA "swamped" journalists with material and then directed them to the highlights. Harwit uncovered specific instances of AFA influence, such as a *Time* magazine article critical of the NASM and authoritatively citing an *Air Force*

Magazine analysis of the script as a primary source. AFA personnel liaisoned with members of Congress and their staffs. They appeared frequently in the media. As stated, they sent out volumes and volumes of material—hundreds of copies of reports and compilations.

Harwit speculates that the AFA must have spent $100,000 to wage this aspect of the campaign, in addition to committing the full-time efforts of four people. Aubin suggests a much more modest operation: $10,000. He says that he and his chief of media relations, Jack Giese, handled the bulk of the media contacts, and John Correll generated reports and magazine stories. Aubin explains, "From the standpoint of my department budget, I didn't even feel it. It's just not that expensive when you own your own equipment. We just kept printing as we needed to. Tons of stuff." Whatever the actual costs, Harwit resents this professional lobbying campaign against the museum: "It means doing whatever you can get away with in terms of propaganda. And I think that's how lobbyists think about these things. It's more a matter of technique and trying to win whatever battle you're fighting. Right or wrong. Whether it's selling cigarettes, or it's selling aircraft, or getting a larger budget for the air force."[46]

In his book Harwit also revealed some specific examples of a cozy relationship between the AFA and some members of Congress. For example, Representative Peter Blute (R-Massachussetts) spearheaded a bipartisan letter signed by forty-two congressmen and sent to the Smithsonian head, Robert McCormick Adams, on August 10, 1994. The letter included statistics from a script analysis conducted by *Air Force Magazine* editor Correll that had not yet been published. Moreover, the next month Senator Nancy Kassebaum (R-Kansas) successfully sponsored a "Sense of the Senate Resolution" noting that the script was "revisionist and offensive to many World War II veterans," and cautioning that any exhibit must "reflect appropriate sensitivity" to them. It passed unanimously. Harwit traced the source of the language: it was sent to a Kassebaum aide by the AFA's Aubin. After the resolution was successfully shepherded to completion, the AFA's director wrote to Kassebaum, commending her for her efforts. Harwit concludes, "in a show of deference, they [the AFA] had congratulated Senator Kassebaum for her wisdom in authoring a resolution that they themselves had drafted for her."[47]

Aubin doesn't deny these connections. But he denies that they are as diabolic as Harwit thinks. In the case of the Kassebaum resolution, for instance, Aubin outlines how such a relationship evolves. The AFA issued a press release characterizing this as a "politically correct" exhibition. Next Nancy Kassebaum was quoted in the conservative newspaper the *Washington Times* on the issue. Aubin then swung into action, contacting one of the senator's staffers, furnishing background material, and cultivating the relationship. It was the same thing he was doing with other staffers willing to support the AFA's position. As he sees it, "It's not unusual. [But] Martin Harwit suggests that there's some strange conspiracy or something when a staffer calls an association and asks for some language. I mean, this happens in this town all the time with lobbyists. So yes, I plead guilty."

Aubin dismisses the suggestion that he did anything inappropriate. He was simply doing his job, as he sees it. He blames Harwit for the controversy: "The guy was well-meaning, but he is the most naive individual I've ever seen at the top of such an organization. I mean, this is a political community. And for him to not understand how Congress worked—I just think he was dense, when it came right down to it."

John Correll's extensive content analyses of successive versions of the script and his hard-hitting features in *Air Force Magazine* earned him the mantle of "big hero" to many vets, according to Steve Aubin. In Correll's first such examination, he reported a serious imbalance in what was represented. Forty-nine photos of Japanese casualties overpowered three photographs of American casualties, for example. One aggressive, anti-American statement by the Japanese was compared to eleven aggressive, anti-Japanese statements by Americans. In a memo Correll sent to the AFA director Monroe Hatch, he ended his summary by asking, "Can such ratios be a coincidence?"[48]

The museum responded to this investigation by attempting to come closer to equalizing the ratios. It did so over time—an effort that the AFA found commendable—but this did not obliterate what Correll and Aubin saw as a "structural problem." As Correll characterized it in a report, the NASM had failed to eliminate "A Tilt That Persists." Aubin recalls, "We didn't want to get into the business of telling them editorially what to do or what not to do. . . . We didn't want to get into the thing of 'This should go' and 'That should go.' We thought it was better to make them do it." Correll insists,

We did not dictate a solution. We refused to do this line-by-line review, "Put this in," "Take this out." As we go through and we're giving them our comments, we're saying, "This is typical of the kind of
thing that we see is contributing to imbalance," but we kept trying
to say, "We're not saying you *must* take this out."[49]

Such denials notwithstanding, by persisting in issuing Correll's
analyses, the AFA did appear to be dictating terms. For example, Correll adamantly stated in a report that *"The exhibition will not be acceptable if it fosters any of the following impressions"*: Japanese were victims,
Americans were motivated by racism, or there was anything dishonest or immoral about U.S. use of the bomb, for example (emphasis in
the original). Moreover, when he wrote to the NASM later the same
year, Correll demanded that the curators present a comparable number of photographs of disabled American veterans to balance the photographs of Japanese survivors. "We do not intend to shut up on this
point," he resolutely declared.

These don't sound like suggestions. They sound like warnings—
muscular, bullying, intimidating warnings. Although "censorship"
was not commonly brought up during this controversy, Correll
rushes to disavow that anything like it occurred: "Is it censorship if
we express an opinion? Which is about all we have done."[50]

In the end, one group did conduct a line-by-line script review
with the NASM: representatives of the American Legion met with
Smithsonian and NASM officials for a total of about thirty-six hours
in September 1994.[51] Keep in mind that the museum had already
done a good deal of juggling, incorporating alterations based on the
AFA's critiques into successive versions of the script. The NASM had
even decided to preface the exhibition with a new section called "The
War in the Pacific: An American Perspective," nearly doubling the
original size to ten thousand square feet. This significant addition
provided historical context regarding Japan's aggressive behavior toward its Asian neighbors before the war; it also reviewed Japan's bru-
tal conduct during the war.

Harwit insists that he remained open, flexible, and conciliatory.
But the AFA's Correll counters that Harwit and the museum were not
compliant: "We said, 'Do this,' 'Do this,' and you know, they kept ignoring everything that we had to say." (This of course contradicts
Correll's general insistence that the AFA was not dictating terms but

merely publicizing problematic areas.) Correll continues to believe that the museum decided to concentrate primarily on "two days in Japan"—and their aftermath. Steve Aubin currently argues that "There was an undertone that had a very warmongering type of attitude. . . . It's not thought control on our part. I think it's thought control on their part."

So while Harwit listened to objections from many quarters and responded to them with concrete adjustments to *The Last Act*, he now perceives his main opponents as somewhat disingenuous and self-serving:

> What the Air Force Association said was, "This is un-American." "You are pro-Japanese." All kinds of other things that I don't think were true. And so trying to discern what the real motivation was, and then take steps to correct the situation to allay the fears of people—the real fears that they have, rather than the ones that they come up with to justify their actions—that was perhaps the most difficult thing. And to some extent I think we never did succeed, perhaps because I think our antagonists were ashamed to say what they really wanted to achieve.

And what might that be? "People would rather argue about some lofty thing like patriotism," Harwit claims. "They won't tell you that it's all about money."

Tom Crouch likewise perceives a great deal of bad faith on the part of the exhibition's major critics: "Martin just [kept] negotiating, and negotiating, and negotiating. . . . And you can make changes you're comfortable with, and at the same time you know you aren't coming within ten miles of what fundamentally bothers them."[52] None of these efforts at conciliation quelled the criticism. They simply provoked more.

Correll and Aubin essentially envisioned a different exhibition, a sweeping one that surveyed over a decade of hostilities before the atomic bombings. In their version, the fateful days of August 1945 would close the story, not begin it. Others imagined an even more radical simplification. For example, a two-page ad placed in the *World War II Times* by the World War II National Commemorative Association pleaded, "Dr. Harwit, Let This Plane Fly Unfettered." Some editorialists echoed the sentiment that the *Enola Gay* be displayed without comment. In this view, it could speak for itself, just as some traditionalists felt western paintings could.[53]

General Tibbetts joined the ranks of those supporting a "no comment" philosophy for structuring the exhibition. An interview and profile published in the *Washington Post* described him as a "private" and "ordinary looking" man, living in a subdivision in Columbus, Ohio. He characterized the mission over Hiroshima as "boring" because everything went as planned, and stated matter-of-factly, "I've never lost a night's sleep over it and I never will. . . . I got nothing to be ashamed of. That's how it was." In an interview he granted to the *Dallas Morning News* and published a week later, he underscored how his age and experience granted authority and demanded respect: "I'm an old gladiator and I'm facing the setting sun," he reflected.[54]

Most important, Tibbetts offered *his* model for the plane's display: "I suggest that the *Enola Gay* be preserved and displayed properly—and alone—for all the world to see. She should be presented as a peacekeeper and as the harbinger of a cold war kept from going 'hot.' . . . Thus far the proposed display of the *Enola Gay* is a package of insults." The phrase "a package of insults" became a rallying cry for many vets. After all, it was the judgment of the man who was there, the man who carried out the orders, the man who in many people's minds successfully delivered the *coup de grâce* to the Japanese campaign. But Tom Crouch argues, "I've always thought anything as exotic and complicated as an airplane is really a social construction. There are few objects that really tell something on their own." Martin Harwit also vigorously dismisses such an approach: "You can't just put the *Enola Gay* out there with airplanes that either flew faster or higher or further than previously. This was a B-29 among four thousand that had been built. There's only one reason why that airplane is in the collections of the Air and Space Museum, and that is because it dropped the bomb on Hiroshima."[55]

The numbers game highlighted just how far apart these sides stood: wrangling over the projected number of casualties, should an American invasion of the Japanese home islands been necessary to force the enemy to surrender, became critical to this controversy. The inflation and deflation of these figures in the exhibition mirrored in general the various versions of this proposed show. (There is great variance as well over reports of the number of lives lost in Hiroshima and Nagasaki.) One newspaper headline at the time proclaimed,

"Truman Had 250,000 Reasons for Dropping the Bomb." This number refers to Truman's estimate, made after the war, of the U.S. deaths that might have occurred during an invasion, plus up to 500,000 wounded. The headline thus translated abstract numbers into individual lives in a simple way, just as the writer Paul Fussell presented his own biography in order to flesh out one of those statistics in particular.

American casualty estimates swing widely from a low of twenty-five thousand to forty-six thousand, to a high of one million. The estimates depend on what sources you consult, when and how these conclusions were reached, and the motives of their proponents (frightening the enemy versus ex post facto justification of using a new destructive technology). The extent to which people become heavily invested in one number becomes clear in a letter written to John Correll by one of the "only five old men": "I just received a summary of the current plans for exhibit. . . . Please note the lack of any reference to Pearl Harbor and the savings of *six million* lives anticipated by the Japanese to be lost in an invasion." (emphasis added). His referent is unclear. Should it be American casualties, it is off the curve. Should it be Japanese casualties, it signifies that the atomic bombs were less destructive of life than conventional warfare would have been. Whichever the case, it invoked the figure that immediately equates to the Holocaust, with its attendant horrors.[56]

The Stanford historian Barton Bernstein lowered his estimates from 229,000 American casualties to 63,000, after restudying the diary of World War II's Admiral William Leahy. (These figures refer to projected dead, wounded, and missing.) Harwit felt that although larger figures might have been true, it was a "kind of speculation that was beyond what a museum could do or show." When the NASM decided to incorporate this lower figure into the exhibition, the American Legion—which had laboriously sifted through the entire script and offered its input—withdrew its support. The Legion stated that this was because it had reviewed what it believed was the final script, until this alteration was introduced. But Mike Neufeld believes that the national leadership of the American Legion had underestimated how worked up veterans had become over *The Last Act*, and the group was looking for a way out of cooperating further with the museum. This was not an issue that was worth risking the support of its membership.[57]

Once a sizable body of veterans became upset about what they heard was in the offing, Martin Harwit describes the equivalent of the so-called blue wall of silence going up; no veterans' groups were willing to support the NASM publicly. The American Legion later claimed that the NASM treated it with a patronizing attitude: "They talked to us like our heads were screwed on. They underestimated the Legion." Moreover, an article in another Legion publication argued, "no one seems to be happy with the exhibit, and therefore it is eminently important to save the Smithsonian Institution from itself."[58] The quote hauntingly evokes the hawkish sentiment from the Vietnam War that should U.S. forces need to destroy villages in order to save their inhabitants from communism—so be it.

According to Tom Crouch, veterans wanted their "master narrative" to hold sway. Michael Neufeld agrees:

> They wanted a story that was their story about the bomb, and they may even have actually believed their own rhetoric that they were producing the true or the unbiased story. But in fact what they were trying to do was force down everybody's throats one particular version of the story: the bomb ended the war, saved a million lives, or five million lives, or whatever number they wanted to pick—end of discussion. No other point of view was possible, or even should be allowed to be expressed in a public museum.

Crouch and Neufeld aimed to present a diversity of viewpoints, both pro- and anti-bomb. While they admit they may have inadvertently worded things a certain way in early versions that sounded biased, or left certain things out, they sought to broaden the perspective on this event. That objective was undercut when Smithsonian secretary Heyman bowed to the critics and declared, "In this important anniversary year, veterans and their families were expecting—and rightly so—that the nation would honor and commemorate their valor and sacrifice. They were not looking for analysis, and frankly, we did not give enough thought to the intense feelings such an analysis would evoke." Michael Neufeld believes it was not possible to look at the impact of the bomb or debate the decision to drop it. Not at this time, not in this context. He says, with both sadness and resignation,

> I think the political realities were such that in a national museum, in the center of the capital, with the *Enola Gay* icon right there in the

same space with the survivor stories, there wasn't any real way you could bring all those things together and politically survive. To me it became obvious that about the only exhibit that you could do is one that essentially defends or advocates the correctness of using the bomb.[59]

Following are some voices we've heard elsewhere. They reveal the range and passions of reactions to this exhibition. These responses highlight the fact that knowing a person's perspective on one controversy does not enable you to predict what position they will take on another. Joseph Noble, for example, championed controversial exhibitions in his time and understands what it's like to be a museum official under fire. Yet he does not support the curators in this instance. Noble believes that the Smithsonian was wrong with *The Last Act*. He "could have vomited" over what the NASM proposed to present: "You can't tell anybody that's lived through World War II that we shouldn't have dropped the atomic bomb." Here, generational fidelity defeats professional identity. (In addition, Noble's wife was at Pearl Harbor when the Japanese attacked in 1941.)

The English-born Freud critic Peter J. Swales, no stranger to being labeled a revisionist, sides with the veteran/opponents on this one: as the son of a World War II vet, he rejects what he assumes was the curators' revisionist view of the conflict:

[M]y poor old man, my poor father would have been very harrowed and distressed if somebody tried to revise the history of World War II. And suggested that Britain was crazy to take on the German Navy or something like that. Whatever revisionist thesis. Because I mean, you know, people . . . gave their bloody lives to defend certain ideals of freedom, and yes, including freedom of speech, against the likes of fascist idiots like Adolf Hitler and Mussolini. . . . [So] I can understand why there were people protesting.[60]

And yet, with the Freud exhibition proposed to open at the Library of Congress in 1996 (see chapter 4), Swales *insisted* on a revisionist view being represented.

What about Benny Andrews, who led the protests against *Harlem on My Mind*? He summarily dismisses the veterans' objections. "I was in the military too," he notes, "and I look at these people who become professional veterans. They keep wearing their outfits around. Why don't those people take those silly things off? You know, they claim they did something for their country. Okay, you did it. Now get on with your business, instead of being angry."

The issues and emotions that were raised by this exhibition obviously became extremely complex once criticism began to build. Tom Crouch raised an important point to Martin Harwit in a memo: "Do you want to do an exhibition intended to make veterans feel good, or do you want an exhibition that will lead our visitors to think about the consequences of the atomic bombing of Japan? Frankly, I don't think we can do both." Crouch now explains, "I was essentially saying I think you either have to do a show that you think is honest and straightforward and balanced, or you can make these guys happy. And I'd still stick with it, probably even more firmly today than I believed it then."[61] Harwit, however, believed that he could satisfy everyone, which propelled him into tireless negotiations.

As alluded to earlier, there was always a tension between what the curators had in mind and what veterans would have preferred to see. Michael Neufeld puts it simply: "Memorials are one thing. History is another." So while Martin Harwit was trying to please a variety of external factions, he had internal problems to attend to as well. Neufeld and Crouch were unhappy about the rounds of revisions being forced on the exhibition from outside sources. (Strains obviously developed between Harwit and the curators, although they insist that relations remained "decent" and they bear Harwit "no ill will.") By the end, Neufeld reflects, "There was a profound sense of ambivalence because on the one hand, we didn't like to see a show being killed from political pressure. But on the other hand, we felt relief because we didn't like the exhibit anymore, and we didn't really want to be defending it." The curators felt pushed up against a wall, but didn't wish to resign from this particular project. If they did so, critics of the exhibit could seize on that as "evidence" that they were guilty of certain things all along.

The AFA's Stephen Aubin faults Harwit for not ruling his domain more autocratically: "I think Neufeld and Crouch really resented any outside people telling them, the 'all-knowing,' that they should make any changes. Ultimately, Martin Harwit was unwilling to ride herd on his artistes, who just didn't want to bend in terms of their own viewpoints." But that statement fails to recognize how conciliatory the curators had been forced to become. Aubin does, however, recognize the tough balancing act facing the director: "Harwit had to try to satisfy outside groups, and he had internal problems—he had to try to be true to what he believed he should be doing in terms of defending his curators."

Despite their differences, Harwit and his curators were tarred with the same ideological brush. They were all accused of being "politically correct." An article in a California newspaper—based in conservative Orange County—derided the "cultural commissars" who had taken charge of the Smithsonian. Typical of a number of such articles at the time, the writer ticked off a litany of outrageous exhibitions that had sullied those hallowed halls: *Science in American Life* (presenting the triumphs as well as the failures and problems of scientific developments); *The West as America*; and even a revamped show about airpower in World War I, in which Snoopy and the Red Baron are critiqued as pop culture diversions from the actual horrors of that war.[62]

The *Wall Street Journal* led with this angle in its own catalogue of horrors, "Snoopy at the Smithsonian." "Culture police." "Ideology police." "The Academic Left." The *Journal*'s editorial writers hurled these insults, and others, at Smithsonian personnel. They ridiculed the museums' "transformation . . . into vehicles for political re-education." They boldly asserted, "It is clear that the cadres at the Smithsonian see themselves as missionaries to a great unwashed public steeped in ignorance and delusion." So while veterans already held a beef against the NASM because of its presumed foot dragging in restoring the *Enola Gay*, this line of attack allowed critics to judge *The Last Act* as part of a string of insults too. The *Journal* traced the source of the problem to Secretary Adams's hiring of "activist curators and administrators" starting in 1984, Martin Harwit included (beginning in 1987). But listen to how Harwit characterizes himself:

> I've never been a political activist. I don't think I've ever marched for anything. I would consider myself fairly conservative. . . . and I think that comes from having been born in Czechoslovakia [and] because of the occupation by Hitler, and seeing my relatives go into concentration camps. . . . I'm very grateful to America for having entered the war and having vanquished the Nazis.

He continues, "When I got called up to serve in the United States Army, after coming to this country [after World War II], I of course served. It wasn't as though I was the kind of person who tried to get out of that or was a pacifist." But to the conspiratorial mind, only a cabal of subversives could have fashioned an exhibition like *The Last Act*.[63]

The conservative columnist and politician Patrick Buchanan sounded a similar alarm. So did House Speaker Newt Gingrich, in a much-quoted harangue: "Political correctness may be OK in some faculty lounge, but . . . the Smithsonian is a treasure that belongs to the American people, and it should not become a plaything for left-wing ideologies." "Politically correct pinheads," another writer opined. "The National Museums of PC," yet another offered. (That journalist cited an "Avenge Pearl Harbor" poster at the *Science in American Life* exhibition as betraying the same bias *The Last Act* allegedly did.) Both John Correll and Stephen Aubin support these claims. Correll was quoted as saying, "people are not interested in counterculture morality pageants put on by academic activists." Aubin reflects, "I viewed it as part of the politically correct stuff. [B]ut we've got to draw the line somewhere. Let's have one victory for common sense here. The point is, you may have your fine little academic theories and all that. Put it in a book."[64]

Michael Neufeld angrily dismisses such charges:

> I think the way the *Wall Street Journal* frames the debate is basically absurd, so I hate to buy into their rhetoric. I mean, it's essentially a paranoid view of academia and of the museum world, where these sort of evil curators and evil academics came in and changed the way things are around. We're just historians, and we were trying to do what we thought was a realistic job of depicting all the sides.

He was also criticized for being Canadian. The implication was that this biased him and automatically disqualified him from being a curator of this exhibition. "Absurd," he claims. "Jingoism." "Xenophobia." Feigning a menacing voice, he warns of being an agent of "our enemy to the north, Canada." For him, "This was a nasty political campaign, and they were looking for any opening whatever to go after us."

Critics disparaged both Neufeld and Crouch because they were too young to have direct experience of the war. The fact that Crouch curated the exhibit on the internment of Japanese Americans also led some critics to question his patriotism or tag him "pro-Japanese." But

"The last time I looked," he notes, "that was the most American show in the National Museum of American History." A *New York Times* editorial urged open discussion of the decision to use the atomic bomb, but slipped into the tendency to characterize one group as intolerant "censors" (veterans), and the other group as extremists who viewed Truman "as a war criminal" and implied that "Hiroshima is America's Auschwitz." Once again, this reduces complex positions to caricature. As Tom Crouch concludes, "There was a sense in which it was a mistake to talk about left wing and right wing in this."[65]

Harwit had to be vigilant on one additional front. Besides answering the complaints of veterans and other critics and preserving a working relationship with his staff, he had to concern himself with the international dimensions of this controversy. Harwit was not dealing with the Romanov jewels. But he was arbitrating some extremely touchy matters with a strategically important American political ally and trading partner. Japanese sensitivities and Japanese objects had to be handled carefully. The headline of a Patrick Buchanan column bellowed "Japan Got What She Deserved."[66] Such sentiments might be tolerated in the realm of renegade politics and journalism. But they were definitely not acceptable in the domains where Martin Harwit was operating.

The Japanese, like the Americans, have struggled for over fifty years to come to terms with the experiences of World War II. Each side nourishes its ambivalences. Each side wrestles with guilt. Each side glosses over some of the more extreme aspects of its conduct. *The Last Act,* as in so many instances of controversial exhibitions, provided a roost upon which these emotions could temporarily alight. An intriguing example of how unresolved issues return as fantasy are Japanese pulp fiction military novels. These books, whose "audience demographic" is men from high school age to their thirties, replay the war with the Japanese as the victors. So-called virtual reality stories pit the Japanese against racist, colonialist aggressors. In one instance, they successfully liberate Japanese Americans held in internment camps in Washington state.[67]

But the lines between reality and wishful thinking have also been blurred in more mainstream endeavors. Until recently, the Japanese Education Ministry reviewed textbooks and mandated extensive alterations, aimed at building consensus for the government. Only in

1997 did Professor Saburo Ienaga win his decades-long battle to end censorship of texts and allow inclusion of explanations of Japanese aggression and atrocities—monstrous massacres of Chinese, medical atrocities against Filipinos, the enslavement of thousands of Korean women as sex slaves, or "comfort women"—before and during World War II. These were some of the same events critics of *The Last Act* wanted to include in the Smithsonian exhibition, and which the museum subsequently incorporated in the massive "War in the Pacific" section.[68]

In August 1994, in the midst of the wrangling over the American exhibit, a new museum opened in Nagasaki, connected to the Peace Memorial Museum. It supplements the tale of the atom bombs and their aftereffects with portrayals of forced laborers in the city's military industries and the infamous Japanese seizure of the Chinese city of Nanking in 1937-38, commonly referred to by Westerners as the "Rape of Nanking." Hundreds of thousands are estimated to have died in the slaughter. The Japanese faced their own version of the numbers game, conceding that various theories propose different death tallies. Moreover, controversy followed this curatorial vision as well. Two years later, museum officials bowed to pressure from nationalists and removed a graphic photograph of a Chinese woman being jostled by Japanese soldiers.[69]

In December 1994, just before the cancellation of *The Last Act*, another drama was playing out elsewhere in America's capital. As part of a series of stamps commemorating the fiftieth anniversary of the end of World War II, a proposed design pictured a mushroom cloud and carried the logo, "Atomic bombs hasten war's end, August 1945." Nagasaki's mayor condemned it as "heartless." Negotiators from the Japanese embassy in Washington, the State Department, the United States Postal Service, and the White House worked to avoid an unpleasant diplomatic flap. In the end, the Postal Service deferred to the wishes of the White House and substituted a picture of Truman announcing the war's end.[70]

The Japanese media decried the Smithsonian's scaled-back exhibition of the *Enola Gay*. The new plan invalidated complex negotiations between Harwit, Japanese museum officials, and the mayors of Hiroshima and Nagasaki for the loan of materials and planned videotaped testimonies by these officials about the bomb's legacy. Japanese journalists reported that the *Enola Gay* had become a "holy relic," about which there could be no critical discussion. That reopened old wounds and reignited old debates among the Japanese. In a letter to the editor of the *Japan Times*, an economics professor at Nagasaki University argued that European colonial powers should apologize first for *their* atrocities before World War II, before they can expect Japan to apologize for the war. That's another definition of balance. Before the abbreviated exhibition went up, the mayor of Nagasaki stated publicly that along with the Holocaust, the American bombings of the two Japanese cities were the greatest crimes of the twentieth century. He argued, emotionally, "This is tantamount to killing a flea with a sledgehammer. It can hardly be called a justified act, even in wartime."[71]

The victims' perspective did prevail in one venue, however. American University in Washington, D.C., hosted an exhibit at the same time the Smithsonian unveiled the restored *Enola Gay*, focusing on the aftermath and human consequences of the bombings. *Constructing a Peaceful World: Beyond Hiroshima and Nagasaki* featured twenty-five artifacts (including the lunch box with carbonized food and the watch, frozen in time, slated to appear at the NASM) with accompanying photos and text, plus three thirty-minute videos produced by the Hiroshima Peace Culture Foundation. Two *hibakusha* (bomb survivors) also spoke. The exhibit was already planned in conjunction with a summer program on nuclear history; the cancellation at the NASM made certain items available for their show. Presenting this exhibition reiterates what happened in the aftermath of *Harlem on My Mind* and *Back of the Big House*—one exhibit compensated for the deficits of another. It even received an endorsement from an American Legion spokesman, who stated, "It's fundamentally different because AU is a private institution. The Smithsonian is a public institution, where the impression is that anything it says is official history."[72]

These struggles were not only engaged on paper and in meeting rooms. Martin Harwit reports that protestors annually threw red liquid on rockets at the NASM on or around the anniversary of the bombings of Japan. Not surprisingly, then, someone splashed the fiftieth anniversary exhibit with red paint during previews. (Echoes of the scratching of ten paintings at the Metropolitan Museum of Art during the *Harlem on My Mind* controversy?) On opening day twenty-

FIG. 19. Smiley-faced *Enola Gay* editorial cartoon. AUTH © 1995 *The Philadelphia Inquirer.* Reprinted with permission of Universal Press Syndicate. All rights reserved.

one people were arrested during a demonstration in the museum, some of them bearing signs urging "Never Again" or "No More Hiroshimas." Four days later, the NASM closed for ninety minutes after three protestors poured a pint of human blood and two bags of ashes on the *Enola Gay*'s fuselage. They were charged with felony destruction of government property and found guilty.[73]

The Fellowship of Reconciliation and Physicians for Social Responsibility both deplored the presentation of the plane without analysis. A coalition of historians condemned the display as representing "historical cleansing," and the Organization of American Historians censured it for becoming *"patriotically* correct." Both groups accused the NASM of "caving in." From Harwit's perspective, "I was quite disappointed in the historians because what they wrote in the op-ed pieces they did usually was not supportive of what we were trying to do in the exhibition. They tended to tout their own books and their own theories."[74]

The severely abridged exhibition of the *Enola Gay* remains at the NASM. Tellingly, it is entitled *The "Enola Gay": Something More Than an Airplane.* The introductory text reads, in part: "It was an airplane like so many others that rolled off the wartime assembly lines by the thousands; an advanced bomber for its day, but only one among many of its breed. Fifty years later it seems almost larger than life; as much an icon, now, as an airplane." Smithsonian secretary Heyman acknowledges in the statement at the entrance that this is a scaled-down version, the result of a controversy. But all other traces of the debate have been excised. The concluding video juxtaposes vintage photographs of the youthful, hardy B-29 crew with their aging faces and their recollections. General Tibbetts cautions that you cannot play "What if?" when looking back at World War II or its ending. Instead, he emphasizes the heroics and patriotism that "succeeded in bringing that great carnage to an end, and everybody got to go home"—Paul Fussell included.

The *Baltimore Sun* took a swipe at the exhibition when it opened, calling it "Enola Lite, 97-percent controversy free." A *Washington Post* writer dubbed the Smithsonian the "pablum museum" and commented, "This is the new mood in the revolutionized Washington: When in doubt, bail out. Hit the ejection button. Cave. Do what the 49ers never, never, never do: punt."[75]

The *Enola Gay* was endowed with particular meanings in 1945. It has taken on additional ones much more recently. Whether people know a great deal or just a little about the controversy at the National Air and Space Museum during 1994 and 1995, the *Enola Gay* has become the touchstone in the public's mind when they think of controversial museum exhibitions, as it has for curators throughout the country.

It is impossible to precisely measure the impact of *The Last Act* on the principal players or future shows. The Air Force Association's Stephen Aubin, who even now feels that the exhibition wasn't balanced enough to pass muster as a freshman college paper, declares, "Some people said, 'Well, that [the controversy] could have a chilling effect.' Well, if it has a chilling effect on some of the scholarship we saw coming out, then good." Indeed, in some instances the consequences are clear. A proposed NASM exhibition on airpower during the Vietnam

War, a general overview of aviation's involvement in that conflict, was shelved because of the struggle surrounding the *Enola Gay*. Although Tom Crouch reports that it was "fairly far down the pipeline," that it had had a great deal of veteran involvement in the planning stages, and that no controversy was expected, the Smithsonian administration didn't wish to take any additional chances at the same time the display of the *Enola Gay* was generating such criticism. He reports, "There are no immediate plans to breathe new life into it." Michael Neufeld adds, "It may never come back because of the desire not to take on any more touchy subjects."

Neufeld and Crouch recognize that this exhibition changed them. It changed the museum too. However, the difference is partly the result of the change in leadership that followed Martin Harwit's resignation, and not any specific new policies that govern the development of exhibitions. According to Tom Crouch, "I honestly think there's a sense in which once Martin went away, stakeholders in this place said, 'Oh, okay, these guys have been through hell. Let's rebuild and be nice.' But the rest of the [Smithsonian] institution suffered, and continues to, to some extent." As for the personal impact, Crouch concedes it has been "a career-altering experience." "Michael and I have become a part of the history of Hiroshima. We will never escape the *Enola Gay* controversy."

Michael Neufeld echoes these sentiments:

> It's a different world, it's a different leadership in this museum, and we're not going to do what Harwit attempted to do, that's for sure. . . . [Moreover] The museum community as a whole has suffered from the controversy because it really discouraged innovative or challenging history exhibits. I mean, they'll come back gradually, but it sent a message out there that it was dangerous to do these things. It hasn't been healthy.

What is more, the personal consequences are apparent to him too: "Any attack article [on exhibitions] invokes *Enola Gay*. It just keeps coming back to haunt us."

Martin Harwit claims that being thick-skinned helped him to endure all this turmoil. Since his resignation he has been short-listed for a number of jobs, but has been told that having been embroiled in such a controversy was a liability. So he has concentrated on writing and on consulting as an astrophysicist. Yet somewhat surprisingly, he affirms upon reflection,

> The directorship of the Air and Space Museum was the best job I ever had. There's just no doubt. Throw in the *Enola Gay* controversy and it doesn't make any difference. I'm sort of spoiled. Doing exhibitions, having eight to ten million people come in each year and look at what you're trying to teach them; you know, that's very heady.

Some creative soul penned the following in the fourth volume of the comment books used for *The West as America*: "Mama don't let your babies grow up to be curators." The expression is cute, obviously mimicking Willie Nelson's advice against aspiring to become a cowboy. But does this mean that curators are lowlifes? Or does it mean that theirs is a perilous profession? Like the art showcased in *The West as America*, and like the *Enola Gay*, it is open to multiple interpretations.

7

The Postmodern Exhibition

Cut on the Bias, or Is *Enola Gay* a Verb?

MUSEUMS ARE NO longer dead zones or monuments to the past. Nor are they simply vanity sites, tributes to wealth, power, or the self-congratulations of mankind lording over other animal species, or of one race of humans reigning over another. Museums are now noisy, contentious, and extremely vital places.

This book has been an exploration of displays of power. As we have seen time and again, displays of power represent both action and reaction. Displays of power have always been what museums do. But exhibitions today commonly reflect the interests of groups that are ideologically different from those previously in control—groups that are only recently flexing their muscle, having just elbowed their way into the cultural spotlight. To be sure, new viewpoints are being expressed in established institutions, channelled along disparate racial, ethnic, and doctrinal lines. But old voices are just as frequently being raised to fight back their challenge.

Yet remarkably, some observers view exhibition controversies simply as a slight arrhythmia in an otherwise healthy and vigorous museum world. To hear the *New York Times* tell it, for example, these are the "glory days." A feature story that sprawled across nearly two entire pages of one Sunday edition touts the boom, the blockbuster, the healthy bottom line for museums. Photos show hordes of visitors lolling on the steps of the Metropolitan Museum of Art, where nearly thirty years earlier crowds gathered to protest *Harlem on My Mind*. Vibrant banners overhead announce an exhibit of the work of the art world celebs Georgia O'Keefe and Alfred Stieglitz and the debut of the new Chinese Galleries. (In full color: the *New York Times*, like museums, is extremely market-savvy these days.) Or we see people queuing up to view the work of Picasso at the National Gallery of Art in Washington, D.C. He beat out all other competitors in the race for big numbers during the 1997 season. Still others dine, buy things, schmooze at corporate-sponsored events, or simply relax in the tranquility of museums throughout the country. Nowhere in this status report is any mention made of controversy.

The same author trumpets the prosperity awash in this world in another *New York Times* article. A box score of the top fifteen exhibitions of 1997 reports relative performance stats as if they were sports scores. Picasso, the champion, appears twice: *Picasso: The Early Years* packs in the crowds in both Washington and Boston. Other heavy hitters appear as well: Renoir and Monet; ancient cultures like Byzantium or Egypt; and even dazzling merchandise representing a more contemporary concept of civilization, courtesy of Cartier. Idea-driven exhibitions or any hint of trouble are noticeably absent in this roster.[1] The impression advanced instead is that museums are flush and self-satisfied—everything is copacetic.

Moreover, Joan Rosenbaum, the director of the Jewish Museum in New York City, concedes that conflictual episodes like the *Enola Gay* and others don't really shape her thinking. Nor do they impact on how she does her job day-to-day. Her museum is a host site for *Sigmund Freud: Conflict and Culture.* But the fierce debate it provoked in the planning stages doesn't concern her. She is primarily preoccupied with matters internal to the museum's operation: management issues, fund raising, dealing with her board of directors. She shares the mundane, unglamorous details of her job:

> The daily life of a director is sufficient to eclipse whatever you heard last week [about this or that controversy], I have to tell you. You deal with staff turnover. You deal with an emergency plumbing problem. The fact that something came in wildly over budget, that we're being offered a show that we had never planned for, and we'd have to move the whole schedule around. That someone very prominent and very wealthy is suddenly interested in the board, and how can we engage them? I mean, those are the things that have a certain urgency.

Only once or twice a year, when she attends conferences of her professional peers, can Rosenbaum find the time to focus on any larger political issues buffeting her world.[2]

William Truettner, the embattled curator of *The West as America,* believes that the troubles over the past few years represent merely a tiny blip on the cultural radar screen: "By and large, there are thousands of exhibitions that go on every year that are absolutely standard shows, and that haven't raised an eyebrow."[3] Even so, the troublesome ones have attracted considerable attention; some people even argue that these disputes have commanded more notice than they deserve. David Lackey, for example, whose firm designed *Gaelic Gotham,* was simultaneously working on a project in Chiapas, Mexico. From his perspective, "I wish it [social conflict] were more in the streets, quite honestly. I call it the 'taming of society.' Museums are relatively safe places. Having traveled around the world a great deal, these controversies seem somewhat trivial."[4]

As noted at the beginning of this book, controversies over museum exhibitions vividly demonstrate that symbolic politics has displaced other political struggles over issues of race, representation, and inequality—struggles that could possibly alter the real conditions of people's lives. At the end of the day, we are still dealing with exhibitions, not natural disasters, revolutions, or even new public policies.

Even the most radical curator working in the most innovative museum is subject to many conservative pressures. There is the weight of institutional history, like the aristocratic legacy symbolized by the Museum of the City of New York's extensive silver collection. And fiscal constraints increasingly intrude on curatorial decision making. Although William Truettner of the National Museum of American Art believes that the number of museum controversies has not been significant, he concedes that their impact has. He states, "I'm a bit depressed at the moment. Five years ago this institution was set to turn in a new direction. I think it had a great opportunity and lost it. And now it's more concerned with fund raising than what it presents to the public."

Both Truettner and Harry R. Rubenstein of the Smithsonian's National Museum of American History note that their museums now must scramble more and more for the funds they require to present their shows. According to Rubenstein, "Only the smallest shows don't require fund raising." His museum is in keen competition with others for "a pool of money that's getting smaller and smaller." Michael S. Roth, who curated the Freud exhibition, notes that "In a period of increased scarcity for cultural support, the nature of decision making by administrators changes. That's obvious. . . . What you get is a narrowing of the vision."[5]

Finally, organizations like museums have a tremendous will to persist. Most museum officials will readily jettison a burdensome exhibition concept like ballast from an overloaded ship, should it seem essential to insure their future. Today they will likely consider what to bring aboard their program much more carefully in the first place. Legacy, finances, and endurance operate like the sturdy lines that tether a hot air balloon to guarantee that it not break loose and destroy itself.

Scholars subscribe to certain ideologies and myths, just as museum personnel, and the combatants in the various battles in this book subscribe to theirs. My own credo includes a belief in the free exchange of ideas. It includes a belief in the right to present a distinct point of view, sustained by evidence, and yet acknowledging alternative explanations and points of view. It includes the right to make a fool of yourself, to be wrong, to be rebutted.

I strongly identified with the critics of exhibitions when I interviewed many of them: the general drift of their politics, their sense of exclusion, their keen desire to be heard, their support of ideals such as balance, fairness, and community participation, and especially their passion. Still and all, my allegiance to principles of authorship and open inquiry and my belief that you cannot and should not "protect" people from making up their own minds about what they see trumped my other convictions and emotions. No matter how autocratic, bumbling, or acquiescent curators and museum officials have been—and granted, they have made many mistakes and many enemies—their right to proceed with their vision needs to be staunchly defended. Should opponents challenge what they present through spirited debate, written refutations, or even boisterous demonstrations—so be it. And so much the better. But attempts by various factions to radically reconstruct exhibitions to their own liking before they have gone up, to intimidate and threaten curators, museum employees, or supporters, or even to derail shows that they do not like are intolerable in a free society.

This book pushes beyond Matthew Arnold's concern with "the best that has been thought and said in the world."[6] It demonstrates that culture—and the struggles over it—can reveal us at our most un-flattering, too, and that it is important to pay attention to such clashes. As is the case with all the partisans I've presented, my own preoccupations are intricately entangled with my sense of identity and my own particular preferences and convictions.

Some journalists and museum officials may deny that anything is amiss in the world of museums today. Even so, it is difficult to ignore the news of fresh controversies that surface regularly. For example, two controversies developed at the Ellis Island Immigration Museum within six months of one another in 1998. An exhibition about the massacre of Armenians by Ottoman Turks in 1915 became problem-atic when officials of the National Park Service (which administers the site) requested that the organizer of *Armenia: Memories from My Home* remove some photographs and text. The officials claimed that the images were "gruesome and gory" and inappropriate for the many children who visit there. A compromise was reached after much hand-wringing, and some of the disputed images were re-stored.[7] Meanwhile, the legitimacy of classifying these events as genocide continues to be debated.

No sooner had that exhibition come down than another one be-came problematic. *America's Concentration Camps: Remembering the Japanese American Experience* addressed the imprisoning of Japanese Americans in internment camps during World War II. Along with vi-sual documentation in the museum, curators reassembled a barracks, a guard tower, and barbed wire fence from Heart Mountain, Wyoming, outside on the grounds. The Smithsonian's Tom Crouch had used the term "concentration camp" in *A More Perfect Union*, which he curated in 1987. It caused no problems at that time. But in the spring of 1998, some Jewish groups contested its applicability to this other group's experience (the executive director of the American Jewish Committee declared that the term "deserves protection").

Ellis Island's superintendent feared that use of this label in this context could offend the metropolitan area's large Jewish population. She demanded a name change. That mobilized the intervention of Senator Daniel Inouye, which eventually resulted in a conciliation be-tween Jewish and Japanese American groups. "Concentration camp" was retained, while a detailed discussion of its origins and its appli-cability to various experiences was included. One commentator

FIG. 20. *America's Concentration Camps: Remembering the Japanese American Experience,* 1998. Installation photograph by Kevin Daley, National Park Service. Courtesy of the Statue of Liberty-Ellis Island Foundation, Inc.

wisely observed that this was an example of a group sensing it was in danger of forfeiting something that has become central to its identity. He understood that for some Jews this curatorial decision posed the possibility that they might be "losing their singular lexicon of anguish."[8] This example points up once again the complexities of reception, and how it varies from time to time and place to place.

Just months before, the Smithsonian Institution became embroiled in a similar tussle. The Smithsonian was slated to host a lecture series as part of the fiftieth anniversary commemoration of the founding of the modern state of Israel. The roster included a wide range of voices: scholars, writers, Orthodox and conservative political Jewish spokespeople, as well as Arabs. But a plurality of voices can be threatening to certain people. Representative Michael P. Forbes (R-New York) wrote to Smithsonian secretary I. Michael Heyman that this was "going to be an *Enola Gay* controversy," and that the program represented a "leftist approach" to Israel. Moreover, as if proceeding according to a dog-eared script, the media stirred up people's emotions. The *New York Post* editorially denounced the Smithsonian and accused it of bias. Later, the enraged author of a letter to the editor reiterated the major complaints veterans had directed against the *Enola Gay* exhibit, and once again invoked the passage from the first draft of the script regarding a Japanese "war of vengeance."

That preliminary National Air and Space Museum document had been written four years prior. As we know, curators subsequently edited it to avoid misinterpretation. Yet it was still being shamefully manipulated for ideological purposes rather than being put to rest. Heyman once again capitulated to political, media, and public pressure: he ordered the Smithsonian to disassociate itself from a group that had become defined as a controversial collaborator, and to produce a lecture series on its own.[9] The *Enola Gay* experience thus provides a benchmark against which many other exhibitions are subsequently measured.

The question arises, "What *is* the Smithsonian—or any public institution—willing to do nowadays?" Are museum officials running scared? Playing it safe? Frank Rich of the *New York Times* answers in the affirmative. He opened his scathing review of *America's Smithsonian*, the Institution's 150th anniversary exhibition in 1996, with a dismissal that would make any curator cringe: "There are some shows so dull they can't even give the tickets away." When the traveling show reached Manhattan—one of twelve projected sites it bombed with audiences; a behemoth 100,000-square-foot exhibition did a spectacular belly flop. But why?

The exhibition was a mishmash, an amorphous assortment of items from the Smithsonian's collections, much like a selection of musical greatest hits peddled on late-night television. It invited comparison with children's flip books, where a kid can construct new characters by randomly turning the selections of heads, torsos, and legs. You could imaginatively cluster Lincoln's top hat, Theodore Roosevelt's chaps, Franklin D. Roosevelt's lap robe, Eleanor Roosevelt's fur coat, and George Washington's battle sword and scabbard into a *fabulous* [a-]historical ensemble. You'd be dressed to take a fantasy voyage in a Mercury spacecraft or a 1948 Tucker automobile, or to view a smattering of artworks, gems and jewelry, manmade artifacts from around the world, and specimens from the natural world.

America's Smithsonian was the antithesis of *The West as America.* The one exhibition left it completely up to the viewer to furnish any interpretations. The other preached a party line, according to its harshest critics. Because the curators played it safe in this instance, it would be impossible to fault *America's Smithsonian* for theoretical heavy-handedness; no curatorial point of view was apparent. Objects appeared to have been chosen for their celebrity value or their sheer visual appeal. Like *People* magazine's "fifty most beautiful people" of the year, these objects were all surface, no depth; thus they were accorded a shallow equivalency.

This sort of display is relatively immune from political attack, although it is not necessarily satisfying to the public or to experienced critics of exhibitions. To the exhibit designer David Lackey,

> It was really disappointing. It's troublesome to see an exhibition that comes across almost like "Ripley's Believe It or Not." . . . The Smithsonian did an exhibition on [founder] John Smithson in the 1980s that was absolutely splendid. It linked his travels around the world and understanding different cultures, and [demonstrated] how that collection was based. It was a link to an incredible human journey, an odyssey. And I never felt this exhibition had that depth. . . . For example, the beetles were like specimens of gems. They looked almost interchangeable.

Just as significant as the Smithsonian's choice of what to display and how to display it was the prominence of its "proud partners," corporate sponsors such as the Intel Corporation, MCI Communications Corporation, Discover® Card, and TWA. Each procured a huge space in the exhibit to pitch itself. MCI's "cyber playground," for example, offered Internet connections and free long-distance phone calls. These were infomercials, blatant self-promotions on a large scale. Their presence highlights both the increased dependence of museums upon corporate support and the blandness of many of the resulting exhibitions.

America's Smithsonian was conceived before the *Enola Gay* controversy had fully played out. It was the inaugural exhibition of a new regime. But the *Enola Gay* was connected to *America's Smithsonian* in a vital way. Martin Harwit insists that Secretary Heyman was charged with a new priority when he assumed office. It was up to him to secure financial stability for the Smithsonian, both from the private sector and from Congress, whose contributions have decreased over recent years. It took Harwit a long time to "get it": the struggle over the *Enola Gay* was as much about money as it was about important principles. In fact, a *Washington Post* article disclosed that the controversy at the NASM over the proposed exhibit of the *Enola Gay* was thwarting the Smithsonian's efforts to convince corporate supporters to sign on to *America's Smithsonian. The Last Act* not only threatened the economic interests of the military and the aerospace industries. The debate it engendered also made it more difficult for the Smithsonian to raise funds on its own behalf.[10] When museums are forced to hustle more and more for their income, it is certain to have an impact on the decisions they make about what to present to the public.

Equally as troubling is what does *not* make it onto the walls—after *The West as America,* after the *Enola Gay* and all the other controversies of the past half dozen years, in a time when museums are no longer overlooked and undervalued by large segments of the public. The public, along with critics, can judge what appears within their range of vision. But the inchoate fears of controversy that can coalesce into self-censorship generally remain hidden from audiences and researchers alike. Robert Macdonald, the director of the Museum of the City of New York, reflects on the conflicts at other institutions:

> Curators and officials at the Smithsonian and the Library of Congress were definitely afraid. They have jobs to protect, [and] the "culture wars," as they're called, had come down to where they were fearful of speaking what they believed to be true, because they would lose their jobs. . . . I was shocked, but I don't blame them at all. They have families to feed.

We have discovered how the controversy over *The West as America* caused the National Museum of American Art to beef up its internal regulations and carefully weigh in advance what it presents to the public. Moreover, the negative coverage of the Library of Congress after the conflict over *Back of the Big House* sent that institution reeling too. For the LOC associate librarian Winston Tabb, the fallout served as a wake-up call:

> One of the things this uncovered for us was that we didn't have an adequate system in place for the planning of exhibitions and letting

people in the Library know what was coming. We learned from this and have taken very active steps to remedy [the situation]. And that's the reason I'd say we've had no such difficulties since that time.

The LOC has, of course, faced controversy since then. But in the case of *Sigmund Freud: Conflict and Culture*, it was much more prepared to stand tough in the face of intense scrutiny and criticism. For Jill Brett, the LOC public affairs officer, "The Library stood by the Freud exhibit, which was the right thing to do. And it's the same exhibit we were going to do, not a changed one because of the voices raised against it."

What exactly has Winston Tabb instituted? A group of senior managers now oversees a double review process. First, they must approve the creation and scheduling of any exhibition. Second, closer to the projected opening date, the team reviews the images, objects, and anything else associated with the show, including educational and public programs and even the merchandise to be sold. This way, senior managers know exactly what's going on in every respect. According to Tabb, *Back of the Big House* likely "accelerated" the development of an administrative structure he would have put into place anyway.[11]

The impact of controversies ripples out in circles far beyond their point of origin. For example, an exhibit of the work of the late-nineteenth- and early-twentieth-century western landscape artist Thomas Moran opened at the Gilcrease Museum in Tulsa, Oklahoma, in 1998. As a reviewer noted, it was the best opportunity to publicly examine this painter's work since *The West as America* in 1991. But the curatorial choices were strikingly different in this latter case. Rather than link artists like Moran to ideologies of nationalist expansion and exploitation of the land and its original inhabitants, this exhibition displayed a light interpretive touch. It opted for a "noncontentious, 'here-it-is' approach," sidestepping the ideological minefield that the curators of *The West as America* hurtled through. The assistant to the museum director explained, "People are becoming more gun-shy. I think we're being more contemplative and cautious."[12] As with *Harlem on My Mind*, when a daring curatorial leap forward is met with loud disapproval, a judicious institutional drawing back may follow in its wake. Certain subjects and certain treatments of them may simply prove to be not worth the headache.

∎

This book has continuously noted the pivotal role the media play in museum controversies. Journalists are always looking for a good angle. Controversy provides it. "Censorship" is one such angle. "Political correctness" is another. But at what point do angles become slants? How do they sharpen some details while they diminish others? That is, how do angles in fact round off the edges of a story, forcing it into a predetermined shape? Media coverage of museums has breathed life into disputes that might otherwise have remained arcane conflicts. It simplifies and packages these struggles for general public consumption. The intense hunger for a good story has generated a number of extreme illustrations of media professionals actively constructing their accounts.

In the case of *Gaelic Gotham*, for example, recall the political activist Brendan Fay's charge that "fucking ethics of journalism were crossed" when a reporter initiated the call for a boycott of the exhibition. That exposed the slender lines between community newspapers, community membership, and journalistic advocacy. During the *Enola Gay* episode, a large number of special interest publications relentlessly hammered away at the National Air and Space Museum. This campaign was incited and supported in vital respects by the Air Force Association's exposés. The activities of this powerful lobbying organization, coupled with multiple channels to spread the message, helped generate a groundswell of dissent against the curators and their ideas. It is the most extreme example of a crusade waged against a museum and a proposed program. What is more, journalists working for more mainstream media also fed the fury by largely reproducing what the critics alleged, rather than thoroughly checking out the story for themselves or questioning how those ideas were filtered through certain lenses.

Museum directors such as Elizabeth Broun and Martin Harwit were simply out of their league in mounting public relations counterattacks. That wasn't an ordinary part of their duties. Recall Broun's sense of being unequal to the task: "You don't want to go to war with people who buy their ink by the barrel." Recall, too, that the LOC's Jill Brett described the media pouncing on the story of the Freud exhibition as if it were "red meat." That was the reaction of someone whose job it is to reach out to and interact with the media. Troubleshooting the debate over the Freud exhibition was a sobering professional experience for her, and it taught her colleague Irene

Chambers something too: "The story takes on a life of its own, and it's out there, and people are talking about something on the basis of one reporter's story. I guess I've known this all along, but this time brought it all home. And then people are talking on the basis of something that wasn't true, and they're responding to each other."[13]

One additional key phrase surfaced in some of these controversies: "the community," or "community participation." But whose voices do you listen to? How can you be sure who they represent? How seriously do you take them? "Community" became a particularly sensitive point in relation to *Harlem on My Mind, Back of the Big House,* and *Gaelic Gotham.* The Hunter College history professor Ed O'Donnell, one of the curators of *Gaelic Gotham,* pinpoints a fundamental problem with confronting individuals and coalitions who claim to speak for others. He argues that in communities based on ethnicity, religion, or sexual orientation, "There's a segment that has a strong sense of itself, and begins to speak for the group. Those subgroups tend to be more motivated and more organized, while most [other] people are out there trying to put food on the table, and go through everyday life. [This privileging of identity] is not their burning passion."

Jack Salzman, another member of the curatorial team for *Gaelic Gotham,* argues that

> Shows, like books, like everything else, get done by smart people. And those people are smart not because of their race, ethnicity, or gender. They're just smart. The real issue that has to do with race and gender and ethnicity is that too many people, too many women, too many people of color (to use a not-very-meaningful term), have been excluded from the realm of being smart.

But while Salzman is displeased that discrimination in the past has blocked opportunities for certain people, he voices doubts about the advisability of acceding to the demands of those whose credentials are based solely on group affiliation, not specific museum expertise:

> I know there are people who believe that these shows are to be done with the community. I just don't agree with that. It seems to me that you wind up just trying to cater to a community, and that the responsibility is to come up with the best and smartest show you can.

. . . If communities were always involved, then how do you ever get anything done?

Robert Macdonald, the director of the Museum of the City of New York, stakes out an important philosophical and tactical response to various constituencies that are extremely vocal about expressing themselves and pressing their demands. Realistically, that sort of confrontational stance is not likely to wane in the near future. Macdonald asserts,

> We have to listen to as many voices as we can hear. But we have to select those voices that are going to be heard in our galleries, and that's the challenge. So you have to try to be as inclusive as you can in listening. But you have to have the intellectual courage to select what goes up on your walls. Then you have the responsibility to stand by it.

Macdonald made many enemies during the struggle to bring *Gaelic Gotham* to completion. Time and again, they remarked on his combativeness and what they perceived to be Macdonald's stubborn refusal to listen to opposing views. In other words, his personality may have prevented his ideas about curating a show from receiving their best test. But Macdonald's premise makes a great deal of sense and holds a great deal of promise. It requires that museum personnel clearly cordon off the preliminary, fact-finding stages from the exhibition-building stages. Community input would be welcomed in the first instance. Professional criteria would prevail in the second phase, where the curatorial vision could proceed without interference. All parties should be clear about what the ground rules are throughout the process.

Macdonald's ideas are echoed by Tom Crouch. As a curator of *The Last Act*, Crouch was drawn into a protracted struggle, largely not of his own making. He witnessed firsthand how repeated attempts to assimilate outside demands failed to quiet the critics. Once tinkering with the script was allowed, the outcome became less and less acceptable to *all* the parties. Looking back, Crouch now realizes, "I think one of the lessons I learned is that fairly close to the beginning of the controversy, what you ought to do is find ground that you're comfortable on, dig your heels in, and see what happens. I think there's a lot of truth to that."

The costs of not doing that in the case of the *Enola Gay* exhibition were that National Air and Space Museum personnel endured months and months of attacks and were forced to smooth critics' ruffled feathers continuously. The ultimate result, of course, was losing control over the show and being forced to settle for something entirely different from what they'd originally conceived. Not only that, but capitulation has led to repeated unpleasantness: NASM personnel are judged to be either ideologues or wimps. Moreover, new exhibitions proposed anywhere can become targets for fresh attacks by opponents emboldened by the collapse of *The Last Act*. Despite the denials of people like Joan Rosenbaum, exhibition controversies *do* have an impact.

One of the best examples is what happened when the Smithsonian's National Museum of American History was planning an exhibition on sweatshops in 1997. It was projected to have a sweep of almost two hundred years. The highlight would be the display of artifacts seized in the 1995 government raid of a sweatshop in El Monte, California, including sewing-machine workstations and sections of the razor wire that surrounded the building. Shockingly, this was in the United States itself, and it was now—not in some crowded, turn-of-the-century tenement eighty or a hundred years ago on New York City's Lower East Side, or in some developing country.[14]

But the executive director of the California Fashion Association (an apparel trade group) issued this chilling warning in 1997: "We cannot stand idly by," she cautioned. "We want to turn this exhibit plan into another *Enola Gay*." Wielding this earlier episode like a club, she appeared hellbent on halting *Between a Rock and a Hard Place: A History of American Sweatshops, 1820-Present* before it opened to public view. As the co-curator Harry Rubenstein ponders, "All of a sudden it makes *Enola Gay* into a verb. Which is sort of an interesting creation."[15]

Fashion designers cut fabric against its grain or bias so that it will hang in dramatically different ways. The co-curators Peter Liebhold and Harry Rubenstein did something similar with their material. Like Robert Macdonald, they work in a post–*Enola Gay* museum environment. But Liebhold and Rubenstein's achievement is probably a better test of how to pitch your camp under these changed conditions than *Gaelic Gotham* was. Their strategy for presenting a controversial

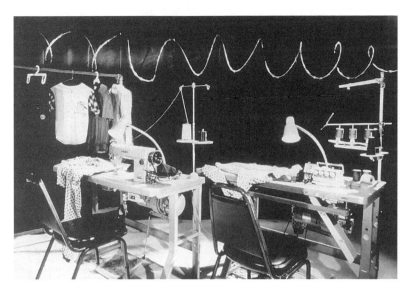

FIG. 21. Artifacts from the El Monte Sweatshop in the exhibit *Between a Rock and a Hard Place: A History of American Sweatshops, 1820–present*, 1998. Installation photograph by Eric Long. National Museum of American History. Used by permission.

FIG. 22. Jacob Riis, *Necktie Workshop in Division Street Tenement, New York*, 1887. Courtesy of the Library of Congress.

topic such as sweatshops was to insist on "different styles of conversation" or different voices within the exhibition. It too was "cut on the bias."

The historical section employed a curatorial voice. But they felt that using only this voice in the exhibition would be a mistake. Therefore, the El Monte section used the voices of the participants, be they workers or law enforcement agents. "The Fashion Food Chain" (which addressed the range of manufacturing alternatives) had the dry, authoritative voice of a textbook. Furthermore, a video presented the industry voice, while a "national leaders" section gave six individuals representing manufacturers, labor, government, community groups, and others the opportunity to offer their written comments.

Liebhold and Rubenstein cast a wide net to collect their information. But they carefully controlled the script. They subjected it to academic review, both within and outside the museum. Otherwise, it was "very closely held," explains Liebhold. "We wanted to avoid one of the pitfalls that we saw from *Enola Gay*, which is where people were going to nitpick specific words, and not respond in a more general kind of fashion." Did anyone actually request or demand a copy of this script? "Only a couple of people had the courage to ask," Liebhold explains. "We made it clear that we were not going to [let it out]." And Harry Rubenstein adds,

> In this climate, we were just afraid. And in some ways it's a shame, because many times when we were developing the script we would wonder how a group would perceive something. They could be the best ones to find mistakes in your work. But people working in public history feel under attack, and therefore we can't share the material because this could jeopardize the project as a whole.

Once the story of the industry's displeasure broke in the media, the curators offered logical defenses of their approach. Yet had a political groundswell formed against *Between a Rock and a Hard Place*, these arguments would not have mattered much. In this instance, several key politicos rallied to support the exhibition. Representative George Miller (D-California) circulated a "Dear Colleague" letter in Congress and initiated a letter to Smithsonian secretary I. Michael Heyman, signed by forty-five of his colleagues. At a regents' meeting, three of the nine members of the Smithsonian governing board spoke up in favor of the NMAH's plans. The Smithsonian administration stood firm this time.

These were demonstrations of support that never materialized for *The Last Act*. Veterans have a certified claim on American support and good will. Congress is one of the most important champions of their cause. Vets also boast a number of powerful lobbying groups, and they have the strength of numbers. When vets felt they were going to be presented unfairly in a Smithsonian exhibition, they could rally plenty of supporters to their side. But the topic of sweat-shops does not activate claims of unfair representation that scores and scores of people will reflexively believe. For most of those who heard about the exhibition in advance, the stakes were not that high. They were willing to adopt a wait-and-see attitude.

Harry Rubenstein explains, "We were under huge amounts of pressure, which is maybe different than [being] under fire," as Martin Harwit, Tom Crouch, and Michael Neufeld were a few years earlier with the *Enola Gay*. Peter Liebhold reflects, "Museums are a different place to work, post–*Enola Gay*. There were a number of exciting, inter-esting shows [before that] exploring the bounds of what type of mate-rial would be talked about in museums. And I think most people re-treated from it."

Liebhold and Rubenstein took care that a wide range of voices would come through in *Between a Rock and Hard Place*. They represent a new wave of curatorship that is increasingly sensitive to the multi-ple voices connected to their subjects and the diversity of their audi-ences. For example, one of the much-denounced group of wall texts accompanying *The West as America* raised the question "What's Wrong with the Language We Use?" The curators discussed the im-plications of employing either the generic "Indian," the racist "Injun," or a precise descriptor such as "Oglala Sioux." Moreover, these curators acknowledged that not everyone viewing *The West as America* would be like themselves. "When these works were painted," they wrote, "their intended audience was almost certainly white. Many of us here today, however, are not white. Some of us, in fact, may be stubbornly unvanished Indians."

In important respects, *The West as America* curators presaged the approach taken in the George Gustav Heye Center of the Smithson-ian's National Museum of the American Indian, which opened in New York City in 1994. The *process* of curating the exhibitions in this museum has been brought to the surface, much as the design of the Centre Georges Pompidou in Paris brought that building's mechanical systems to the outside rather than burying them within. "Selectors" of particular objects in Heye Center exhibitions are explicitly listed, along with their specific tribal affiliations. Three major interpretive approaches are emphasized: the anthropological, the art historical, and the native view. Every printed statement is identified by the person making it, as well as the perspective they represent.

The meaning of objects is magnified by native interpretations. The sensation of the objects themselves is enhanced by recorded voices and authentic music. The galleries are seen as places for dialogue. They are also seen as places where viewpoints may clash.

Other museums have followed this lead. A 1997 exhibition at the Yale University Art Gallery focused on objects produced by a tribe of people on Africa's Ivory Coast. *Baule: African Art/Western Eyes* sought to amplify the viewer's experience too. The four sections of the show corresponded to four native meanings of "to see": private, public, sacred, or secular artifacts. Field photographs and soundtracks helped reproduce natural settings. Documentary films further enlarged the context. Moreover, this art museum presented life-sized Baule environments, smudging the line between art and ethnography. It transcended conventional connoisseurship, offering an enhanced milieu where disconnected items customarily have been displayed instead.[16]

The West as America, the National Museum of the American Indian, and *Baule* have changed the way objects are presented and have enlarged the museum visitor's understanding of them. By doing so, museums are acknowledging that we live in an increasingly multicultural society and a multinational world. Because this recognition is relatively recent, it proceeds with fits and starts. It generates both profundities and follies. All too often, it involves a zero-sum game, where opponents see only victory or defeat—not the possibility of compromise. When one group fears that its power is slipping away, a visible way to stave the flow is to challenge various types of public representation. As we've seen, all too often that has meant that museums have been caught in the crossfire.

In New York, near the Brooklyn-Queens border, another multicultural vision unfolds quietly and unintentionally. Cypress Hills cemetery, the final resting place of Jackie Robinson and Mae West, has become a multiethnic neighborhood that has few counterparts in the world of the living. A Puerto Rican woman duplicates the Jewish ritual of leaving small stones at a gravesite. A Chinese mourner adapts an ancient tradition to the New World by leaving a plate of White Castle hamburgers for a loved one at another spot. Greeks, Lithuanians, and East Indians have found a home there too.

Like so many other features of New York City life, this mosaic is fabricated from need, not desire: with land so scarce and costly, it is not as simple as it once was to establish ethnically, racially, and religiously segregated burial grounds. The dead jostle one another over space in New York, just as the living do. But now their bodies could end up lying next to others whom they might never have had much opportunity (or desire) to associate with while they were alive. Moreover, the Museum of the City of New York presented a photo essay on such current burial practices in 1997, one additional example of the way contemporary museums have fixed on significant social phenomena.[17]

Museums have become places where conflicts over some of the most vital issues regarding national character and group identity—the struggle between universalism and particularism—regularly break out. These conflicts are displays of power, the result of groups flexing their muscles to express who they are or to beat back the claims of others. Even if such controversies were to cease immediately, they will remain an important artifact of an era of extraordinary social change and self-examination in America.

Interviews

All interviews were conducted by the author. Over two-thirds of them were face-to-face; the remainder were by telephone. They ranged in length from approximately three-quarters to over three hours. All were tape recorded and transcribed, except for two. Any unattributed quotes in the text derive from these interviews. Briefer telephone conversations were held with other individuals, and are duly noted. Identifying information reflects each interviewee's status or position at the time they spoke with the author.

Benny Andrews, artist and community activist, May 8, 1997.

Anonymous member of Ad Hoc Committee of Concerned Irish-American New Yorkers, October 23, 1997.

Stephen P. Aubin, Director of Communications, Air Force Association, April 2, 1998.

Harold Blum, Executive Director, the Sigmund Freud Archives, Inc., and Clinical Professor of Psychiatry, New York University, July 1, 1997.

Jill Brett, Public Affairs Officer, Library of Congress, December 15, 1997.

Elizabeth Broun, Director, the Smithsonian Institution's National Museum of American Art, February 9, 1998.

Angela Carter, community activist and owner of the Irish Bookshop (New York City), March 16, 1997.

Marion R. Casey, Ph.D. candidate in history, New York University, December 8, 1997.

Irene (Burnham) Chambers, Chief of Interpretive Programs Office, Library of Congress, December 15, 1997.

John T. Correll, Editor in Chief, *Air Force Magazine*, March 30, 1998.

Brother Emmett Corry, O.S.F., retired professor and Director of the Division of Library and Information Science, St. John's University, and research archivist, October 17, 1997.

Frederick Crews, Professor Emeritus of English, University of California–Berkeley, September 7, 1997.

Tom D. Crouch, Chair of Aeronautics Department, the Smithsonian Institution's National Air and Space Museum, April 8, 1998.

Nancy Curtin, Associate Professor of History, Fordham University, September 11, 1997.

Diane Dillon, Assistant Professor of Art History, Northwestern University, January 26, 1998.

Morris Eagle, Professor of Psychiatry, the Derner Institute of Advanced Psychological Studies, Adelphi University, June 5, 1997.

Brendan Fay, Irish gay activist and educator, February 28, 1997.

Sophie Freud, Professor Emerita of Social Work, Chair of Human Behavior Sequence, Simmons College, September 6, 1997.

Thelma Golden, curator, Whitney Museum of American Art, November 13, 1997.

Martin O. Harwit, astrophysicist and former Director, the Smithsonian Institution's National Air and Space Museum, March 19, 1998.

Melinda Hunt, public artist, March 8, 1997.

Elizabeth Johns, Silfen Term Professor of the History of Art and Chair of Art History Department, University of Pennsylvania, December 23, 1997.

Peggy King Jorde, Project Executive, African Burial Ground Memorialization Office, August 14, 1997.

Joni Louise Kinsey, Associate Professor of Art History, University of Iowa, December 16, 1997.

David Lackey, exhibition designer, Whirlwind and Company, April 28, 1997.

David Levinthal, photographer, March 9, 1997.

Peter Liebhold, museum specialist, the Smithsonian Institution's National Museum of American History, April 8, 1998.

Margot Lovejoy, Professor of Art, Purchase College, SUNY, August 20, 1997.

Robert R. Macdonald, Director, Museum of the City of New York, June 17, 1997.

Bernadette McCauley, Assistant Professor of History, Hunter College, CUNY, June 20, 1997.

John McInerney, clinical social worker and member of Ad Hoc Committee of Concerned Irish-American New Yorkers, November 9, 1997.

Jane McNamara, Associate Head, Education and Programs, Museum of the City of New York, and team member, *Gaelic Gotham*, March 13, 1997.

Helena Mulkerns, writer and freelance journalist, November 29, 1997.

Patrick T. Murphy, Director, Institute of Contemporary Art (Philadelphia), March 26, 1997.

Frank Naughton, Professor and Chair of Sociology and Anthropology Department, Kean College of New Jersey, October 15, 1997.

Alex Nemerov, Assistant Professor of Art History, Stanford University, December 17, 1997.

Michael J. Neufeld, curator, the Smithsonian Institution's National Air and Space Museum, April 8, 1998.

Joseph Noble, Director Emeritus, Museum of the City of New York, May 1, 1997.

Edward T. O'Donnell, Assistant Professor of History, Hunter College, CUNY, April 3, 1997.

B. Byron Price, Executive Director, Buffalo Bill Historical Center, February 11, 1998.

Jan Ramirez, Deputy Director, Programs and Collections, Museum of the City of New York, and Project Director, *Gaelic Gotham,* March 13, 1997.

Joan Rosenbaum, Director, the Jewish Museum (New York City), October 9, 1997.

Michael S. Roth, Associate Director, the Getty Center for the History of Art and the Humanities, September 26, 1997.

Harry R. Rubenstein, museum specialist, the Smithsonian Institution's National Museum of American History, April 8, 1998.

Jack Salzman, Deputy Director, Education, Media and Public Programs, the Jewish Museum (New York City), May 5, 1997.

Julie Schimmel, Associate Professor of Humanities and Religious Studies, Northern Arizona University, December 28, 1997.

Allon Schoener, curator, January 18, 1997.

Peter J. Swales, independent scholar and Freud critic, May 15, 1997.

Winston Tabb, Associate Librarian for Library Services, Library of Congress, December 15, 1997.

William Truettner, Curator of Painting and Sculpture, the Smithsonian Institution's National Museum of American Art, February 9, 1998.

John Michael Vlach, curator and Professor of American Studies and Anthropology, George Washington University, April 20, 1997.

Fred Wilson, artist, January 23, 1997.

Sherrill D. Wilson, Director, Office of Public Education and Interpretation of the African Burial Ground, August 5, 1997.

Notes

NOTES TO CHAPTER I

1. Quoted in Patricia Leigh Brown, "Though the Body's Still Warm, the Cold War Is Collectible," *New York Times*, January 2, 1992, C1; and *East Side Story*, written by Dana Ranga and Andrew Horn, directed by Dana Ranga (Kino International, 1997).

2. As the decade has progressed, the term "culture wars" has come under increasing criticism. For a collection of critical articles that find fault with the oversimplified and "overheated" cast of such rhetoric, see Rhys H. Williams, ed., *Cultural Wars in American Politics* (Hawthorne, NY: Aldine de Gruyter, 1997). See also Alan Wolfe, *One Nation, After All* (New York: Viking, 1998), where the author argues that the American middle class is not morally divided by a culture war (he found evidence of such a split only in relation to homosexuality), but that an impassioned battle *has* been waged by intellectuals.

3. Evette Cardona, "Uproaring Twenties," *NewCity* (Chicago), March 7, 1991, 7; and Mari Yamaguchi, "War Museum Shuns Atrocities," *Kansas City Star*, February 11, 1996, A16.

4. For the "victory culture," see Tom Engelhardt, *The End of Victory Culture: Cold War America and the Disillusioning of a Generation* (New York: Basic Books, 1995).

5. Telephone conversation, April 17, 1997.

6. See "A Museum Enshrines a Simpler Era's Dreams," *New York Times*, January 21, 1993, B8.

7. Author's interview, March 26, 1997.

8. Robert Sullivan, "Trouble in Paradigms," *Museum News* 71 (1), January–February 1992, 41. The American Museum of Natural History in New York City debuted its new Hall of Biodiversity in the spring of 1998, embodying this newer, interdependent philosophy.

9. See Donna Haraway, "Teddy Bear Patriarchy: Taxidermy in the Garden of Eden, New York City, 1908–1936," in *Primate Visions: Gender, Race, and Nature in the World of Modern Science* (New York: Routledge, 1989); and William Claiborne, "The Skeleton in the Museum's Closet," *Washington Post*,

April 5, 1992, F1. The boy, Minik, was seriously traumatized by the event. See also Phillips Verner Bradford and Harvey Blume, *Ota Benga: The Pygmy in the Zoo* (New York: St. Martin's, 1992) for a related account of an African who was first displayed at the 1904 St. Louis World's Fair, and later at the Bronx Zoo. Significantly, one of the authors is the grandson of Ota's captor. Institutional *mea culpas* have resulted in reconfigured exhibits and rewritten wall texts that reflect the current era's biases, and are upsetting to many visitors for going too far in another ideological direction; see, e.g., Michael Shanahan, "Smithsonian Updates Itself—Not to All Tastes," *Oregonian*, August 24, 1994, A3.

10. See Judith H. Dobrzynski, "Art(?) to Go: Museum Shops Broaden Wares, at a Profit," *New York Times*, December 10, 1997, A1.

11. Calvin Tomkins, *Merchants and Masterpieces: The Story of the Metropolitan Museum of Art* (New York: Henry Holt, 1989 [1970]), 23–24.

12. See Lisa W. Foderaro, "Museums Step Up Their Retailing to Turn Art into Revenue," *New York Times*, February 18, 1997, B5; Glenn Collins, "A Museum Markets Endangered Species to a Mass Audience," *New York Times*, March 13, 1997, D21; Carol Vogel, "Artful Back-Scratching Hitches Couture Names to Needy Museums," *New York Times*, January 4, 1997, 13; and Michael Kimmelman, "Does It Really Matter Who Sponsors a Show?" *New York Times*, May 19, 1996, H33.

In 1997 San Diego's Natural History Museum displayed film clips and props from *Jurassic Park*. The popular exhibition was underwritten by Burger King and General Mills, both of whom had marketing tie-ins with the sequel *The Lost World*; see Denise Gellene, "Museums—the Sequel: Dinosaurs for Dollars," *Los Angeles Times*, June 27, 1997, D1. Also in 1997 Chicago's Field Museum of Natural History paid over $8 million at auction for "Sue," a tyrannosaurus rex skeleton. With funds coming primarily from Fortune 500 corporate sponsors, the museum hopes to create a permanent blockbuster; see Stevenson Swanson, "Museums' Corporate Ties Rattle Some Bones," *Chicago Tribune*, October 12, 1997, sec. 1, 1.

13. Author's interview, March 13, 1997.

14. Ibid.

15. Author's interview, August 5, 1997.

16. Edward T. Linenthal, and Tom Engelhardt, eds., *History Wars: The Enola Gay and Other Battles for the American Past* (New York: Metropolitan Books, 1996), 23.

17. Duncan F. Cameron, "The Museum: A Temple or the Forum," *Journal of World History* 14 (1), 1972, 189, 199. Linenthal does not cite Cameron, even though he employs the same terms.

18. Quoted in Herschel B. Chipp, *Guernica: History, Transformations, Meanings* (Berkeley: University of California Press, 1988), 44.

19. "Repainting Begins on Rainbow Tank," *Boston Sunday Globe*, October 3, 1993, 10.

20. Author's interview, January 23, 1997.

21. Kobena Mercer, "Looking for Trouble," in *The Lesbian and Gay Studies Reader*, ed. Henry Abelove, Michele Barale, and David M. Halperin (New York: Routledge, 1993), 359.

22. Theodor Adorno, with Else Frenkel-Brunswik, Daniel J. Levinson, and R. Nevitt Sanford, *The Authoritarian Personality* (New York: Harper and Row, 1950); Eviatar Zerubavel, *The Fine Line: Making Distinctions in Everyday Life* (New York: Free Press, 1991); Anne Roiphe, "Us and Them, or The Virtue of Rudeness," *New York Observer*, May 1, 1995, 5; and James Davison Hunter, *Culture Wars: The Struggle to Define America* (New York: Basic Books, 1991), 43–46. Hunter has come under particular fire for his characterization of a bipolar ideological division. Survey and ethnographic data point to more complex divisions, and find that the rhetoric of a few social movement leaders may be more polarized than the attitudes of the general public; see Williams, 1997.

23. Janet Malcolm, "The Silent Woman-III," *New Yorker*, August 23 and 30, 1993, 148.

24. *New Art Examiner*, November 1995, 20–23. See also *"That* Girl! The Saga Continues," *New Art Examiner*, January 1996, 9; "Why Barbie's Show Lacks Substance," *New York Times*, December 11, 1995, A11, and "The Barbie Exhibition: Show but Don't Tell," *Curator Magazine* 39 (1), May 1996: 15–18.

NOTES TO CHAPTER 2

1. Jerry Tallmer, "The Show on Everyone's Mind," *New York Post Magazine*, January 25, 1969, 4.

2. Grace Glueck, "The Total Involvement of Thomas Hoving," *New York Times Magazine*, December 8, 1968, 45–46.

3 Thomas P. F. Hoving, *Making the Mummies Dance: Inside the Metropolitan Museum* (New York: Simon and Schuster, 1993), facing p. 128.

4. Author's interview, May 1, 1997. All subsequent unattributed quotes are from that interview.

5. This husband-and-wife team is best known for their eponymous chair. But Schoener's work shares obvious connections with the pair's manifold experiments with film, graphics, and exhibitions from the 1940s through the 1970s.

6. Author's interview, January 18, 1997. All subsequent unattributed quotes are from that interview.

7. *New York Amsterdam News*, January 11, 1969, 16.

8. Quoted in full in Robert G. Weisbord, and Arthur Stein, *Bittersweet*

Encounter: The Afro-American and the American Jew (Westport, CT: Negro Universities Press, 1970), 169–70.

9. Fred Ferretti, "New York's Black Anti-Semitism Scare," *Columbia Journalism Review*, 8 (3), fall, 1969, 22–23.

10. Joseph Berger, "Albert Shanker, 68, Combative Leader of Teachers, Dies," *New York Times*, February 23, 1997, 1; Steven R. Weisman, "A City at War," *New York Times*, March 1, 1997, 22.

11. Press release, November 16, 1967.

12. Quoted in Grace Glueck, "Adam C., Mother Brown, Malcolm X," *New York Times*, January 12, 1969, D26. Harold Rosenberg captured the sense of tumult in the museum world at that time—the growing emphasis on events rather than objects—in his essay "Museum of the New," in *Artworks and Packages* (New York: Dell, 1971 [1969]). This desacralization of museums caused Rosenberg to draw a comparison with movie theaters and bowling alleys.

13. Allon Schoener to author, February 3, 1997.

14. Ishmael Reed, "The Black Artist: 'Calling a Spade a Spade,'" *Arts Magazine* 41, May 1967, 49.

15. Quoted in Grace Glueck, "Negroes' Art Is What's In Just Now," *New York Times*, February 27, 1969, 34.

16. Henri Ghent, "White Is Not Superior," *New York Times*, December 8, 1968, 39.

17. Author's interview, May 8, 1997. All subsequent unattributed quotes are from that interview.

18. Hoving, 1993, 166–67; and author's interview with Schoener, January 18, 1997. In a fax I received from Mr. Hoving in July 1997, he declined to be interviewed, after I had made three requests. He stated, "I have recorded my memories very adequately in 'Mummies.'"

19. Author's interview, January 18, 1997. A *shabbas goy* is a Gentile who is hired to turn on lights and stove burners and perform other household tasks for observant Jews who are prohibited from doing "work" on the Sabbath. "Haryou" stood for Harlem Youth Opportunities Unlimited.

20. *New York Times,* January 31, 1969, 21.

21. The poem is reprinted in its entirety in "Anti-Semitism in the New York City School Controversy," a report of the Anti-Defamation League of B'nai B'rith, January 1969; see also Jack Gould, "Free Speech and the Right to Abuse It," *New York Times*, February 2, 1969, D19; and Julius Lester, *Lovesong: Becoming a Jew* (New York: Henry Holt, 1988), 47–65. Host Julius Lester, a black man, later converted to Judaism, embracing the religion of his German Jewish great-grandfather.

22. Ibid., 56–57.

23. In *Mummies,* Hoving states that he "embellished the truth" when he

wrote about this maid and chauffeur, although it's not clear if he made them up or merely misrepresented them (1993, 168). Allon Schoener doesn't believe they ever existed (author's interview, January 18, 1997).

24. Quoted in Jay Levin, "Met on Guard to Avert New Vandalism," *New York Post*, January 17, 1969.

25. "Harlem off Our Mind?" *New York Times*, January 31, 1969, 38; and Loyle Hairston, "Harlem on Whose Mind?" *New York Amsterdam News*, March 8, 1969, 23.

26. "One Vote for Thomas P. F. Hoving," *Art News* 68 (3), March 1969, 23.

27. "Books Withdrawn from Met's 'Harlem' Exhibit," *Publishers Weekly*, March 17, 1969, 32–33.

28. David Vestal, "Can Whitey Do a Beautiful Black Picture Show?" *Popular Photography* 64 (5), May 1969, 122, and author's interview with Benny Andrews, May 8, 1997.

29. Author's interview, May 8, 1997, and Camille Billops, interview #2 with Reginald Gammon, October 15, 1995, in *Artist and Influence,* vol.15, ed. James V. Hatch, Leo Hamalian, and Judy Blum (New York: Hatch-Billops Collection, 1966), 120.

30. Quoted in Glueck, "Total Involvement," 1968, 104; Camille Billops, interview #1 with Reginald Gammon, January 30, 1974, in Hatch et al., 1966, 108; and M. S. Handler, "75 Artists Urge Closing of Museum's 'Insulting' Harlem Exhibit," *New York Times*, January 23, 1969, 14.

31. Lerone Bennett, Jr., "Nat's Last White Man," in *William Styron's Nat Turner: Ten Black Writers Respond*, ed. John Henrik Clarke (Boston: Beacon Press, 1968), 5; Alvin F. Poussaint, "'The Confessions of Nat Turner' and the Dilemma of William Styron," in Clarke, 1968, 19; Ernest Kaiser, "The Failure of William Styron," in Clarke, 1968, 57; Charles V. Hamilton, "Our Nat Turner and William Styron's Creation," in Clarke, 1968, 73; and "Call It 'Nat Turner'; Won't Be Picketed," *New York Amsterdam News*, February 15, 1969, 1.

32. See photo illustrating "Harlem: Sold Out by Massa Hoving?" *Modern Photography*, May 1969, 64; Hairston, 1969 (Hairston, incidentally, was one of the contributors to the "rebuttal book" to *Nat Turner*); James R. Mellow, "The Electric Uncle Tom," *New Leader*, March 3, 1969, 28–29; author's interview, May 8, 1997; and Charles Wright, "Harlem at the Met: For Lap Dogs Only," *Village Voice*, January 30, 1969, 17. Schoener recalls, "We talked about the whole business of 'Tom-ism' all the time. And you know, they [his black assistants] were not Toms" (author's interview, January 18, 1997). Reflecting the polarization of the time, a writer in the *Village Voice* suggested "Uncle Jake" as a pejorative for those young leftist Jews who were embarrassed by their Jewishness and who were willing to take up every political cause except that of the Jews and Israel (January 13, 1969, 26). It was a period when undiluted "essences" were esteemed.

33. "What's Going On Here?" *New York Amsterdam News*, February 1, 1969, 14.

34. Rudy Johnson, "Two Harlem Pastors Disagree on Exhibit," *New York Times*, January 20, 1969, A22. Note that a photo of a confirmation class at Powell's church was prominently featured in the exhibition.

35. Telephone conversation, June 13, 1997.

36. Author's interview, January 23, 1997.

37. See John A. Williams, ed., *The Black Photographers Annual*, vol. 4, (Brooklyn, NY: Another View, 1980), 49–50. Information about both Bey and Van DerZee derives from this source, and additional information about Van DerZee comes from Reginald McGhee, ed., *The World of James Van DerZee: A Visual Record of Black Americans* (New York: Grove, 1969). Besides Van Ellison's catalogue essay and the interview in the Van DerZee book, I am unaware of anything else she published. A letter sent to her home address in Harlem in April 1997 was returned by the post office marked "deceased."

38. Author's interview, May 8, 1997. Benny Andrews was something of an exception: he was a little older (in his late thirties), he *was* showing in a gallery, and he had two young children at the time (who sometimes accompanied him to demonstrations).

39. Jesse H. Walker, "A Black Art Show Is at the Museum," *New York Amsterdam News*, February 8, 1997, 1.

40. Lawrence Alloway, "Art," *Nation*, February 3, 1969, 157.

41. "The Black Artist in America: A Symposium," in *The Metropolitan Museum of Art Bulletin* 27 (5), January 1969, 259. The entire issue was devoted to questions of race, art, and social action, and included an extensive nine-page bibliography on a wide range of aspects of life in Harlem.

42. Allon Schoener, editor's foreword to *Harlem on My Mind: Cultural Capital of Black America, 1900–1968* (New York: New Press, 1995 [1968]), n. p.

43. John Canaday, "Getting Harlem off My Mind," *New York Times*, January 12, 1969, D25.

44. Arlene Croce, "Discussing the Undiscussable," *New Yorker*, December 26, 1994–January 2, 1995, 54–55.

45. Katherine Kuh, "What's an Art Museum For?" *Saturday Review*, February 22, 1969, 58–59; and Hilton Kramer, "Politicizing the Metropolitan Museum," *New York Times*, January 26, 1969, D31.

46. A. D. Coleman, "Latent Image: Christmas Gift," *Village Voice*, January 23, 1969, 15.

47. Telephone conversation, June 24, 1997.

48. See "James Van DerZee" and "Roy DeCarava: 'Thru Black Eyes,'" reprinted in A. D. Coleman, *Light Readings: A Photography Critic's Writings, 1968–1978* (New York: Oxford University Press, 1979), 18, 27; and Coleman, 1969.

49. Author's telephone conversation; and Coleman, 1979, 10. I am grateful to Marilyn McLaren for a conversation in which we serendipitously uncovered this divergence between the two versions.

50. Eugene D. Genovese, "Harlem on His Back: An Historian Looks at Hoving's Harlem," *Artforum* 7 (6), February 1969, 34–37.

51. See "Bruce Davidson: *East 100th Street,*" in Coleman, 1979, 45–48.

52. Amy Goldin, "Harlem Out of Mind," *Art News* 68 (3), March 1969, 53; Alloway, 1969, 156; and Mellow, 1969, 28.

53. Goldin, 1969, 53.

54. Grace Glueck, "Art: 'Harlem on My Mind' in Slides, Tapes and Photos," *New York Times*, January 17, 1969, 28; and Mellow, 1969, 29.

55. See "Steps toward a First Step," *New York Times*, January 19, 1969, D15; "Can Black and White Artists Still Work Together?" *New York Times*, February 2, 1969, sec. 2, p. 1; and Sylviane Gold, "Seeking a Theater Varied as a Rainbow," *New York Times*, February 23, 1997, H5.

56. Quoted in Ferretti, 1969, 21, 28.

57. Wright, 1969. The song (New York: I. Berlin, 1933) was included in the musical review *As Thousands Cheer.*

58. Elisabeth Bumiller, "Harlem on Her Mind," *New York Times,* March 28, 1997, B1; and Amy M. Spindler, "Taking Stereotyping to a New Level in Fashion," *New York Times*, June 3, 1997, A21.

59. Author's interview, November 13, 1997.

60. John Michael Vlach, *Back of the Big House: The Architecture of Plantation Slavery* (Chapel Hill: University of North Carolina Press, 1993), xiii.

61. Ibid., xiv.

62. This and other unattributed quotes by Vlach derive from a presentation I heard him give at the opening of the exhibition at the Unitarian Universalist Congregation at Shelter Rock, Manhasset, New York, on April 20, 1997, and from an interview I conducted with him afterwards. Shelter Rock was the eleventh site for this exhibition.

63. Holly Selby, "Slavery Exhibit Has New Home," *Baltimore Sun*, December 29, 1995, 1E; and Linton Weeks, "The Continuing Hurt of History," *Washington Post*, December 22, 1995, C10. Jill Brett, the LOC public affairs officer, used the figure of sixty as the "official," albeit unscientific, count of objectors; author's interview, December 15, 1997.

64. "A Library on Tiptoe," *Washington Post*, December 22, 1995, A18; and "The False Peace of Blissful Ignorance," *Chicago Tribune*, December 29, 1995, 20.

65. Author's interviews, December 15, 1997. The same day I conducted these interviews, I picked up a copy of the *Baltimore Sun* to read on my return trip. An article featured a new book commemorating the centennial of the LOC's Special Collections, *Eyes of the Nation*. The journalist quotes Vincent

Varga, the book's photo editor, about the process of selecting images: "'we all agreed that the Library of Congress is about telling the truth. We,' he says, underlining his strong identification with the library, 'we are ultimately the First Amendment. This is the First Amendment made manifest, the Library of Congress, the embodiment of the First Amendment.'" Carl Schoettler, "Compiling the Nation's Photo Album," *Baltimore Sun*, December 15, 1997, 3D. But some people would not be able to endorse this enthusiastic pronouncement, in light of the LOC's banishment of the slavery exhibition.

66. Kate Mulligan, "Life on Plantations as Lived by the Slaves," *Washington Times*, February 1, 1996, M8.

67. Mary Ann French, "The Fertile Ground of 'Plantation,'" *Washington Post*, January 18, 1996, C2; and Weeks, 1995.

68. "A Library on Tiptoe," 1995.

69. David Nicholson, "The Costs of Cultural Blackmail," *Washington Post*, December 24, 1995, C2; and Karen Lange, "Library of Congress Fracas Spotlights UNC Press Book," *Chapel Hill Herald*, December 22, 1995, 1.

70. Todd Gitlin, "The Big Mouse," *New Republic*, January 22, 1996, 14.

71. Winston Tabb, "Rest of the Story," *Chicago Tribune*, January 22, 1996, 14. Essentially the same letter ran in the *Pittsburgh Post-Gazette*, January 20, 1996. According to Jill Brett, her office sent out this letter whenever critical articles appeared across the country. Tabb became the "point man" in this controversy, and this was the sanctioned response.

72. Quotations excerpted from "Comments: From Viewers of the Exhibit *The Cultural Landscape of the Plantation*," Martin Luther King, Jr. Memorial Library, January 1996.

73. *Gazette*, January 5 and 19, 1996.

74. Author's interviews, April 20 and December 15, 1997. Tabb adds that the LOC's *African-American Odyssey*, which opened in February 1998, is its largest survey ever of African American materials, and another reason he was willing to abandon *Back of the Big House*. For the record, a secretary told me that Tabb had been employed at the LOC for about twenty-five years.

NOTES TO CHAPTER 3

1. Also spelled "cingulum," from the Latin for belt or girdle. The English put a wooden contraption around the neck of Irish children in the nineteenth century when they dared to use their native language. Such devices are also referred to as a "tally stick" or "bata scór" in Irish. My thanks to Angela Carter of the Irish Bookshop, New York City, for providing this information.

2. Robert Trussell, "Michael Flatley Is Lord of the Cash," *Kansas City Star*, September 28, 1997, L4.

3. James Bradley, "A Fading Tile in the Gorgeous Mosaic?" *Irish Echo*,

August 18–24, 1993. "The gorgeous mosaic" was a phrase popularized by New York City Mayor David Dinkins to characterize how different ethnic groups fit together in the city while retaining their distinctiveness, superseding the idea of a melting pot. See also Mary Cantwell, "St. Patrick's Gallimaufry," *New York Times*, February 13, 1993, 20.

4. *New York Post*, January 11, 1993.

5. Pete Hamill, "The Suppressors of Freedom: Curse of the Irish," *New York Post*, March 14, 1991, 30; and Jimmy Breslin, "The Cardinal Sins of Irish Catholics," *New York Newsday*, March 19, 1991, 3.

6. Andrew M. Greeley, "On Irish Catholics, Breslin Writes Baloney," *New York Newsday*, March 2, 1991, 67.

7. Clyde Haberman, "The Irish Finally Stop to Remember," *New York Times*, March 18, 1997, B1; and Christine S. Cozzens, "Tracing Tragedy in Ireland," *New York Times*, June 1, 1997, xx 13. A similar campaign to include the famine in school curricula is under way in New Jersey.

8. In his memoir about growing up in the comfortable suburbs of New Jersey and learning about his family's suffering during the mass slaughter of Armenians by Turks in 1915, the poet Peter Balakian quotes an aunt telling him about a talk she gave in 1940 commemorating the twenty-fifth anniversary of the event: "We didn't use the term *genocide* then, we said The Massacres." But now referring to genocide, and drawing multiple comparisons to the Holocaust, Balakian aims to inform his readers about a horrific historical episode that has been largely unremarked. Using the suitably contemporary terms, he may help plant this harrowing chapter into the public's consciousness more firmly than the facts alone have done. See Peter Balakian, *Black Dog of Fate: An American Son Uncovers His Armenian Past* (New York: Basic Books, 1997), 177.

9. "Catholic Pogrom Continues," letter to the editor, *Irish Echo*, February 10–16, 1993, 10 (emphasis added).

10. Betty Liu Ebron, "Irish Eyes Will Smile at Her Exhibit," *New York Daily News*, March 18, 1993, 23.

11. Author's interview, June 17, 1997. All subsequent unattributed quotes are from that interview.

12. Author's interview, March 13, 1997. All subsequent unattributed quotes are from that interview.

13. Marion R. Casey, statement of responsibilities, January 2, 1995. After a telephone conversation on January 10 with Gary Roth, the deputy director for programs and special projects, Casey faxed a list of tasks to the museum.

14. Author's interviews with Angela Carter, March 16, 1997, and Frank Naughton, October 15, 1997. All subsequent unattributed quotes are from those interviews.

15. Author's interview, April 3, 1997. All subsequent unattributed

quotes are from that interview. To be perfectly candid, there were moments when I felt that the struggle between Marion Casey and the museum was being recapitulated between her and myself when I requested an interview from her for this book. I wrote her five letters over a seven-month period; no other interviewee required that amount of contact. I also asked other interviewees to pass along my continued interest in speaking with her. Once, when I believed we were close to hammering down a date, she balked after I met her request to provide a list of the people I had spoken with thus far. She judged it to be top-heavy with people "on the museum's side." My first letter to Marion Casey was sent on March 1, 1997. We finally met on December 8, and she was very generous in allowing me to see and photocopy relevant documents. She also furnished additional ones I requested later on.

16. Author's interview with Macdonald, June 17, 1997.

17. Ibid. In a letter to the editor, Marion Casey calculated that she was paid less than five dollars an hour, without benefits. However, the "unfairness" angle is somewhat misleading: she was contracted to complete certain assignments; she was *not* a salaried employee of the museum. See "Casey Addresses Director's 'Distortions,'" *Irish Echo*, September 13–19, 1995, 9.

18. Author's interview, November 29, 1997. All subsequent unattributed quotes are from that interview.

19. Author's interviews, March 16 and October 17, 1997. All subsequent unattributed quotes are from those interviews.

20. Author's interviews, June 17, April 3, and May 5, 1997.

21. Author's interview, April 28, 1997. All subsequent unattributed quotes are from that interview.

22. Ray O'Hanlon, "Just Don't Mention the War," *Irish Echo*, January 24–30, 1996.

23. Author's interview, December 8, 1997. All subsequent unattributed quotes are from that interview.

24. "Museum Bait and Switch," *Irish Echo*, August 9–15, 1995, 9.

25. Telephone conversation, October 9, 1997. The phrases "bait and switch" and "follow the money" also surface in a set of notes Marion Casey wrote to herself, summarizing the controversy in February 1996. These are simply two examples of ideas that were repeated with a self-confirming regularity within a group of like-minded individuals.

26. Emmett Corry, O.S.F., to New York Irish History Roundtable members, January 15, 1996.

27. Author's interview, October 23, 1997. All subsequent unattributed quotes are from that interview.

28. Author's interviews. I have seen copies of two letters sent by Corry to NEH Chairman Hackney.

29. Several of the community critics of *Gaelic Gotham*, including Marion

Casey, find great irony in the fact that in 1987, as president of the American Association of Museums, Robert Macdonald appointed a committee to frame an ethics code for museums. The irony, for them, stems from their belief that he conducted himself in a very *un*ethical manner in dealing with them and with this exhibition.

30. In a letter to a member of the Irish History roundtable, King pledged to help the roundtable "regain control of its creation," confirming the group's proprietary claims.

31. John Kuo Wei Tchen in Council for Scholarly Evaluation of *Gaelic Gotham, The Gaelic Gotham Report* (New York: New York Irish History Roundtable, 1997), 45.

32. Author's interviews, October 23 and June 17, 1997. Marion Casey produced two extensive analyses of the budget for *Gaelic Gotham* after she was no longer associated with the project. Both seem to have provided the basis for others' critique of the show's finances. The version she produced in March 1996, just as *Gaelic Gotham* opened, reads like a "field guide": "When you go to see the exhibition . . . see if you can figure out where all the money went—I don't see evidence of three quarters of a million dollars, or even of the NEH's $250,000, in *Gaelic Gotham*." She states she prepared it for a journalist prior to his reviewing the exhibition; personal communication, December 23, 1997.

33. Author's interview, May 5, 1997. Robert Macdonald said the same thing to me about my being the first person to sit down and try to get the complete story, as did Jan Ramirez (although she had some contact with individuals in the community, such as Brendan Fay, because of her role as project director).

34. Author's interview, March 16, 1997. Ladies' Mile was a concentration of department stores in the Chelsea section of Manhattan, fashionable from the mid-nineteenth century until World War I, the Gilded Age refers to the decades after the Civil War, characterized by greed, vulgar taste, and the relentless pursuit of material goods.

35. Author's interview, February 28, 1997. All subsequent unattributed quotes are from that interview.

36. Telephone conversation, October 22, 1997.

37. Author's interviews, February 28, November 9, and October 15, 1997.

38. John O'Mahony, "1996: Time of the Troubles," *New York Post*, December 21, 1995, 56. See also Helena Mulkerns and Harry Keaney, "Irish Ire Erupts over New York Show," *Irish Echo*, January 17–23, 1996, 1, 29.

39. Edward O'Donnell, "'Gaelic Gotham' Team Comprises Top Scholars," *Irish Echo*, January 31-February 6, 1996, 12, and author's interview, April 3, 1997.

40. Mulkerns and Keaney, 1996.

41. *The Gaelic Gotham Report*, 1997, 5; the January 31-February 6, 1996, issue of the *Irish Echo* published three letters to the editor protesting the charge of anti-Semitism as "groundless" and an "invention"; author's interview, December 8, 1997.

42. Author's interviews, May 5, March 13, and June 20, 1997.

43. Brendan Fay et al. to Robert Macdonald, December 9, 1995; and Robert Macdonald to Brendan Fay, December 12, 1995.

44. Press release, January 11, 1996; Angela Carter to Brendan Fay, December 19, 1995; Brendan Fay to Jan Ramirez, January 11, 1996; and author's interview, November 9, 1997. The reference to "simian-faced hordes" calls up crude stereotypes of the Irish, which were explored in *Gaelic Gotham*; the "Big House," according to McInerney, is a phrase commonly used among the Irish to characterize their colonization by the British.

45. Author's interviews, June 17 and September 11, 1997. All subsequent unattributed quotes are from those interviews.

46. Marion Casey, form letter, June 29, 1995; and author's interview, December 8, 1997.

47. Author's interviews, June 20, April 3, and March 13, 1997. Casey consulted an attorney very early on: January 9, 1995, when she first suspected that the MCNY might seek to replace her. She considered bringing actions based on her intellectual property rights and defamation (on the part of Macdonald). She had a lawyer send a letter to the MCNY on her behalf for the first time exactly five months later; author's interview, December 8, 1997.

48. Author's interviews, March 13 and April 28, 1997; and *Gaelic Gotham: A History of the Irish in New York* (exhibition script) (New York: Museum of the City of New York, 1996), 65.

49. Quoted in Thomas Cahill, *How the Irish Saved Civilization* (New York: Doubleday, 1995), 129.

50. Emmett Corry, "MCNY Director Still Doesn't Get It," *Irish Echo*, September 20–26, 1995, 9.

51. Recall, too, that Candice Van Ellison wrote of tension between the black community and the Irish in the catalogue to *Harlem on My Mind*, because the Irish have a long history of working as New York City cops. They are often "The Man."

52. Marion R. Casey, "How to Ruin a Good Exhibition," *Wall Street Journal*, April 10, 1996, A17; and author's interviews, December 8, October 15, May 5, and September 11, 1997.

53. Jan Ramirez notes that the Irish consul, along with three members of the Irish American community, took up Macdonald's offer to view the exhibition model and the entire range of related materials, courtesy of David Lackey and members of the project team. After this "walk-through," they left

convinced that this was a professional effort. Except for representatives of an ad hoc committee that sponsors an annual St. Patrick's ball, who almost moved their event from the MCNY because of the controversy but were also impressed when they viewed the entire setup, no one else availed themselves of this opportunity to preview the MCNY's plans; author's interviews, March 31 and April 28, 1997.

54. John T. McInerney to Robert Macdonald, January 5, 1996; and author's interviews, March 16, February 28, June 17, and March 13, 1997. The published version of the script contains the following "disclaimer," addressing these very issues: "This publication presents the text of *Gaelic Gotham: A History of the Irish in New York*. The rich visual, audio, and video elements of the actual exhibition cannot be experienced herein" (v).

55. *The Gaelic Gotham Report*, 1997, 63.

56. Kevin McHugh, "Museum Ignores Request to Furnish 'Gotham' Script," *Irish Echo*, February 7–13, 1996, 36; and author's interview, June 17, 1997.

57. Author's interview, June 17, 1997; and quoted in "Fighting Irish," *New York Times*, February 13, 1996, A20. Macdonald's first use of this statement appears to be in a letter sent to Brother Emmett Corry in his capacity as president of the New York Irish History Roundtable, April 18, 1995.

58. Angela Carter to Brendan Fay, December 10, 1995; and author's interviews, November 29 and October 17, 1997.

59. Telephone conversation, October 9, 1997; and author's interview, September 11, 1997.

60. Author's interview, May 1, 1997.

61. Cited in Joseph Veach Noble, "VD: An Educational Exhibit," *Curator Magazine* 17 (3), 1974, 202, and author's interview, May 1, 1997.

62. Helena Mulkerns, "The Silence of the Walls," *Irish Echo*, April 24–30, 1996, 35; and Casey, "How to Ruin," 1996. Non-Irish joined the chorus too: Tchen characterized this as a clash between a "very well-established Knickerbocker elite" and "the great unwashed"; *The Gaelic Gotham Report*, 1997, 40–41.

63. "The New York Irish," *Irish Times*, March 25, 1996.

64. Mulkerns and Keaney, 1996; and Angela Carter to Brendan Fay.

65. Kevin Kenny, "Taking Care of the Irish," *American Quarterly* 49 (4), December 1997, 820, 822.

66. *The Gaelic Gotham Report*, 1997, 34, 39.

67. Joe Carroll, "Controversy Breaks Out over 'Gaelic Gotham,'" *Irish Times*, May 25, 1997, 9.

68. *The Gaelic Gotham Report*, 1997, 87; and author's interview, October 15, 1997. The report was released on May 15, 1997. Seven months later, Frank Naughton reported that nearly four hundred copies had been distributed,

primarily to groups and organizations interested in historical exhibits in museums and public history. It was primarily funded through the New York Irish History Roundtable.

69. Marion Casey was not a member of the Council for Scholarly Evaluation of *Gaelic Gotham*. She did, however, furnish them copies of all her correspondence and the documents she had compiled. She also reviewed the report in draft form.

70. *The Gaelic Gotham Report*, 1997, 69; and author's interviews, October 17 and October 15, 1997.

71. Author's interview, April 3, 1997; Marion R. Casey, "Who Sets the Cultural Agenda?" *Irish Echo*, February 21–27, 1996, 9; and Mulkerns, 1996.

72. Peter McDermott, "'Gaelic Gotham': A Stimulus for Further Thinking," *Irish Echo*, March 27-April 2, 1996, 25; Mulkerns and Keaney, 1996; and Mulkerns, 1996.

73. Author's interview, November 29, 1997. Mulkerns states that "wetback" is used to characterize Irish who are "just off the boat," just as it denigratingly refers to other newly arrived immigrants.

74. John McGinnis, "Irish-Americans and What Might Have Been," *Wall Street Journal*, March 19, 1996, 70. Several of the community activists spontaneously mentioned that they were not personally connected to McGinnis. The chairman of the board and the president of the MCNY rebutted McGinnis's charges in a letter published March 28, 1996. It is the only time they publicly joined in this battle.

75. Mulkerns and Keaney, 1996; and *Gaelic Gotham: A History of the Irish in New York*, 1996, 110.

76. Author's interviews, February 28 and October 23, 1997. Fay declined the MCNY's invitation to deliver the Mark Ouderkirk Memorial lecture in a lengthy and very critical letter he sent to Jan Ramirez, January 11, 1996 (the day of the meeting at Fitzpatrick's Hotel).

77. Telephone conversation, November 3, 1997.

78. See Joe O'Neill, "Stanford Band Skit Provokes Outrage," *Irish Echo*, October 15–21, 1997, 1. The incident even prompted debate among the readers of Ann Landers; see "Stanford Band Gets Praise, Shame," *Kansas City Star*, February 8, 1998, G4.

NOTES TO CHAPTER 4

1. "Psychiatry's Depression," *Time*, April 2, 1979, 74; "Is Freud Dead?" *Time*, November 29, 1993; "Is God Dead?" *Time*, April 8, 1966; and Paul Gray, "The Assault on Freud," *Time*, November 29, 1993, 47. According to both Peter J. Swales and Frederick Crews, the Gray article was "a rip-off" of Crews's article on current critical scholarship on Freud, "The Unknown

Freud," *New York Review of Books,* November 18, 1993 (author's interviews, May 15 and September 7, 1997). Crews collected this essay along with "The Revenge of the Repressed" on the recovered-memory movement (*New York Review of Books,* December 1, 1994), the exchange of letters that followed each, and "Afterword: Confessions of a Freud Basher" in *The Memory Wars: Freud's Legacy in Dispute* (New York: New York Review of Books, 1995).

2. Jeffrey Moussaieff Masson, *The Assault on Truth: Freud's Suppression of the Seduction Theory* (New York: Farrar, Straus and Giroux, 1984); and quoted in Janet Malcolm, *In the Freud Archives* (New York: Knopf, 1984), 50–51.

3. Janet Malcolm, *Psychoanalysis: The Impossible Profession* (New York: Knopf, 1981), 107.

4. Author's interview, June 5, 1997. All subsequent unattributed quotes are from that interview.

5. Quoted in Malcolm, 1984, 19.

6. Ibid., 33, 38. Masson unsuccessfully sued Malcolm in two libel trials.

7. Ibid., 114, 135. The bulk of part 2 is about Swales, although it has been overshadowed by the subsequent dispute between Masson and Malcolm.

8. Author's interview, May 15, 1997. All subsequent unattributed quotes are from that interview.

9. Ibid. See also Peter J. Swales, "Freud, Minna Bernays, and the Conquest of Rome: New Light on the Origins of Psychoanalysis," *New American Review* 1, 1982, 1–23.

10. Malcolm, 1984, 124.

11. Author's interview, May 15, 1997; see also Malcolm, 1984, 118.

12. Malcolm, 1984, 96, 98, 106–7, 111.

13. Irvin Molotsky, "Freud Show Delayed amid Criticism," *New York Times,* December 6, 1995, A18; and Henry P. Schwartz, "Sigourney Awards to Gill, Neubauer, Schafer, Stone," *American Psychoanalyst* 29 (1), 1995, 9. As it turned out, Freud's consulting couch was too fragile to travel, but a Persian rug that draped it was displayed.

14. Author's interview, July 1, 1997; and Molotsky, 1995. At Blum's request, this interview was recorded by note-taking, not by audio tape. All subsequent unattributed quotes are from that interview.

15. Peter J. Swales transcribed a recording made by someone who attended and later gave him the tape.

16. Author's interview, September 7, 1997. All subsequent unattributed quotes are from that interview. *The Sins of the Fathers: Hawthorne's Psychological Themes* was published by Oxford University Press.

17. The essay "Analysis Terminable" appears in *Skeptical Engagements* (New York: Oxford University Press, 1986). The University of California Press reissued *The Sins of the Fathers;* quotation, 284.

18. Quoted in Dinitia Smith, "Freud May Be Dead, but His Critics Still Kick," *New York Times*, December 10, 1995, E14.

19. Michel Foucault, *The History of Sexuality,* vol. 1, *An Introduction* (New York: Vintage Books, 1980), 45 (emphasis in the original).

20. Author's interview, March 26, 1997.

21. Peter J. Swales to Oliver Sacks, June 12, 1997. The reference to Nazis and "Freudian Jews" was made by the French Lacanian psychoanalyst Elisabeth Roudenesco, in a letter bolstered by 180 signatures, portraying a petition Swales sent to the LOC as a work of extreme violence and fascistic tendencies (discussed shortly). Swales characterizes this as "a disgusting moment in the history of scholarship," noting that at least half of his petitioners were Jewish, and some others were married to Jews.

22. Author's interview, September 26, 1997. All subsequent unattributed quotes are from that interview.

23. Frederick Crews to Marvin Kranz, June 7, 1995; and author's interview, September 7, 1997.

24. Peter J. Swales to Marvin Kranz, July 11, 1995; and author's interview, May 15, 1997.

25. Author's interview, May 15, 1997. A good example of the philosophical differences among the signatories comes from Morris Eagle: "Who gives a shit whether Freud slept with Minna? I'm interested in theory, conceptual critiques, and empirical findings. I'm not interested in Freud the person, and how good or bad a guy he was" (author's interview), June 5, 1997.

26. Author's interview, May 15, 1997; and Swales et al. to James Hutson, July 31, 1997.

27. Peter J. Swales to signatories, July 28, 1995.

28. Frederick Eberstadt to James Billington, October 17, 1995; Barry Silverstein to Michael Roth, October 11, 1995; and Sonu Shamdasani to Michael Roth, October 11, 1995. An odd historical footnote to the Cold War: while the stock of psychoanalysis may be declining in value throughout the West, it now enjoys a bull market in Russia, where it was effectively banned under communist rule; see Alessandra Stanley, "Freud in Russia: Return of the Repressed," *New York Times*, December 11, 1996, A1.

29. Daniel Zalewski, "Fissures at an Exhibition," *Lingua Franca*, November–December 1995, 74.

30. Ibid., 77.

31. See Julia M. Klein, "Museum's Freudian Flip Brings Calls of Censorship," *Philadelphia Inquirer*, December 10, 1995, D1.

32. Smith, 1995.

33. Author's interview, September 6, 1997. All subsequent unattributed quotes are from that interview.

34. Peter Swales to Oliver Sacks, January 19, 1996; Oliver Sacks to Peter Swales, January 23, 1996.

35. February 9, 1996 (emphasis added) (http://plaza.interport.net/nypsan/sfa_loc.html).

36. Morris Eagle, "From the President's Desk," *Psychologist Psychoanalyst* (official publication of Division 39 of the American Psychological Association) 16 (2), spring 1996, 7.

37. "Clash of the Super Egos," *Daily Telegraph* (London), December 7, 1995, 19; Peter Swales to Russ Powell, February 22, 1996; and Peter Swales to various recipients, March 4, 1996. During my interview with him, Swales also described this as a "passion play." He was resolute that anyone attributing malevolent motives to the petition was "depraved" and among the "intellectual lowlife of the Western Hemisphere." He also termed some of those contributing to the exhibition catalogue, whose work differs from his own, "fucking jerks."

38. Author's interviews, June 5, September 6, May 15, and September 7, 1997. For two examples where "Freud basher" figures prominently, see Martin Levin, "Freud-Bashers Open Fire on Father. Hmmm," *Globe and Mail* (Toronto), January 4, 1996; and Edith Kurzweil, "Politically Correct Freud?" *Partisan Review* 43 (2), 1996, 236–41.

39. Note, for example, Jonathan Lear: "Obsessing about Freud *the man* is a way of keeping Freud *the meaning* at bay" (emphasis in the original), in "The Shrink Is In," *New Republic*, December 25, 1995, 25.

40. "Historical Shows on Trial: Who Judges?" *New York Times*, February 11, 1996, sec. 2, 26.

41. Zalewski, 1995, 77.

42. Marc Fisher, "Under Attack, Library Shelves Freud Exhibit," *Washington Post*, December 5, 1995, A1; and Peter J. Swales to James Billington, March 4, 1996.

43. Author's interviews, December 15, 1997.

44. Malcolm, 1984, 90, 110.

45. Peter Swales to Oliver Sacks, January 19, 1996.

46. February 11, 1996, document 167, Swales dossier.

47. See Michael S. Roth, "The Freud Flap," *Tikkun*, March–April 1996, 41; Richard Karel, "Library of Congress Freud Exhibit Derailed by Money Problems, Conflict," *American Psychiatric News*, January 5, 1996, 33; and Peter J. Swales to Winston Tabb, June 18, 1996.

48. See Marc Fisher, "The Rewriting on the Wall? A Library of Congress Exhibit on German Resistance Provokes Debate about History and Museums," *Washington Post*, July 24, 1994, G1; and letters to the editor, *Washington Post*, July 31, 1994, G2.

49. "Library Postpones Freud Exhibition," *Gazette* (Library of Congress) 6 (45), December 8, 1995, 15; and Harriet I. Basseches (with Nancy R. Goodman), "Grassroots Group Boosts Freud Exhibit Momentum," *American Psychoanalyst* 30 (3), 1996, 33. According to Irene Chambers, the magnitude of the funds coming from Austria were exaggerated; they "wouldn't have gotten us anywhere near doing this exhibition"; author's interview, December 15, 1997.

50. Peter J. Swales to Marc Fisher, November 29, 1995. Swales also condemns the LOC, a public institution, for accepting material subject to restrictions imposed by private parties.

51. Quoted in Courtney Leatherman, "Whither Civility?" *Chronicle of Higher Education*, March 8, 1996, A22.

52. Peter Swales to Oliver Sacks, January 19, 1996; and author's interview, May 15, 1997.

53. See Ronald M. Benson, "Task Force Helps Keep Freud Exhibit Alive," *American Psychoanalyst* 30 (3), 1996, 32–33.

54. Author's interview, October 9, 1997.

55. Author's interview, May 15, 1997.

56. See Frederick Crews to Michael S. Roth, June 5, 1996; and Peter J. Swales to Richard Camer (editor, *Clinical Psychiatry News*), April 19, 1996. Swales's acutely angry follow-up letter about a phrase that was omitted from his published letter to the editor severely chastised the man for deleting Swales's middle initial. In the documents I have seen, Swales sometimes uses it, and sometimes does not. I have attempted to carefully honor his own self-presentation. I am confident he will let me know if I've erred.

57. Author's interview, July 1, 1997; and Zalewski, 1995, 77.

58. Crews, 1995, 293.

59. Author's interview, December 15, 1997.

NOTES TO CHAPTER 5

1. The Poppers' ideas have attracted a good deal of attention. See two articles in the *New York Times Magazine:* Anne Mathews, "The Poppers and the Plains," June 24, 1990, 24; and Jon Margolis, "The Reopening of the Frontier," October 5, 1995, 51–57. See also Camilo José Vergara, *The New American Ghetto* (New Brunswick: Rutgers University Press, 1995).

2. Richard Bernstein, "Unsettling the Old West," *New York Times Magazine*, March 18, 1990, 56, 59.

3. See Edmund Newton, "Columbus and Rose Parade Prove to Be Thorny Mixture," *Los Angeles Times*, October 12, 1991, B1; Michael S. Arnold, "Protestors Stop Mock Landing of Columbus," *Los Angeles Times*, October 12, 1992, A3; and Fox Butterfield, "Columbus Runs into Storm in Boston," *New York Times*, October 11, 1992, A18.

4. C. Carr, "Chris Crossed: Highs and Lows on the Quincentennial Trail," *Village Voice*, October 27, 1992, 45.

5. Quoted in Mark Sussman, "Celebrating the New World Order: Festival and War in New York," TDR (*The Drama Review*) 39 (2), summer 1995, 10. Ironically, of course, things were not so clear-cut: Hussein retained power, and hostilities threatened to break out again in the region in subsequent years.

6. See Julie Jolin, "Out of the Storm," *Chicago Tribune*, June 23, 1991, sec. 12, 14; and Sussman, 1995, 15. There were some dissenters from this euphoric celebration, but they were carefully cordoned off from the celebrants.

7. Quoted in "Conflict Emerges over Custer Park," *New York Times*, October 13, 1991, A37.

8. Elizabeth Broun, "Foreword" to *The West as America: Reinterpreting Images of the Frontier, 1820–1920*, ed. William H. Truettner (Washington, D.C.: Smithsonian Institution Press, 1991), ix. The American studies professor Bryan J. Wolf quipped, "We must hang a palette and paint brush next to the Winchester rifle"; "How the West Was Hung, or, *When I Hear the Word 'Culture' I Take Out My Checkbook*," *American Quarterly* 44 (3), September 1992, 423.

9. William H. Truettner and Alex Nemerov, "More Bark Than Bite: Thoughts on the Traditional—and Not Very Historical—Approach to Western Art," *Journal of Arizona History*, autumn 1992, 319.

10. Although I have not investigated this point thoroughly, while researching the battle over the exhibition of the *Enola Gay* (chapter 6), I discovered that a 1975 exhibition of drawings by Japanese atomic bomb survivors also incorporated comment books—obviously years before the NMAA did; see Japanese Broadcasting Corporation (NHK), *Unforgettable Fire: Pictures Drawn by Atomic Bomb Survivors* (New York: Pantheon, 1977).

11. "Showdown at 'The West as America' Exhibition," *American Art* 5 (3), summer 1991, 2. I have examined all four comment books and have selected quotes from each. A selection was also reprinted in "Vox Populi," *New York Times*, July 7, 1991, H25, and in the *American Art* article. That article states that 199 comments praised the wall texts; 177 were negative. The Yale professor Alan Trachtenberg contradicts this finding, asserting that "appreciative comments were outnumbered about three to one," although he never specifies how he reached his conclusion; see "Contesting the West," *Art in America*, September 1991, 119.

12. See Evan Thomas, "Time to Circle the Wagons," *Newsweek*, May 27, 1991, 70; Martin F. Nolan, "Shootout at the PC Corral," *Boston Globe*, June 16, 1991, A35; Robert Hughes, "How the West Was Spun," *Time*, May 13, 1991, 79; and Charles Krauthammer, "Westward Hokum," *Washington Post*, May 31, 1991, A19. All these articles appeared at least two months after the show's

opening and after the controversy had evolved; they were not instantaneous reviews.

Alexander Cockburn quoted from Boorstin's book *The Americans: The Democratic Experience* (1973) to demonstrate how this exhibit opposed this historian's viewpoint: Boorstin wrote of western ranchers, "Their great opportunity was to use apparently useless land that belonged to nobody." "The P.C. File: Native Intelligence," *Nation*, June 24, 1991, 838.

13. Hughes, 1991; Kay Larson, "How the West Was Done," *New York*, June 17, 1991, 79; and Kenneth Baker, "Why Western Art Show Drives Some Folks Wild," *San Francisco Chronicle*, July 4, 1991, E1. This show remained a target for a very long time. Nearly three years after it opened, a critic rejected the interpretations by Alex Nemerov as "sheer fantasy"; see the review of several exhibition catalogues on western art by Andrew Wilton in *Burlington Magazine*, February 1994, 120.

14. Ken Ringle, "Political Correctness: Art's New Frontier," *Washington Post*, March 31, 1991, G1. Ringle was similarly dismissive of both Ric Burns's PBS documentary *The Way West* in 1995 and Ken Burns's documentary *The West* in 1996. The first he deemed a "revisionist guilt trip," while the latter "wanders as aimlessly and endlessly as a longhorn on loco weed"; see "Westward Ho-Hum! On PBS, a Saddle-Sore History Lesson," *Washington Post*, May 8, 1995, D1, and "Westward, Whoa!" *Washington Post*, September 15, 1996, G8.

15. Author's interview, December 17, 1997. All subsequent unattributed quotes are from that interview.

16. Nolan, 1991, A37. In an article crammed with humorous phrases, many straight from classic westerns of the silver screen, Nolan derided this "tabloid television" view of western art: "As principles of art criticism go, there seems to be a wheel missing off this Conestoga."

17. Author's interviews, December 28 and December 17, 1997, and comment book 2.

18. Author's interview, December 28, 1997. Schimmel argued in her essay that depictions of Indians mutated from noble savages to violent aggressors to the "doomed Indian," in accord with white interests and fears.

19. Author's interview, December 23, 1997. All subsequent unattributed quotes are from that interview.

20. Krauthammer, 1991; and comment books 1, 2, and 3.

21. Author's interviews, December 23, December 17, December 28, and December 16, 1997.

22. Author's interview, February 9, 1998. All subsequent unattributed quotes are from that interview.

23. Author's interview, December 23, 1997. Johns's perspective is consistent with her earlier work. She published a monograph on Thomas Eakins in

1983 where she closely examined primary documents regarding the artist's time and place, late-nineteenth-century Philadelphia. In a later essay about Eakins, she took a swipe at other art historians who employ revisionist theories to analyze the man and his work, especially regarding homosexual desire: "The evidence of letters and photographs indicates that Eakins *was* sloppy about sexual decorum. All else is oral tradition." "*Swimming*: Thomas Eakins, the Twenty-ninth Bather," in *Thomas Eakins and the Swimming Picture*, ed. Doreen Bolger and Sarah Cash (Fort Worth, TX: Amon Carter Museum, 1996), 79. (I am grateful to James Boyles for alerting me to this important reference.)

Other observers find provocative hints of the possibility of homosexual desire or behavior in incidents in Eakins's biography and in his paintings and photographs, even though solid evidence has not been uncovered. Another critic captures the agitated state of Eakins scholarship, caught between two different approaches: "To miss seeing the appetite for men's bodies is to fail to accept Eakins; to make that appetite into an identity is to fail to understand him." Adam Gopnik, "Eakins in the Wilderness," *New Yorker*, December 26, 1994–January 2, 1995, 87.

Johns, like other principals in museum controversies, brought with her a distinctive history of theoretical preferences and previous academic debates.

24. Nemerov affirms that he draws from the methodologies of literary theory and psychoanalysis. He is especially interested in how unconscious meanings find their way into works of art. One of the earliest comments in comment book 1 noted, "If I want Freud, I'll go to a hospital/clinic. If I want Indians, I'll go West." It is also worth mentioning that another writer declared, "Let John Berger die already." The writings of Berger, a self-declared Marxist cultural critic, are obviously similar to the views dominant in *The West as America*.

One of Nemerov's most intriguing discussions centers on N. C. Wyeth's 1916 oil painting *Wild Bill Hickok at Cards*. While he notes the affinities to Caravaggio's *Supper at Emmaus* (c. 1600), his analysis also raises the possibility that Wyeth was reflexively commenting on the role of the artist in this work. In this respect, Wyeth becomes a character similar to the writer W. W. Beauchamp in the movie *Unforgiven*.

25. Author's interviews, February 9, 1998.

26. Author's interviews, February 9, 1998, and December 17, 1997. Barbara Kruger emerged in the 1980s with her signature black-and-white photo montages of words and text, edged with red (one of her most familiar images was created for an abortion rights march in 1989, "Your body is a battleground"). A reviewer once remarked, "Ms. Kruger is using language to push the viewer about." Roberta Smith, "Barbara Kruger's Large-Scale Self-Expression," *New York Times*, January 11, 1991, C12.

Nemerov found the Couse painting to be "lurid." It depicts a bound and sleeping (or unconscious) white woman being guarded by an Indian, amid "phallic objects" that make the situation erotic. Couse's granddaughter strongly disputed Nemerov's interpretation, accusing him of "twist[ing] the intent" of the work. Where Nemerov saw fears of miscegenation, Virginia Couse Leavitt fathomed an appreciation of cultural differences. See the entry for *The Captive* in *Eanger Irving Couse: Image Maker for America* (Albuquerque, NM: Albuquerque Museum, 1991), 66–67. Once again, I thank James Boyles for alerting me to an important reference.

27. Author's interview, December 16, 1997; and comment book 1.

28. Trachtenberg, 1991, 121, 122; William H. Truettner, "For Museum Audiences: The *Morning of a New Day?*" in *Exhibiting Dilemmas: Issues of Representation at the Smithsonian*, ed. Amy Henderson and Adrienne L. Kaeppler (Washington, D.C.: Smithsonian Institution Press, 1997), 39, 43; and author's interview, February 9, 1998.

29. Author's interview, February 9, 1998. Comments like "I feel as if I've been hit over the head by an ideological hammer" (comment book 2) directly led to the changes.

30. Author's interview, December 17, 1997. Bill Truettner provided me with complete sets of the wall texts, both the old and new versions. All the quotations that follow come from these materials.

31. To bolster his allegorical interpretation, Alex Nemerov quoted directly from Remington's own writing about his hatred of various other racial groups, including Jews, Indians, Chinese, Italians, and Germans. From Nemerov's perspective, early-twentieth-century paintings displaced battles between labor and capital onto the frontier; immigrants and workers "became" savages and redskins. See Truettner, ed., 1991, 297–98.

32. See, e.g., Eric Foner and Jon Weiner, "Fighting for the West," *Nation*, July 29–August 5, 1991, 165; and Paul Mattick, Jr., "At the Waterhole," *Arts Magazine*, November 1991, p 23.

33. See Thomas, 1991; and Steven C. Dubin, *Arresting Images: Impolitic Art and Uncivil Actions* (New York: Routledge, 1992) for a discussion of "the politics of diversion."

34. B. Byron Price, "Field Notes: 'Cutting for Sign': Museums and Western Revisionism," *Western Historical Quarterly* 24 (2), May 1993, 232.

35. Author's interview, February 11, 1998. Jane Tompkins, a professor of English, analyzed her visit to the Cody institution in "At the Buffalo Bill Museum, June 1988," in *West of Everything: The Inner Life of Westerns* (New York: Oxford University Press, 1992). She deems Frederic Remington's paintings "imperialist and racist," is extremely put off by the displays of weaponry and stuffed animal trophies, and left "full of moral outrage" (she recants that response after she reads about Buffalo Bill the man). But Tompkins asserts more

than she argues. She is especially peeved by the paucity of information provided on the wall texts. Yet it is highly unlikely that the museum's interpretations of these works would satisfy her, particularly because she visited before
The West as America influenced the presentation of this material.

36. Author's interview, January 26, 1998. All subsequent unattributed
quotes are from that interview.

37. Ibid.; and Wim de Wit, *Grand Illusions: Chicago's World's Fair of 1893*
(Chicago: Chicago Historical Society, 1993).

38. Author's interviews, February 9, 1998. See also *Revisiting the White
City: American Art at the 1893 World's Fair*, organized by Carolyn Kinder Carr
and George Gurney (Washington, D.C.: National Museum of American Art
and National Portrait Gallery, 1993).

39. Telephone conversation, January 15, 1998; and see Martin A. Berger,
"Modernity and Gender in Thomas Eakins's *Swimming*," *American Art* 11 (3)
fall 1997, 32–47. This is the painting formerly known as *The Swimming Hole*.

40. Author's interview December 23, 1997. Jack Smith, a columnist for
the *Los Angeles Times*, also visited the Autry Museum. He walked through the
exhibits, and understood that the main message was that western life had
been greatly romanticized. Yet "I do not give up easily my belief that the
American West was much as it is portrayed in Western movies." Like the
writer in the comment book whose great-grandfather was a sheriff in Kansas,
Smith would not be swayed by a new interpretation. See "Sold Out on the
Romanticized Sagas of the Old West," July 18, 1991, E1.

NOTES TO CHAPTER 6

1. The unusual name became the stuff of parody and absurdity. A newspaper in Crystal Lake, Illinois, headlined an article "Atomic Bombers Criticize Enola Homosexual Exhibit" ("PC Run Amok," *Washington Post*, September 30, 1994, 1); *Washington City Paper* ran a story entitled "*Enola Gay* Bashing" (September 23, 1994, 8); and an editorial cartoonist pictured the B–29
fuselage tagged "Enola Sexually Undifferentiated" (*Oregonian*, September 30,
1994).

2. Tom Engelhardt, *The End of Victory Culture: Cold War America and the
Disillusioning of a Generation* (New York: Basic Books, 1995).

3. See Steven C. Dubin, *Arresting Images: Impolitic Art and Uncivil Actions*
(New York: Routledge, 1992). A fierce debate broke out in 1996 when the
Phoenix Art Museum staged *Old Glory: The American Flag in Contemporary
Art*. Included was Tyler's piece, as well as a flag made from human hair and
flesh, and another draped in a toilet.

4. Margot A. Henriksen, *Dr. Strangelove's America: Society and Culture in
the Atomic Age* (Berkeley: University of California Press, 1997).

5. Kristin E. Hussey, "Hiroshima, Nagasaki a Mystery to Americans," *Washington Times,* March 3, 1995, A2. In 1998 I informally polled an upper-level class ("Mass Media and Popular Culture") about the president and the bomb. Only two out of approximately forty students answered correctly "Truman"; one of them was old enough to be alive at the time the event occurred.

6. William H. Truettner and Alexander Nemerov, "What You See Is Not Necessarily What You Get: New Meaning in Images of the Old West," *Montana: The Magazine of Western History* 42 (3), summer 1992, 72.

7. "The *Enola Gay* Exhibit a Mainstream Victory," *Mobile Register,* January 6, 1995, 6A; and Herbert Molloy Mason, Jr., "Proudly Display the *Enola Gay,*" *VFW,* March 1995, 21. To younger people, Jane Fonda is best known as an actress, a fitness guru, or the daughter of Henry, sister of Peter, aunt of Bridget, or wife of Ted Turner. For many people alive during the Vietnam War era, however, she remains "Hanoi Jane," despised for allegedly undercutting the U.S. military by traveling to the North Vietnamese capital and meeting with enemy leaders.

8. Pat Choate, *Agents of Influence: How Japan Manipulates America's Political and Economic System* (New York: Knopf, 1990); and quoted in "Hollings 'Joke' Angers A-Bomb Survivors but Tokyo Plays It Down," *Los Angeles Times,* March 5, 1992, A9.

9. Vincent Canby, "Japan Unfolds through Many Images," *New York Times,* June 14, 1992, H1; and quoted in Jane Galbraith, "Group Takes 'Rising Sun' Protest Public," *Los Angeles Times,* April 7, 1993, F1. The intense competition between the two countries was also addressed in the 1986 movie *Gung Ho,* where a Japanese car maker takes over an abandoned American auto plant.

10. See David E. Sanger, "Gloom Lifts in U.S. and Falls on Japan," *New York Times,* December 29, 1992, A4.

11. See *Journal of American History* 82 (3), December 1995.

12. See, for example, Thomas F. Gieryn, "Balancing Acts: Science, *Enola Gay* and History Wars at the Smithsonian," in *The Politics of Display: Museums, Science, Culture,* ed. Sharon MacDonald (London: Routledge, 1998); and Vera L. Zolberg, "Museums as Contested Sites of Remembrance: The *Enola Gay* Affair," in *Theorizing Museums: Representing Identity and Diversity in a Changing World,* ed. Sharon MacDonald and Gordon Fyfe (Oxford: Blackwell, 1996).

13. Edward T. Linenthal and Tom Engelhardt, *History Wars: The* Enola Gay *and Other Battles for the American Past* (New York: Metropolitan Books, 1996); Philip Nobile, *Judgment at the Smithsonian—The Bombing of Hiroshima and Nagasaki: The Uncensored Script of the Smithsonian's Fiftieth Anniversary Exhibit of the* Enola Gay (New York: Marlowe and Company, 1995); and Martin Harwit, *An Exhibit Denied: Lobbying the History of the* Enola Gay (New York:

Copernicus, 1996). These sources present events chronologically, while I have chosen to organize my account thematically.

14. Nicholas D. Kristof, "Shoichi Yokoi, 82, Is Dead; Japan Soldier Hid 27 Years," *New York Times*, September 26, 1997, D19.

15. Ken Ringle, "At Ground Zero," *Washington Post*, September 26, 1994, A1. Note that this was not Ringle's only article on this subject, that others such as George F. Will cited his reportage, and that Ringle explicitly referred to *The West as America* in this important piece.

Michael Neufeld points out the *reductio ad absurdum* of such an argument: once everyone connected to an era dies off, history can no longer be written about; author's interview, April 8, 1998.

16. Paul Fussell, *Thank God for the Atom Bomb and Other Essays* (New York: Ballantine, 1988), 6, 3, 10.

17. Tony Capaccio, and Uday Mohan, "Missing the Target," *American Journalism Review*, July-August 1995, 21; Michael S. Sherry, "Patriotic Orthodoxy and American Decline," in Linenthal and Engelhardt, 1996, 109; and Edward T. Linenthal, "Anatomy of a Controversy," in Linenthal and Engelhardt, 1996, 13.

18. See Harwit, 1996, 228–33; author's interview, March 19, 1998; Thomas Sowell, "The Right to Infiltrate," *Forbes*, March 13, 1995, 74; "Smithsonian Exhibit Angers Veterans," *Nashville Tennessean*, July 25, 1994.

19. Author's interview, March 19, 1998. All subsequent unattributed quotes are from that interview.

20. Quoted in Richard M. Kohn, "History at Risk: The Case of the *Enola Gay*," in Linenthal and Engelhardt, 1996, 151.

21. For a compelling look at how race factored into the Pacific theater of war, on both the American and Japanese sides, see John W. Dower, *War without Mercy: Race and Power in the Pacific War* (New York: Pantheon, 1986). One of the issues this exhibition raised was whether the Japanese were already near defeat, without the dropping of the bombs, an idea substantiated by a 1946 U.S. Strategic Bombing Survey.

22. Quoted in Harwit, 1996, 133. The full text of the congressional letter is quoted on 373. The idea that the decision to drop the atomic bomb was "morally unambiguous" surfaced repeatedly. For example, the air force historian Richard Hallion, at an earlier stage of the debate: "Dealing with a morally unambiguous subject, why did they have to produce two and maybe three scripts to get it right?"; quoted in R. Emmett Tyrrell, Jr., "Hiroshima and the Hectoring Herd," *Washington Times*, September 2, 1994, A18. On the other hand, Robert J. Lifton and Greg Mitchell argue that Hiroshima remains a "raw nerve" for Americans precisely because we have never reconciled our conflicting emotions about what occurred there; see *Hiroshima in America: Fifty Years of Denial* (New York: G. Putnam's Sons, 1995).

23. David E. Sanger, "Enola Gay and Little Boy, Exactly 50 Years Later," *New York Times*, August 6, 1995, XX3.

24. See Gus Gugliotta, *Washington Post*, May 31, 1994, 1B; Robert L. Koenig, *Arkansas Democrat Gazette*, July 1, 1994, 2A; and Tom Webb, *San Antonio Express-News*, May 15, 1995, 3.

25. See, for example, Elizabeth Herbert, "Exhibit Bombs with Vets," *Sun Chronicle* (Attleboro, MA), August 14, 1994; "This Show Might Bomb Pre-opening," *Times Herald Record* (Middletown, NY), August 11, 1994.

26. See "Exhibit Torpedoed," *Tulsa World*, January 31, 1995, 1; Col. Charles D. Cooper, USAF-Ret., "The *Enola Gay*—Mission Aborted," *Retired Officer*, March 1995, 4; and Karen de Witt, "Exhibit's Wings Clipped," *Sarasota Herald-Tribune*, January 31, 1995, 1A.

27. Mark Johnson, "An Indelicate Balance," *Tampa Tribune*, May 2, 1994, 1.

28. Harwit, 1996, 239; and author's interview, April 2, 1998. All subsequent unattributed quotes are from that interview. Crouch and Neufeld acknowledge that leaks occurred, but this is obviously a sensitive subject with them. They are not surprised, however. With such a controversial subject, it would be folly to expect that "everybody would be on the same page," Crouch argues; author's interview, April 8, 1998.

29. Quoted in Harwit, 1996, 242. Besides Harwit's concern over critics taking a quote out of context, he was acutely aware that it is a distortion of the curators' intentions to separate the written elements from an exhibition and subject them to analysis, when the gestalt is made up of audio and visual elements as well. See Harwit, 1996, 215; and chapter 3 on *Gaelic Gotham*.

30. Author's interview, April 8, 1998; all subsequent unattributed quotes are from that interview. The issue of "balance" is the central focus of Gieryn's 1998 "symmetric analysis of the symmetric rhetoric" (220) used by the opposing parties in this episode. But by focusing on rhetorical strategies, Gieryn fails to place this struggle within a broad sociohistorical context: Why did it break out when it did? Why over these issues? He also downplays the role of the media; the importance of this taking place in Washington, D.C., and the objectives of opportunistic politicians; and the mobilizing of varying degrees of power by different groups.

31. See "War and the Smithsonian," *Wall Street Journal*, August 29, 1994, A10; and Harwit, 1996, 317.

32. See Ken Ringle, "A-Bomb Exhibit Plan Revamped," *Washington Post*, August 30, 1994, C1; and Harwit, 1996, 53.

33. Japanese Broadcasting Corporation, *Unforgettable Fire: Pictures Drawn by Atomic Bomb Survivors* (New York: Pantheon, 1977) features a selection of drawings by middle-aged and elderly Japanese survivors of the atomic bombing of Hiroshima. Through their portrayals and written descrip-

tions, the horrific human costs of this event become painfully apparent: there are repeated references to skin hanging off bodies, maggots festering in wounds, dead horses littering the streets, babies clutching onto severely injured or dead mothers. It is difficult to imagine that anyone—except the most hardened viewer—could fail to be moved.

34. Harwit, 1996, 276; Capaccio and Mohan, 1995, 19; and author's interview, April 8, 1998. According to one report, the Smithsonian received over thirty thousand angry letters; see Joel Achenbach, "*Enola Gay* Exhibit: Plane and Simple," *Washington Post*, June 28, 1995, 1.

35. Author's interview, April 2, 1998; Capaccio and Mohan, 1995, 20; and author's interview, April 8, 1998.

36. Harwit, 1996, 127, 146, 133.

37. Ibid., and quoted by Paul Boyer, "Whose History Is It Anyway? Memory, Politics, and Historical Scholarship," in Linenthal and Engelhardt, 1996, 116. It is worth noting that Herbert Mason shares the anti-intellectual bias of many of the critics (his article seems to snarl when it mentions that all the curators are Ph.D.'s [p. 21]), and dubs the Smithsonian the "Institution of Political Correctness" (p. 22). Stephen Aubin, himself a Ph.D., decries what he sees as "this chasm between the real elite academic crowd and the public."

38. According to Tom Crouch, the most vocal opponent of this exhibition was Lillian Baker, the reactionary author of *Dishonoring America: The Falsification of World War II History* (Medford, OR: Webb Research Group, 1994). He reports that she once had to be removed forcibly from a congressional hearing; author's interview, April 8, 1998.

39. *A More Perfect Union* remains on view at the National Museum of American History, and a version is also touring the country.

40. Sowell, 1995. For an additional, distinct statement of the battle between "cultural elites" and "cultural conservatives" over the arts and humanities, see the editorial "The Kulchur Warriors Hit the Beach," *Washington Times*, January 30, 1995, A20.

41. Mike Feinsilber, "Enola Gay Exhibit May Be Cut Back," *Sarasota Herald-Tribune*, January 28, 1995, 8B; Rowan Scarborough, "Museum Director's Job on the Line," *Washington Times*, January 25, 1995, A1; Dubin, 1992, 130, 148, 241; and Philip M. Crane, "Abolish the Arts Agency," *New York Times*, June 6, 1990, A27. Armey was also a signatory, along with twenty-three of his congressional colleagues, to a letter of complaint sent to Smithsonian Secretary Robert McCormick Adams, August 10, 1994.

42. See Rowan Scarborough, "Smithsonian under Siege on Hill," *Washington Times*, May 12, 1995, A15; Michael E. Ruane, "Senators Assail Enola Gay Exhibit," *Philadelphia Inquirer*, May 19, 1995, A14; and Kohn, 1996, 162.

43. Quoted in Harwit, 1996, 387; author's interview, March 19, 1998; and "Smithsonian Apologizes for 'Historically Inaccurate' Display," *Japan Times*,

May 20, 1995, 5. Harwit wrote that Heyman's office had given him only four or five days to tender his resignation; 1996, 422. A former Marine, Solomon was known for his combative style in the halls of Congress too. During his career he supported a constitutional amendment against flag burning, opposed gun control, and condemned antiwar protestors during the Persian Gulf crisis in 1991. As with his fellow congressional critics, Solomon's stance on the *Enola Gay* issue harmonized with other positions he had taken.

44. *Today Show,* April 1, 1998; and author's interviews, April 2 and March 19, 1998.

45. Harwit, 1996, 13–14, 95–96, 129, 144.

46. Author's interviews, March 19 and April 2, 1998. Correll admits that the AFA has not devoted more time and effort to any other issue; author's interview, March 30, 1998.

47. Harwit, 1996, 252, 257, 259–60, 275. Robert McCormick Adams served as Smithsonian secretary from 1984 until mid-September 1994, when he was succeeded by I. Michael Heyman. Their respective tenures straddled this controversy; Heyman was in office for the critical last year.

48. John Correll memo to Monroe Hatch, April 7, 1994, collected in John T. Correll, *Revisionism Gone Wrong: Analysis of the Enola Gay Controversy, March 1994-December 1996* (Arlington, VA: Air Force Association, 1996).

49. *The Smithsonian Plan for the* Enola Gay: *A Report on the Revisions,* June 28, 1994, in Correll, 1996; and author's interviews, March 30 and April 2, 1998.

50. John T. Correll, "Developments in the *Enola Gay* Controversy," August 22, 1994; John T. Correll to Col. Tom Alison, USAF, Ret., NASM, December 28, 1994, in Correll, 1996; and author's interview, March 30, 1998. The AFA, in its continued concern over what it deemed to be a partisan exhibition, suggested that the original curators be scuttled and replaced with ones who were veterans of military service.

51. "How the American Legion Held Sway on Enola Gay," *American Legion,* May 1995, 36.

52. Author's interviews, March 19, March 30, and April 8, 1998. Harwit even appointed a "Tiger Team" of advisers, including many retired servicemen.

54. *World War II Times,* August–September 1994; and James L. Pattillo, "Museum's Plans Are a National Disgrace," *Santa Barbara News-Press,* August 14, 1994.

54. Eugene L. Meyer, "Target: Smithsonian," *Washington Post,* January 30, 1995, D1; "Interview: Paul W. Tibbets," *Dallas Morning News,* February 5, 1995, 2J.

55. Brig. Gen. Paul Tibbets, "Display the Enola Gay in the Context of a

World at War," *Sun Herald* (Biloxi, MS), June 26, 1994, B5; and author's interviews, April 8 and March 19, 1998.

56. Chalmers M. Roberts, "Truman Had 250,000 Reasons for Dropping the Bomb," *Philadelphia Inquirer,* August 27, 1994, A7; Rowan Scarborough, "A-Bomb Exhibit Pared to Essentials," *Washington Times*, January 27, 1995, A1; Tony Capaccio, "Pentagon A-Bomb Exhibit Includes Suspect Casualty Claims," *Defense Week*, August 7, 1995, 1, 9, 11; and Harwit, 1996, 200. Estimates of the total number of victims of the Nazis is also a sensitive issue, which was fiercely debated during the establishment of the Holocaust Memorial Museum in Washington, D.C. Some Jews balked at including non-Jewish victims, fearing a "slippery slope toward forgetfulness." The noted writer and Holocaust survivor Elie Wiesel presented it like this: "It's true; there were others as well. So they said eleven million, 6 [million] of whom are Jews. If this goes on, the next step will be 11, including 6, and in a couple of years, they won't even speak of the 6. They will speak only of 11 million. See the progression? 6 million plus 5, then 11 including 6, and then only 11"; see Edward T. Linenthal, *Preserving Memory: The Struggle to Create America's Holocaust Museum* (New York: Viking, 1995), 53. Any other historical interpretation would both insult the memory of the dead and have profound repercussions for the living.

57. Author's interviews, March 19 and April 8, 1998. Harwit believes that Truman would have never ordered an invasion that might have cost 500,000 to one million American lives; the public outcry would simply have been too great after such a bloodbath.

58. "How the American Legion Held Sway," 1995, 35; and Julie A. Rhoad, "The Proposed *Enola Gay* Exhibit: Is It an Accurate Portrayal of History?" *American Legion Auxiliary*, January–February 1995, 12.

59. Author's interviews, April 8, 1998; and quoted in Michael Killian, "Furor over Enola Gay Exhibit Forces Smithsonian to Cancel It," *Santa Barbara News-Press*, January 31, 1995, A1.

60. Author's interview, May 15, 1997.

61. Quoted in Harwit, 1996, 189; and author's interview, April 8, 1998.

62. See Marilyn Duff, "The 'Culture Commissars' at the Smithsonian," *Orange County Register*, November 13, 1994, 4.

63. "Snoopy at the Smithsonian," *Wall Street Journal*, October 25, 1994, A16; and author's interview, March 19, 1998.

64. Pat Buchanan, "A Long March to Revile America's Past," *Washington Times*, November 7, 1994, A21; quoted in Joyce Price, "Smithsonian's Slant to Stop, Gingrich Says," *Washington Times*, January 28, 1995, A1; Tyrrell, 1994; John Leo, "The National Museums of PC," *U.S. News & World Report*, October 10, 1994, 21; quoted in Mike Wallace, "The Battle of the Enola Gay," *Museum*

News, July–August 1995, 9; and author's interview, April 2, 1998. In a singular instance of name-calling from "the other side," Philip Nobile called critics of the exhibition "deniers" (1995).

65. Author's interviews, April 8, 1998; and "Hiroshima, 50 Years Later," *New York Times*, August 6, 1995, E14.

66. *Nashville Tennessean*, February 12, 1995. Harwit reports that one of the many messages that came into the museum from the general public at this time was a postcard that read, "I wish we had dropped another five bombs on those yellow-bellied slant-eyed little bastards"; as the next reference indicates, some individuals on both sides of the Pacific obviously keep fighting this war; author's interview, March 19, 1998.

67. Andrew Pollack, "Japanese Refight the War, and Win, in Pulp Fiction," *New York Times*, March 4, 1995, A1.

68. David E. Sanger, "Molding Textbooks to Mold Consensus," *New York Times*, November 22, 1992, E5; and Nicholas D. Kristof, "Japan Bars Censorship of Atrocities in Texts," *New York Times*, August 30, 1997, A4.

69. David E. Sanger, "Museum's A-Bomb Message: There's More to It," *New York Times*, August 4, 1994, A4; and Nicholas D. Kristof, "Today's History Lesson: What Rape of Nanjing?" *New York Times*, July 4, 1996, A4. The planning for a Japanese national war museum, scheduled to open in 1999, has been marked by fierce debates. Officials have decided to exclude references to Japanese war atrocities; see Mari Yamaguchi, "War Museum Shuns Atrocities," *Kansas City Star*, February 11, 1996, A16.

70. Andrew Pollack, "Japan Protests U.S. Stamp on A-Bombs," *New York Times*, December 4, 1994, A25; and Todd S. Purdum, "At White House Behest, Postal Service Scraps A-Bomb Stamp," *New York Times*, December 9, 1994, A19.

71. T. R. Reid, "Japanese Media Decry *Enola Gay* Exhibition," *Washington Post*, June 29, 1995, A32; Dipak Basu, "The West Should Apologize First," *Japan Times*, May 10, 1995; and Teresa Watanabe, "A-Bomb Unnecessary, Japanese Mayors Say," *San Jose Mercury-News*, March 16, 1995.

72. See Eugene L. Meyer, "2 Exhibits to Mark A-Bombings," *Washington Post*, June 21, 1995, D1; Phillip P. Pan, "AU Offers a View of A-Bombs' Horrors," *Washington Post*, July 9, 1995, B2; and Gerald Mizejewski, "View from Hiroshima," *Washington Times*, July 8, 1995, A1.

73. Harwit, 1996, 152; Rowan Scarborough, "Enola Gay Exhibit Splattered with Red Paint Before Opening," *Washington Times*, June 21, 1995, 6; Lonnae O'Neal Parker, "Enola Gay Exhibit Opens to Protest," *Washington Post*, June 29, 1995, C3; Jim Keary, "Enola Gay Painted with Blood," *Washington Times*, July 3, 1995, C3; and Kristan Metzler, "Vandals Found Guilty in Protest of Enola Gay," *Washington Times*, August 3, 1995, C4.

74. Harwit, 1996, 343–44; Kai Bird, "Enola Gay: 'Patriotically Correct,'" *Washington Post*, July 7, 1995, A21; and author's interview, March 19, 1998.

75. Arthur Hirsch,"Enola Gay Exhibit Opens without an Agenda," *Baltimore Sun*, June 28, 1995, 1D; and Joel Achenbach, "Exhibit A: The Pablum Museum," *Washington Post*, February 1, 1995, D1.

NOTES TO CHAPTER 7

1. See Judith H. Dobrzynski, "Glory Days for the Art Museum," *New York Times*, October 5, 1997, AR1; and idem, "Museums Paint Prosperity by Numbers," *New York Times*, February 26, 1998, E1. Idea-driven versus object-driven museums and exhibitions are a much-remarked-upon trend in museum literature today; see Amy Henderson and Adrienne L. Kaeppler, eds., *Exhibiting Dilemmas: Issues of Representation at the Smithsonian* (Washington, D.C.: Smithsonian Institution Press, 1997).

2. Author's interview, October 9, 1997.

3. Author's interview, February 9, 1998.

4. Author's interview, April 28, 1997. All subsequent unattributed quotes are from that interview.

5. Author's interviews, February 9, 1998, April 8, 1998, and September 26, 1997. All subsequent unattributed quotes are from those interviews.

6. Matthew Arnold, *Culture and Anarchy* (New Haven: Yale University Press, 1994 [1869]).

7. See Somini Sengupta, "At Ellis Island Museum, Dispute on Armenia Show," *New York Times*, September 11, 1997, B3; and idem, "Ellis Island, Yielding, Permits Photos of Armenian Massacre," *New York Times*, October 14, 1997, B2.

8. See Somini Sengupta, "What Is a Concentration Camp? Exhibit Prompts a Debate," *New York Times*, March 8, 1998, A35; idem, "Accord on Term 'Concentration Camp,'" *New York Times*, March 10, 1998, B4; and Clyde Haberman, "Defending Jews' Lexicon of Anguish," *New York Times*, March 13, 1998, B1.

9. See Lizette Alvarez, "After Criticism, Smithsonian Revises Plan for Israel Event," *New York Times*, January 7, 1998, A12; Michael Keller, "Does the Smithsonian Hate Israel?" *New York Post*, January 2, 1998, 26; and Anthony Lewis, "Silencing Other Ideas," *New York Times*, January 12, 1998, A21.

10. Author's interview, March 19, 1998; Martin Harwit, *An Exhibit Denied: Lobbying the History of the* Enola Gay (New York: Copernicus, 1996), 357, 379, 428; and Eugene L. Meyer, "Smithsonian May Drop A-Bomb Exhibit," *Washington Post*, January 27, 1995, A1. Days before *The Last Act* was canceled, Meyer reports that only one corporate sponsor had signed on to *America's*

Smithsonian, with a requisite $10 million pledge. Moreover, it wished to remain anonymous because of the *Enola Gay* controversy. *America's Smithsonian* completed three-fourths of its proposed twelve-city tour. The Smithsonian public affairs office reports that corporate support ran out, and fund raising efforts in the three remaining cities were insufficient to continue the venture; telephone conversation, May 1, 1998. Martin Harwit reports that the Smithsonian suffered a major economic loss on *America's Smithsonian*—$20 million, perhaps much more; author's interview, March 19, 1998.

11. Author's interviews, December 15, 1997. All subsequent unattributed quotes are from those interviews.

12. Quoted in Alice Thorson, "Natural Passion," *Kansas City Star,* February 15, 1998, J3.

13. Author's interviews, February 9, 1998, and December 15, 1997.

14. Sweatshops have been the subject of many recent investigations. Accusations have been made against Wal-Mart, Disney, Guess?, the signature clothing line of Kathie Lee Gifford, and others, for using exploitative labor conditions to manufacture their goods. A particularly sobering investigation "followed the money" gained from the sale of baseball caps manufactured in the Dominican Republic, bearing the names of elite American universities. The caps retail for twenty dollars, but workers receive approximately eight cents per item; see Bob Herbert, "Sweatshop U.," *New York Times,* April 12, 1998, WK13. For a similar global economic perspective on Barbie see Eyal Press, "Barbie's Betrayal: The Toy Industry's Broken Workers," *Nation,* September 30, 1996, 10.

15. Quoted in George White, "Plan for a Sweatshop Exhibition Draws Fire," *Los Angeles Times,* September 11, 1997, A1; and author's interview, April 8, 1998.

16. See the review by Holland Cotter, "Beyond Beauty, Art That Takes Action," *New York Times,* September 28, 1997, AR35.

17. See Celia W. Dugger, "Outward Bound from the Mosaic," *New York Times,* October 28, 1997, B1.

Index

About the Author

STEVEN C. DUBIN directs the Media, Society, and Arts Program at Purchase College, State University of New York. He received his Ph.D. in sociology at the University of Chicago. In addition, he did postdoctoral work at both the University of Chicago and Yale University. He is the author of *Bureaucratizing the Muse: Public Funds and the Cultural Worker* (University of Chicago Press, 1987) and *Arresting Images: Impolitic Art and Uncivil Actions* (Routledge, 1992). *Arresting Images* was chosen as a Notable Book of the Year by the *New York Times* and cited by the Gustavus Myers Center for the Study of Human Rights as an Outstanding Book.

Mr. Dubin has written and lectured widely on public funding of the arts, censorship, controversial art, obscenity, and popular culture. His articles and reviews have appeared in *Contemporary Sociology, American Journal of Sociology, Urban Life, Social Problems, Social Forces, Sociological Inquiry, Symbolic Interaction, Visual Anthropology, Journal of Aesthetic Education, Journal of Arts Management and Law, Curator Magazine, Nation,* and *New Art Examiner.*